A Word from the Lost

Remarks on James Nayler's
*Love to the Lost And a Hand held forth to
the Helpless To Lead out of the Dark*

David Lewis

INNER LIGHT BOOKS

SAN FRANCISCO, CALIFORNIA

2019

A WORD FROM THE LOST

Editor: Charles Martin
Copy editor: Kathy McKay
Layout and design: Matt Kelsey

Published by Inner Light Books

San Francisco, California

www.innerlightbooks.com

editor@innerlightbooks.com

Library of Congress Control Number: 2019940912

ISBN 978-1-7328239-7-6 (hardcover)
ISBN 978-1-7328239-8-3 (paperback)
ISBN 978-1-7328239-9-0 (eBook)

Chapter 13, 'Concerning Good Works', first appeared as 'Faith and Works' in *Quaker Voices* 9, no. 1 (2018): 7–11.

Appendix B, the James Nayler chronology, is adapted from David Neelon's *James Nayler: Revolutionary to Prophet* (Becket, MA: Leadings Press, 2009). Used with the permission of David Neelon.

Contents

About This Work

This is a commentary on *Love to the Lost*, a pamphlet published by the early Quaker James Nayler in February 1656. It explores Nayler's theology as described in this pamphlet written prior to his blasphemy conviction, a theology that is similar to that of other early Quakers. I have put Nayler's thought into its historical and biographical context. My main purpose has been to contrast his thought with the published 'disciplines' (descriptions of Quaker faith and practice) issued by London (later Britain) Yearly Meeting in order to show how his writings are reflected in or challenged by later views of the Religious Society of Friends. See the bibliography for a discussion of these books of discipline published over the years and a list of the abbreviations used for the ones cited most frequently in this book.

The commentary is divided into twenty-four short chapters. Fourteen of these reflect on individual chapters from *Love to the Lost*. In between these are eight chapters on aspects of James Nayler's life and its context. These are intended to give present-day readers some insight into what may have been in his mind as he wrote. To help readers navigate around unfamiliar history, I have provided a note on the wars during the period 1637–1653 (see appendix A) and a chronology of James Nayler's life (see appendix B).

I hope the comparison of Nayler's writings with the disciplines of British Quakers will explain Nayler to a modern audience, illustrate the Quaker journey since 1652, and allow me to make some reflections on the present condition of British Quakerism. I have used the books of discipline as a bridge between Quakers over the centuries, exploring the changes in emphasis and hoping to find the continuities.

This work is by a white male Quaker. If the text at times is insufficiently inclusive and exhibits gender bias, please forgive me. Part of the reason is the sources. The women's voices in this book are mostly there because white men in the past have authorized their speaking and writing. I am also British. The text only rarely references the disciplines of other yearly meetings, and consequently my comments may appear very Anglocentric. This does not mean I think British Quakerism has all the answers or voices the 'correct' Quaker theology when compared to other yearly meetings. On the contrary, as my title suggests, we may well be lost.

Nor do I think Nayler had all the answers. It is not easy to be sure what Nayler meant. Several mountain ranges stand between us and Nayler: the changed thinking of the Enlightenment about God and the universe; the aesthetic revolution of the Romantics; and the postmodern and liberal Quaker scepticism about whether absolute and certain 'Truth' exists. Most of us lack his deep Christian background. Modern British Friends probably understand more about Buddhism and Celtic mysticism, for example, than about the theological mix of Reformation Europe. We are strung out along a spectrum from a firm belief in Christ as saviour (Christocentric) through to a belief that all faiths point towards the same God (universalist) to doubts about the existence of any God (nontheist) view. We might think Nayler was at the Christocentric end. However, I have found that if we 'translate' his words into our present-day Quaker cultures, his thoughts and spiritual experiences are similar to modern reflections on God and the Light.

Introduction to James Nayler

I first met James Nayler in the pages of Christopher Hill's 1972 history *The World Turned Upside Down*. There, he is depicted as a tragic figure, misunderstood because his ideas were before his time and tragic because his 'side' lost what most readers would know as the 'English civil wars' and because he personally lost an internecine battle for power within the early Quakers. Hill portrays him as a political scapegoat hung out to dry by a Quaker establishment intent on compromise and survival and since then either ignored or treated with circumspection. Hill introduces Nayler as follows:

> Thus, in [George] Fox's *Journal* James Nayler plays a part only slightly greater than that of Trotsky in official Soviet histories of the Russian Revolution. Yet in the 1650's many regarded Nayler as the 'chief leader', the 'head Quaker in England'. 'He writes all their books', Colonel Cooper told the House of Commons in December 1656. 'Cut off this fellow and you will destroy the sect.'[1]

Hill argues that Fox's message as reported in his *Journal* is a bland Puritanism, exhortations that no Protestant (apart from the paid clergy) of the time could find offensive. Why then did so many thousands gather to hear him, why were so many convinced, why were the authorities so disturbed? Hill argues it was because of the Quaker's revolutionary *social* message and concludes that the hostility was political — the Quakers were viewed as 'roundhead rogues' — and that the spokesperson of this political radicalism, in addition to Edward Burrough, was James Nayler. Nayler was the most powerful preacher the Quakers had; he had the appearance of a simple countryman or shepherd, he spoke with a Yorkshire accent in simple, unscholarly language, and he had experienced what he spoke about.

Nayler was considered by many in the government and among the established clergy as the leader of an organised movement which, from its base in the north of England, had swept with frightening rapidity over the southern counties. It was a movement whose aims were obscure but which had certainly taken over many of the policies of the Levellers; in fact, it was recruiting former Levellers and Ranters as well as Baptists and disaffected soldiers.[2]

Both within and without Quakerism, Nayler is remembered for his 'blasphemous' entry into Bristol. This not only had serious repercussions on Quakerism at the time, but this one event coloured Friends' views of Nayler for the next three hundred years.[3] On Friday 24 October 1656, Nayler and six or seven companions rode into Bedminster, a suburb of Bristol, 'one man with his hat off leading Nayler's horse and one man before with his hat on'. Two horses followed, each carrying a man and woman. It was pouring with rain, and the mud was knee deep. In Bedminster they re-formed: two women, Hannah Stringer and Martha Simmonds, went each side of Nayler's horse, took the reins, and began singing 'Holy, Holy, Holy, hosanna'; John Stringer walked in front, bare-headed. Dorcas Ebury and Thomas Welbeck rode behind, and Simon Carter may have walked there as well. In this manner, they travelled into the centre of Bristol to the White Hart Inn. This was clearly an imitation of Christ's entry into Jerusalem, with Nayler playing the part of Christ. The noise and commotion caused by the procession soon brought out the magistrates, and the entire party was arrested before the women had had time to dry their outer clothes before the inn's fire.

Nayler was the best-known Quaker in England. This was the third performance of the procession. In Glastonbury and Wells (where it was not so wet), the women had thrown garments in front of the horse in place of palm leaves. They were expected in Bristol. One man, George Witherley, cried out to them in Bedminster that 'God required no such thing at their hands'.[4] That was also the opinion of leading Bristol Quakers, who had told the thousand-plus Quakers in the city to have nothing to do with Nayler, even to the extent of not taking him food in prison. Bishop was pleased to report to Margaret Fell that this was obeyed.[5] Furthermore, because the Quakers remained silent, the authorities in Bristol had no reason to arrest or disturb them. The magistrates had no idea what to do with Nayler. They contacted their clerk, who was in Westminster, London, and at his request sent Nayler, Martha Simmonds, John and Hannah Stranger, and Dorcas Ebury up to Westminster to be tried by Parliament.

Nayler's 'blasphemous' entry into Bristol was used by Parliament as an opportunity to attack the whole Quaker movement and to further control and limit religious toleration. It was used by senior Quakers, principally Fox, to insert more order, discipline, and control into the movement. This, argues Hill, closed the door on much that had been courageous and life-giving in the early Quaker movement. The absolute individualism of the appeal to Christ within every person had to be curbed. Quakers ceased to perform miracles, and the movement suffered splits such as Perot's 'hat honour controversy' and the Wilkinson-Story split over the subordination of the individual's light to the sense of the meeting. Nayler himself died in October 1660 after being beaten and robbed outside Huntingdon while walking home. Those who found him recognised him as a Quaker and took him to the home of a local Friend, where he died. His unmarked grave lies in an orchard somewhere near Kings Ripton, a village outside Huntingdon.[6]

Hill's depiction of Nayler entranced me. Nayler was a pre-Marxist revolutionary, a left-libertarian whose vision, described in theological terms because that was all that was available to him and his public, was as relevant to the 1970s as it had been in the 1650s. My reading of *The World Turned Upside Down* brought me to the Friends Meeting in

Rochester, Kent, where I found around six Friends, all about thirty years older than me and none of them revolutionaries. I should not have been surprised. Rosemary Moore describes the Quakers of the 1650s as follows:

> [M]ost Quakers appear to have been of the "middling sort", small businessmen and artisans. . . . [T]he small but influential number of well-to-do adherents would prefer Quakers to other radical groups, as Quakers did not attack property rights.[7]

Nayler's England

The civil wars in the British Isles of the 1640s were the result of political collapse, not revolutionary action; the revolutionary ideas came bubbling up as the carapace of deference and customary order broke down. In this section I set out the long-term trends that historians think may have made 'civil war' inevitable. These are the social and economic trends within which Nayler lived. Appendix A describes the wars themselves in a little more detail.

The economic and social reasons for the collapse were many and varied by locality, but three long-term trends stand out.[8] First, when Nayler was born in 1617/1618, Britain's population was twice as large as it had been one hundred years earlier. This had a tremendous impact on every aspect of society. Importantly, farmers managed to feed the increasing numbers through improvements in techniques and an expansion of the area under cultivation that made wastelands, hillsides, and fens fertile. Land was enclosed and commons were lost, a deprivation that tipped some into destitution and sparked the Digger movement.[9] But the longer- term result was that, unlike in France, there was no demographic crisis and the population was fed, although when Nayler was born people were probably living on a worse diet than that of his grandfather. Food prices, of course, rose, and at first rents did not rise by as much so that profits flowed into the hands of small-scale farmers; by the time Nayler was born, however, the position had reversed and rents had risen considerably, leading to the creation of a new class of landless agricultural labourers.

A second major change was in land ownership. Between 1536 and 1636, the Crown disposed of its own patrimony and that of the church. The number of property transfers doubled between 1536 and 1563. This was the largest transfer of state property into private hands before Margaret Thatcher's 'right to buy' council house legislation in the 1980s. The market boomed as court favourites sold the confiscated estates to those lower down the social scale, who added them to their estates. In addition, the number of those owning land (and so acquiring the social and political prestige that came with it) substantially increased, and not all these owners were instinctive supporters of the monarchy. The number of landowners roughly doubled between 1540 and 1640. It became acceptable to think of land as an investment, similar to goods stored in a London warehouse. As one Puritan moralist put it, 'Landlords made merchandise of their poor tenants. [10] Lawrence Stone notes that '[e]verywhere gentlemen were acquiring substantial holdings of land and were building for themselves a country seat. The house served as a home for family and household, as a centre for the administration of a landed estate, as a political power base from which to dominate the locality.'[11] They bought lands not only from their superiors but also found dubious legal reasons to take over small farmers who had only a traditional feudal title 'copyhold' to their land as well as simple leaseholders unable to pay the rising rents of the 1600s.

Judge Thomas Fell (the protector of early Quakers in the north) was the son of a Lancastrian who bought up land and moved into the new gentry. Swarthmore Hall, his home, was also one of those centres of local dominance. His wife Margaret Askew, who later married George Fox, was from an older family that had held on to their land. It was during these years, especially in the midlands and the south and southwest, that what we think of today as the typical English countryside was created. But even in the northern parts, the gentry class was growing and was building houses. W. G. Hoskins describes the period of 1570 to 1770 as the 'golden age' of the English landscape:

> Before that time life had been hard and comfortless . . . after that time we witness the break-up of the village community. . . . But for those two hundred years — seven human generations — rural England flowered. . . . There were now enough people for an agricultural country at least, and there was time to rest and play. The narrow margin between a hard life and death from starvation   . . . had widened with the bringing into cultivation of millions more acres of land. There was no longer the need to go out at the end of a hard day's farming to hack down more trees and clear more ground: it was all done, all that was worth doing: now there was time to contemplate, and to think beyond the mere utilities of life.[12]

These demographic and economic changes had an impact socially. The explosion of gentry wealth —Stone estimates an increase of 400 percent in a hundred years[13] — meant a decline in their reliance on and deference towards the aristocracy. Increasingly, rents were set by economic, not feudal, considerations; local schools, not the local aristocracy, taught the gentry's children; the state used the gentry, not the aristocrats, as local and sometimes national administrators; and the gentry's purchase of church lands gave many of them a novel religious influence on their locality. Thus, in Nayler's village of West Ardsley (also known as Woodkirk), a family of local landowners called Savile bought the parish lands, once owned by the Black Canons (Dominicans), and the right to nominate the local vicar; in Nayler's time, until 1633 the vicar was a well-known Puritan called Anthony Nutter.[14] The danger for the court was that this rising gentry class had religious ideas at variance with tradition. By 1610, the Anglican church could no longer be sure of the loyalty of its own clergy, and contemporaries thought that a state divided by religion could not survive and that a population divided could not be kept at peace — certainly not with the law enforcement powers available to Charles I. The gentry wanted more political influence, which Charles I's personal rule denied them. By 1640, the quarrel between the House of Commons and the king concerning fundamental constitutional issues such as the impeachment of government ministers or consent to taxation had become intractable. As Stone notes,

> There naturally arose radicals on either flank whose solution took the form of massive enhancement of the traditional powers of the royal prerogative, or an equally massive shift to control and direction by Parliament.[15]

Third, there was no popular memory of the dangers of rebellion and social breakdown. The last peasant uprising had taken place in 1549. The poor were very lightly taxed, and a rudimentary national safety net of relief maintained a measure of social tranquillity. The English governing classes felt sufficiently safe and secure to believe that if they pushed at the boundaries of political acceptability, the house would not fall upon their heads. And, because the 1630s and 1640s was a period when the powers on the Continent were fully involved in fighting each other, England faced no real external threat. Armed conflict became, therefore, a real possibility. Stone explains, 'The avoidance of an explosion for over a century lulled the English elites into a false sense of security, and they were therefore more willing to risk armed confrontation in 1642.'[16]

There is one further factor to be mentioned: climate change. Historians of the period often remarked on its wars, revolutions, droughts, and floods. More recently they have remarked on the evidence that some of this was caused by climate change. The famines, droughts, and floods created social and economic dislocation that governments could not manage. Geoffrey Parker gathered the global evidence together in his book *Global Crisis*. He shows that during the seventeenth century, the earth's climate cooled by about two degrees.[17] It is estimated that between one-quarter and one-third of the human population died, either directly from starvation or indirectly from the consequent social breakdown that led to disease and warfare. From the 1620s onwards, the British Isles suffered a series of droughts, floods, heat, and cold that destroyed harvest after harvest. In the later 1620s, starvation became common across the islands. I have collated some of the evidence in Parker's book below:

1621: Torrential rains destroyed the harvest in Scotland and northern England.

1625, Lincolnshire: '[C]ountry is never in such want as it now is. . . . [Thousands] have sold all they have, even to their bed-straw, and cannot get work to earn any money. Dog's flesh is a dainty dish'. Meanwhile, plague killed 40,000 in London.

1627, Isle of Wight: '[T]he coldness of the summer and great fall of rain in August and September' ruined the harvest (the Isle of Wight usually exported its grain). In 1629, the winter was the coldest and wettest known, killing most of the cattle, while at the same time a smallpox epidemic raged.

1629: '[A] wonderful and great flood as had not been seen of forty years'.

1630: Widespread harvest failure.

1632: The coldest summer 'that any then living ever knew'.

1634: Summer drought.

1635: Intensely cold winter; the River Thames froze over.

1636–1637: Two summers of such intense drought 'that the trees and the land are despoiled of verdure, as if it were a most severe winter'. In 1637, drought was particularly bad in Scotland, where the earth was like iron, and there was plague, an acute shortage of coin, and a universal scarcity of food.[18]

Nayler was a teenager during these years, George Fox a child. Starvation, drought, flood, and insecurity are the backdrop to the civil wars and the 1650s.

1646–51: Every harvest fails through bad weather. In 1648, Wildman, a Leveller, wrote, 'The poor did gather together in troops of 10, 20 and 30 in the roades and seized the corne as it was careying to market, and devided it among themselves before the owner's faces, telling them they could not starve.' In London in 1649 flour reached a price not seen for another fifty years, and more died than were born. The magistrates and clergy of Lancashire wrote, 'There is a very great scarcity and dearth of all provisions, especially of all sorts of grain. . . . It would melt any good heart to see the numerous swarms of begging poore, and the many families that pine away at home . . . and often to hear of some found dead in their houses or in high-wayes for want of bread'.[19]

In London in 1652, 1654, 1656, and 1658, deaths exceeded baptisms. These were the years in which Quakerism reached London. The winter of 1657/1658 was so severe that 'crows' feet froze to their prey'. Oliver Cromwell died on 3 September 1658 and was succeeded by his son Richard. Haselrig, a Republican who opposed the continuation of a protectorate, wrote, 'The people care not what Government they live under, so as they may plough and go to market.'[20]

The return of Charles II on 25 May 1660 brought little respite. The harvests of 1661 and 1662 failed, bringing a marked rise in deaths and fall in marriages; in 1665, the plague killed perhaps 25 percent of London's population, and then in 1666 came the great fire.[21]

I have dwelt on climate because it is rarely mentioned in political histories or in early Quaker pamphlets. Fox's *Journal* makes no mention of the failed harvests when he walked the fields of the midlands. He takes no account of the possibility that the people he met and preached to might be homeless, starving, or refugees from a civil war.

There have been numerous attempts to describe the relative importance of these forces. Many of the histories that have been written mirror the concerns of the author's time as much as they illuminate the seventeenth century. Apart from the Marxist interpretation that so entranced me, other explanations given for the wars include the rise or fall of the gentry; a centralising monarchy versus a Puritan gentry determined to rule in their localities; the wars as the last of Europe's religious contests; and royal incompetence leading to the collapse of the British monarchies. The reality is likely a mixture of these. The environmental, demographic, economic, social, political, and religious changes outlined above make war seem inevitable. How could any society take these blows and continue intact?

Nayler's war

The wars caused immense suffering. Parker estimates that about 7 percent of the total population died (approximately 250,000 people). In comparison, the First World War killed 2.9 percent of the British population. War 'invaded the fields, the yards and the kitchens of the people. It took the linen off their beds and the mirrors off their walls'.[22] Several hundred thousand men and women were maimed, and tens of thousands were taken prisoner and sent as near slaves (bond servants) to colonial America. The effects of the wars may be one reason for the demands for social justice and economic fairness found in early Quaker literature. Young men suffer particularly badly in war, and I do wonder whether the prominence of women in early Quakerism is partly explained by the fact that there were so many widows and single women in the population. In England and Wales, at least 150 towns and 50 villages suffered severe damage, and 200 country houses and 30 churches were destroyed; the cost of the property losses is thought to be about £2 million, and the government took about £30 million in taxes and fines from the population.[23]

War was inevitable once Charles I left London in early 1642, having failed to arrest leading Parliamentarians. Nayler's locality was involved early on. In June 1642, Charles called the north-eastern regional elite to a meeting in a field outside York to put forward his case and appeal for support. Nayler's landlord Thomas Savile was there; Nayler may have been there, too. The outcome was inconclusive as Charles was perceived as aloof and unwilling to negotiate. On 22 August Charles raised the Royal Standard at Nottingham, and both sides moved quickly to secure key commercial and strategic cities. The Royalists, commanded by a cousin of George Savile, occupied Leeds and Wakefield. However, the local Parliamentary forces, led by Thomas Fairfax at the age of only thirty, quickly recruited men.

It seems that Nayler was among these recruits for he appears in a contemporary account as a 'dragooner' (a foot soldier on a horse) in Captain Mildmay's troop at the battle of Leeds, January 1643. His name is mentioned in a pamphlet celebrating the parliamentary victory published a little later. Nayler went on to spend eight or nine years in the army. On 20 May 1643, he became a corporal in Captain Copley's cavalry (Copley was another local landlord). Nayler fought at Wakefield (21 May 1643), Adwalton Moor (30 June–1 July; the Parliamentarians lost), and Nantwich (26 January 1644, against the Irish). A year later he was promoted to quartermaster. Quartermasters in these armies had to fight and then, after each battle, find food, beds, and equipment for the men. He fought at Marston Moor (2 July), the bloodiest battle on English soil, and at the three sieges of

Pontefract (December 1644 to June 1646). In 1646, following a reorganisation of the army, he reported directly to General Thomas Lambert. His final battle was probably Dunbar (3 September 1650).[24] He then left the army because of ill health and returned home to ponder his experiences, plough the land, live with his family, and find a new calling.

The army was a transforming experience for Nayler. The parliamentary armies were an agent of social mobility. Many men were taught to read (the Bible) and write while serving as soldiers and became used to taking part in political discussions led by the aptly named regimental agitators (the equivalent of union shop stewards). Nayler was already able to read and write when he joined the army. The army turned him into a man capable of command and of negotiating with his superiors for free billets and food, a man his superiors thought worthy of consultation on political matters as well as on army organisation. As a result, it is probable that he remained loyal to the army and its political objectives for the rest of his life. However, this was Lambert's Army of the North, not the New Model Army led by Cromwell. The politics Nayler learnt in the army might have been less extreme than those learnt by other Quakers in the New Model. Lambert served the Commonwealth right up to 1660 and was the last of the generals to abandon it (see chapter 20). But he was no radical, and he was suspected by Cromwell and Ireton (Cromwell's son-in-law and advisor) of being a moderate, willing to support Charles's return to the throne under certain circumstances.[25] By 1659, as the pendulum of public opinion swung back towards Royalism, Lambert's army stood firmly for the Commonwealth when its junior officers expelled the Rump Parliament on 15 October 1659.[26]

We have no contemporary explanation from Nayler of why he joined up. He may have been ordered or persuaded by his father's landlord (I wonder where his horse came from), but Thomas Savile claimed to have tried to mediate between the parties. Had his landlord been a Royalist (as Savile's cousin

George was), might Nayler have fought on the other side? Many in his circumstances did. He might have joined through necessity; the Royalist hold on Leeds and Wakefield meant trade was stopped 'so that the people are not able to subsist'[27]; only violence would remove the Royalists and bring in food.

Perhaps it was not immediate necessity that led Nayler to arms but rather his economic position in society. Nayler's earliest biographer describes Nayler's father as a 'sowgelder' and a man neither rich nor poor who 'by his own industry . . . might have lived comfortably'.[28] Does this mean he was not comfortable? Perhaps he lost ownership of his farm. The only reference we have to any Nayler farm comes in the name of a field of nine acres, 'Naylor's wife's ing' (a piece of grassland), on a map created seventy-five years after Nayler's death. Nayler described himself as a 'husbandman', meaning a farmer — but not necessarily one who owned land. He was probably poorer materially than many early Quaker leaders, certainly less well-off than Fox or Edward Burrough. Perhaps the Nayler family could be described, in Christopher Hill's words, as one of those northern peasant families on the way to being proletarians who initially allied themselves with the rising gentry only to turn against them and push the revolution leftwards; but 'because its [the peasantry's] instincts and social aims were to some extent pre-capitalist, looking backward to a stable peasant community, it was bound to be defeated.'[29] Another explanation is that Nayler might have been one of those whose religious beliefs were challenged by the changes made by Archbishop William Laud and whose bitterness, 'the sense that the Protestant cause and therefore God was being betrayed', led him to actively seek armed confrontation.[30] By the mid-1630s, Nayler was among the independents in a separated church (that is, one separate from the local Anglican congregation) at High Haigh near his house.

Turning the world upside down?

The army had turned the political world upside down. Lambert consulted his senior officers in December 1648 about whether the king should be tried for his crimes. Nayler, and the other officers, voted for a trial, meaning they supported Charles's eventual execution. Was Nayler, by joining Fox and the early Quaker movement, hoping for even more radical political and social change? I examine Nayler's politics in another section (see chapter 12), but it is worth looking at the political motivations within the Quaker movement he joined in 1652.

One view of Quaker motives is that of Cromwell's security services, as described in this report to Secretary Thurloe, secretary to the Council of State, whose network of spies and informers was extensive:

> The other cause [of tension] is the comeing of the Quakers, who with their franticke doctrines have made such an impression on the minds of the people of this cittie [Bristol] and places adjacent that it is wonderfull to imagin, and hath also made such a rent in all societies and relations, which, with a publique affront offered to ministers and magistrates, hath caused a division . . . and consequently many broyles and affronts; these quakers being countenanced [supported or tolerated] by the offices of the garrison.[31]

The above describes the arrival of John Audland and Thomas Camm, early Quaker ministers, in Bristol in 1655. Morrill argues that we must be careful not to overestimate the scale of actual disorder; Quakers did not burn down churches, assault priests, or threaten the state with violence. Nevertheless, by 1659 Quakers had replaced Roman Catholics as the bogeymen, 'the apotheosis of the ecclesiastical and social upheaval that was anathema to the provincial traditionalists who hearkened back to the old order.'[32] The 'great fear' of 1641 was that Irish Roman Catholics were about to be employed by Charles I to invade England; in 1659, the fear was that Quakers were about to take up arms to enforce the continuation of the protectorate. [33] Part of the 'revolutionary' label attached to Quakers came from the fears others projected onto them. And part of it was because the Quaker social and political messages — explicit or implied — tapped into a traditional plebeian radicalism found across England. This represented a radicalism that an elite of any religious persuasion would find threatening.

Some of the Quakers' outward testimonies, such as hat honour, objections to tithes, and swearing oaths, were ones that previous religious radicals had also adopted.[34] They were common currency amongst those who objected to the Anglican establishment. Both the establishment and the dissenters mistook these outward signs in Quakers for the usual radicalism. Margaret Spufford, writing about the growth of sects in Cambridgeshire in the seventeenth century, finds Quaker ideas were present before Quakers were there.

> The whole of the Baptists' pastoral work of 1652 and early 1653 before the Quaker missionaries even arrived shows them struggling with villagers who claimed a special revelation and freedom from 'ordinances', whether or not this led them into the Ranter error of justifying sin. . . . [One woman told them,] 'I have received greater manifestations, for God dwelleth in me, and I in him. And now I see that to love, to cloth the naked, and to feed the hungry is enough.'[35]

The Baptist records give the impression that spiritual seeking and unrest was extremely widespread at the very lowest parochial level, amongst women and girls and labourers in the villages, and that the Quaker position was reached, or nearly reached, before the arrival of the Quakers.[36]

The ideas against which the Baptists struggled can be found in Nayler's writings and in almost all early Quaker writings. They were probably current in the families and communities the early Quaker writers came from. Socially, Quakers articulated a radicalism that had been common in English premodern communities for the previous two hundred years, and they built on it to develop a comprehensive critique of the society they lived in. Quakers described this as the Lamb's War. James Nayler wrote a pamphlet under that title in 1657 in which he described this war as wrestling not with flesh and blood

> [b]ut with spiritual wickedness exalted in the hearts of men and women, where God alone should be. . . . [Indeed,] their war is against the whole work and device of the god of this world, his laws, customs, fashions, his inventions, and all which are to add to, or take from the work of God, which was in the beginning; this is all enmity against the lamb and his followers, who entered into the covenant which was in the beginning . . . to take the government to himself, that God may wholly rule in the heart of man, and man wholly live in the work of God.[37]

When Nayler wrote *Love to the Lost,* he was writing for those who were 'lost' spiritually, economically, and politically. And his readers responded in equally diverse ways — spiritually by ecstatic personal transformation; socially by new community interactions; and politically by joining a Commonwealth army and signing petitions. Nayler did want to turn the world upside down, but first he wanted to turn the hearts of his audience inside out.

Doug Gwyn sums up the Lamb's War of the early Quakers as follows:

> Fox and early Friends called the sociospiritual conflict joined in such confrontations "the Lamb's war" . . . They viewed themselves as the faithful vanguard gathered with Christ the Lamb on heavenly Mount Zion (Rev. 14), moving into cosmic conflict against the beast (the state-sponsored church), his false prophet (the enfranchised clergy), and Babylon (adulterated religion and demoralized culture).[38]

Quakers hoped the political turmoil in 1653 and 1659 would provide the conditions needed for the kingdom of God to come into being — with their help. In 1659, non-Quakers believed that Quakers were taking up positions of power in the country — as justices of the peace and army officers — prior to a violent coup. Quakers were looking for a new earth as well as a new heaven. They were defeated by political demands beyond their influence (see chapter 20). The Quaker generation after 1660 was able to build a cohesive religious society that has lasted. But, politically, the experience scarred the Religious Society of Friends for life; Quakers never again took up such strong political positions or allied themselves so closely with the use of violence to achieve their ends.

I think Nayler was less involved politically, less interested in political ends, and less hopeful of the political success of the Quaker movement than other early Quakers such as Edward Burrough or George Fox. Between his first arrest and his imprisonment at Appleby (October 1652 to April 1653 and the disaster of Bristol (October 1656), he kept – just – on the right side of the law. He was careful at Orton in November 1652 not to preach in the church or on the town common, both of which would have been illegal.[39] This is in contrast to other Quaker ministers, including Fox, who deliberately interrupted church services or caused a public disturbance to get their message across.

Nayler's itinerant ministry outside London seems to have been more low-key than that of Fox or others. An account of his early travels dating from some time in 1654 covering five or six weeks in the East Riding of Yorkshire does not mention any interruptions of church services.[40] Large, seemingly pre-planned meetings were held on Sundays at Yarm, Aton, Pickering, and Oustwicke and one in an unnamed woods. The one at Aton was a debate between Nayler, local Baptists, and the local vicar; at Pickering, all were silent until the end. Thursdays were also an occasion for large meetings either in houses or the open air. Other meetings were held in private houses. This is similar to the pattern of visits to outlying farming settlements and villages before coming into the local market town, in this case Chesterfield, that Neelon identifies.[41]

Nayler makes no mention of the 'janglings' and turmoil that is found in Fox's journal for the same year. This probably reflects their different personalities and manner of persuasion. Unlike Fox and many others, Nayler did not court imprisonment. He did not wish to become the most famous, the most 'political', and the most controversial of all the early Quakers, but in the end he did become all of those things.

Introduction to *Love to the Lost*

Love to the Lost was written and published in February 1656, during James Nayler's period of preaching in London between June 1655 and July 1656. He had arrived there to replace Francis Howgill and Edward Burrough as the lead preacher. It was hard and busy work. The Quakers owned the Bull and Mouth in Aldgate, formerly an inn, plus other buildings, including a hall that could hold a thousand people. Three meetings a week were held there at which Nayler was expected to preach. In addition, as Nayler wrote to George Fox in April or May 1656:

> [A] fresh seed is appearing, there is a meeting in the Strand on the first days & great tumults sometimes. . . . At Kingston and Theobalds are constant meetings set up & some sent to them every first day, they are hopeful meetings both, especially that at Theobalds.[1]

Later, in a letter dated in June to Margaret Fell, he wrote, 'I see God will do great work yet here, & truly here is a gallant people, & daily large increase'.[2] In retrospect, he wrote in 1659 that he entered London 'with the greatest fear that ever into any place I came, in spirit foreseeing somewhat to befall therein, but not knowing what it might be.'[3]

We know very little about what Nayler said in his preaching. No one took notes that have survived. We assume what he said differed little from what he wrote. Nayler's experience as a quartermaster in the army enabled him to use *politesse* in high places and common, earthy language to command the low. One of his most critical non-Quaker opponents conceded that he was 'a man of exceeding quick wit and sharp apprehension, enriched with that commendable gift of good oratory and a very delightful melody to his utterance'.[4] I think that in *Love to the Lost* we have the arguments and some of the language he might have used at the Bull and Mouth, calming the crowd saying again and again the same things, destroying Ranting hecklers with a well-timed jibe and Puritan ministers with an unrivalled command of biblical texts and logical argument. Rebecca Travers, then a Baptist, went to hear him dispute with three Baptist ministers and reports (in the third person) that

> they were so far from getting the victory that she could feel his words smote them, that one or two of them confessed they were sick and could hold it no longer, and the third beset him with such confidence . . . but shamed himself in bringing Scriptures that turned against him and she was confounded and ashamed that a Quaker should exceed the learned Baptists.[5]

Nayler could win over, control, and sway a London audience in a way that not even Fox could manage. In private meetings, Nayler was soft-spoken; he used an urbane wit to counter the arguments of learned men and women. In public, he carried a charism and public presence that led observers to call him 'the chief Quaker'.

Love to the Lost was not part of a 'pamphlet war', so it was not addressed to specific groups of people, arguments, or circumstances, although it did attract a response. Because of this, there is a greater likelihood that it reflects Nayler's unforced thinking. Carole Spencer describes it as

> Nayler's most mature and comprehensible under-standing of the Quaker faith as incarnational holiness. . . . [I]t covered all of the main themes in early Quaker theology and provided a foundational text for Nayler's hermeneutic, Christology, and his incarnational eschatology. . . . Nayler described incarnational holiness as a process of transformation using the metaphors of word and seed and numerous other biblical phrases . . .

which builds to a mounting crescendo of resurrection and everlasting rest, in essence divinization.[6]

Spencer argues that Nayler's writings show a debt to the German philosopher Jacob Boehme, whose works were being published by Nayler's publisher, Giles Calvert, throughout the 1650s. 'That Nayler with his acute theological and literate mind would not have sampled this flood of new mystical literature coming from his own publisher seems unlikely.'[7] In addition, Nayler's close friend at the end of his life, Richard Rich, is known to have owned copies of Boehm's works which he lent out. I do not have the expertise to identify whether Boehm influenced *Love to the Lost*, which may have been written before Nayler had had time to absorb Boehm's thought.

My interest is in exploring the extent to which the Religious Society of Friends' later discipline(s) reflect Nayler's thinking and the extent to which the Society has moved away from, or beyond, his writings. Published on 9 February 1656, Nayler's pamphlet is in twenty-five separate sections, starting with 'The Fall of Man' and ending with the 'Resurrection', although the last was only added on the second printing, which is thought to have appeared shortly afterwards. The sections do not refer to each other; each can be read as a stand-alone statement. Because of this, there is some repetition, and I have not tackled all twenty-five sections in this book. These may be the topics he chose to preach on, or the topics that held the most interest for him, or the ones on which Quakers differed the most from other sects or denominations. He did not address certain topics: meetings for worship for business (they had not yet been formalised); the testimonies; the roles of women; the use of silence; and the roles of elders, ministers, or overseers. To contemporary readers, it may appear an incomplete account of Quakerism. This is the Quaker ship before the barnacles, fresh from the shipwright's bench.

The Quaker movement used pamphlets extensively. By 1656, 291 tracts had been published, half of which had been written by just eight men. Many tracts or pamphlets were compilations; Katie Peters has calculated that Nayler's writings can be found in 20 percent of the total.[8] This flood of tracts had two purposes: first to spread the word and reply to opponents and second to maintain the public profile of the ministers and maintain discipline within the meetings they set up. The tracts would be read to the congregations they left behind. The written word came from God in the just the same way as the spoken word did. Edward Burrough wrote in 1654:

> [F]or who Speaks, Writes, or Declares, from the light of God . . . Speaks, Writes, and Declares not as from man . . . but as from God, whose light is spiritual . . . and from this light did the Prophets and Ministers of God . . . Speak, Write, and Declare . . . and from this light . . . did all the holy men of God Write, and Declare.[9]

We should envisage chapters of *Love to the Lost* being read out to meetings in London and elsewhere. Because these words came from God, they were treated in a way similar to Scripture. Quaker opponents complained that Quaker ministers preferred preaching from a passage in a Quaker tract to using verses from the Bible.

The language is unfamiliar to us; some words have different meanings today, and the punctuation and even sentence structure can be strange to our eyes and ears. Nayler's contemporaries complained about the Quaker writing style. Leo Damrosch explains the style as a deliberate attempt

> to interweave scriptural terms and metaphors in order to overwhelm rational resistance by endless variations on a few key words. The inward light could not be demonstrated or even described; it could only be witnessed. The Book of Revelation provided an obvious model. . . . Quaker incantatory rhythms reflected oral practice and, even if intended to persuade readers, did

not originate in a written context. Richard Bauman persuasively describes the "collaborative expectancy" that would have been aroused in an audience by rhythmic energy and repetitive formal patterns, generating "a sense of immediate co-participation in the utterance that would make the listener feel that the minister's words were echoed within himself".[10]

The Quaker experience of God and Light cannot be completely described in a logical pattern of words, just as music or a picture cannot be experienced solely in words. This does not mean that nothing can be said about God — obviously something can, and Quakers do say things. Early Quakers were using word patterns and repetition to create another dimension of experience. Their publications were the most oral and unlearned (in the sense of not using university-taught patterns of discourse) of the period. Sometimes I have struggled with the language. It is the speech of the mid-seventeenth century. The sentence construction and punctuation occasionally need unravelling, and the theological concepts are not familiar to me. But, I have grown to appreciate the thought and passion of James Nayler.

Finally, *Love to the Lost* was written before Nayler and other Quaker preachers in London had experienced the interruptions and accusations of Martha Simmonds and other Quaker women. These interruptions led initially to an attempted 'eldering' of Simmonds and the others and then, when Nayler disavowed that eldering, to a division between him and other Quaker ministers in London that led to Nayler's own breakdown and silence. *Love to the Lost* comes to us without that shadow and arguably without the deeper spirituality that he found after his punishment. This is the fresh new faith with which Nayler travelled England.

Nayler begins the pamphlet as follows:

> The things following which I have declared of are not things of man, nor by man did I receive them, but by

the revelation of Jesus Christ, which is contrary to the wisdom and will of man. (LL 3:48)*

This parallels Paul's words in the opening of Galatians: '*The gospel that was proclaimed by me is not of human origin; for I did not receive it from a human source, nor was I taught it, but I received it through a revelation of Christ Jesus*' (Galatians 1:11–12 NRSV). Nayler goes on to say that only those with a measure of the Spirit will savor these things. Nayler says he has been judged and discerned by the unchanging light of Christ which is the same in man and woman and is a light that will gather all together into one word of faith,

> to believe and speak the same things in the godly conversation, which leads to the end of all rents, schisms, heresies and errors, sects and divisions, into that one name to be baptized where the fulness of God is, blessed forever. (LL 3:48)

Nayler claims that what he says in *Love to the Lost* is the true word of God. Those to whom some things appear dark should not resist them but wait for further understanding. Nayler takes his authority from God; those who disagree with him are simply wrong; and if they persist in disagreeing, then in the evil day they will be made to cry out: 'How have I hated instruction, and resisted the day of healing!' (LL 3:48, a reference to Proverbs 5:12).

I quote extensively in the following chapters from selected sections of *Love to the Lost*, and my chapter titles that are within quotation marks match Nayler's. I then discuss how his theology is reflected in later Quaker disciplines, also referencing works by individual Quakers. In some cases, the distance travelled between Nayler and subsequent Quakers is considerable. But in others, we remain as brothers and

---

* The source of this quote is Nayler's *Love to the Lost*, which is abbreviated throughout this book as LL. See the bibliography for a list of other abbreviations used in parenthetical citations.

sisters. This exploration has helped me understand in greater depth where the British Quaker tradition comes from. I hope it also helps my readers.

1. 'Concerning the Fall of Man'

Nayler describes the fall as a psychological turning away from God. Once that step is taken, humanity is compelled to search for the way back into unity with God. These are Nayler's opening words to the section he titled 'Concerning the Fall of Man':

> In the beginning God made all things good, so did he man, whom then he made in his own image, and placed in him his own wisdom and power, whereby he was completely furnished with dominion, power and authority over the works of God's hands, knowing the nature and use of each creature, by what God had placed in him of himself. (LL 3:50)

This begins as a short paraphrase of Genesis chapter 1 — the first version of the creation myth. However, Nayler adds his own gloss to the gift of dominion, for Genesis does not say that humans knew how to use the creatures and plants. The words 'and placed in him his own wisdom and power' and 'by what God had placed in him of himself' can be extrapolated from *'let us make man in our image, after our likeness'* (Genesis 1:26 KJV) but are not biblical. Nayler then continues with the second version of the creation myth, chapter 2 of Genesis, which introduces the two trees and explains humanity's 'fall'.

> God also made the tree of life in the midst of the garden, and the tree of knowledge of good and evil, and both of these was good in their place, but the tree of knowledge not good for food; therefore did he that made it, forewarn of it, as the thing wherein death was placed, as in the other tree was life. And herein was the blessing and the curse placed, the life and the death, the obedience and the disobedience, election and

reprobation; and these were good for man in their place, while man stood in his place, guided by that which placed him in the good, and forewarned him of the knowledge, and gave him power against it, while he stood in that will which had set all these things in their place, which will was free for God, and from sin, and the will of God and the will of man was one, and at unity with all the creation. (LL 3:50)

Nayler does not paraphrase the second myth. Instead, he develops, using its imagery, his own psychological explanation. He sets a stage, a tableau of perfection. Humans and God have a single will and are in unity with all. There is no searching, no drama, no action, no time, no mention of how the human lives, whether mortal or immortal. Humankind has dominion over all creation, but there is no mention of how that is to be used. Humans, presumably because they were created by God and so are necessarily weaker than God, have been given the power to withstand the temptation of the tree of knowledge as long as they remain in their rightful place. In the wings of the tableau is a figure of division waiting for humankind to seek something other than unity with God. Nayler does not say whether God also made the devil, this figure of division; perhaps the figure or the division is the divide between the bit of God in humans and the created but ungodly human?

But when man looked out into the other, where he [the devil?] ruled who abides not in the truth, wherein the disobedience was received in, of that which was contrary to the will of God to feed upon, then he joined to that which was contrary, wherein the weakness was, and the death, darkness and blindness as to the things of God. (LL 3:50)

There is no mention of the serpent, and the woman is not blamed for the fall, neither by Nayler nor God, though that might be because Nayler does not mention the woman at all! The wickedness is in the tree of knowledge. For Nayler, knowledge of outer things led humans astray by giving them subtlety,

> that which freely he had received of God, but when he grew subtle within himself, and wise to do evil, he lost the will that was free to wait upon in his wisdom and counsel, . . . [and so] he fell, and into the self-inventions which he had chosen in the contrary will, and so entering into the forbidden things became accursed, lost the measure of God, his honor and likeness in things of God. (LL 3:50–51)

In the early seventeenth century, the word 'subtle', in addition to its present meaning of delicate or precise, could mean 'working secretly, taking effect imperceptibly, insidious' (*Shorter Oxford English Dictionary*). Nayler is talking about the gradual corruption or changing of the mind or reason. It is not an outright condemnation of all knowledge but of knowledge we are scarcely aware we know – worldly habits. It seems to be outwardness that leads to the fall. In her commentary on creation stories, Anne Thomas says that George Fox believed there were two ways of knowing, outward and inward.[1] He wrote of eating the forbidden fruit: 'So man did eat: the eye out, the ear out, at last the mouth out too.' Thomas writes that Fox believed the inward Spirit of Christ gave true knowledge and that after the fall the hearing and obeying relationship between humans and God was broken and now 'all stand naked and bare before the living Lord'. The making of clothes from fig leaves was the origin of pride, haughtiness, high-mindedness, and the abominable customs, fashions, and lusts of the world. Fox writes in a letter of 1684:

> So the transgression of the command of God came, when the ear went out after the Serpent, and the eye went after the fruit of the tree, which God forbid them to eat of. So here they came to see their outward shame and nakedness . . . and therefore they went to cover the outward shame.[2]

28

1. 'Concerning the Fall of Man'

The power to resist the attractions of the outward world are within us. If we are distracted by the things of the world and neglect that power, leaving it unnourished, the devil will overcome our minds and souls. Nayler uses an image here of a seed, a God-shaped seed containing the power which God has left. Failure to nourish that seed leads to it drying up and the devil taking over its space— rather like a malign hermit crab.

> [The man] so became led by another seed, wherein God had placed emptiness of himself, which he raised up for dishonor. And here it is that man hath lost his dominion over the devil, by letting him in . . . which now being got in, with a show of God and godliness, into the temple of God the principle part in man, and man having joined with him, now is become his captive, in whom he makes havoc, beguiling him of the life of simplicity and godliness, and perverting his ways, as to the end for which man was made. (LL 3:51)

Note how the devil acts with subtlety, pretending holiness. Nayler gives no explanation as to why humans looked outward and allowed the devil into their heart, specifically into the place in their heart where God had resided and which God had left, leaving an empty God-shaped space. Humans are now driven by another seed wherein God 'placed emptiness of himself' which replaces the seed of wisdom and authority 'and all happiness present and eternal'. The devil got in 'by a show of God and godliness' (LL 3:51). One of Nayler's themes is that the devil blinds Christians to God by pretending to be God, a more congenial and satisfactory God for them than the true one.

Is the search for God purely psychological? Is it a psychological necessity for some and for others of no interest? Can we be satisfied by any power that appears to be God? In later sections, Nayler warns that the devil can appear as God. Something within us drives the search, but what if there is no God and no devil misdirecting the search? No

29

amount of reading Nayler will answer that question, for Nayler does not doubt the existence of God. He also believes most men and women are compelled to search but have failed and are lost.

The section continues with a description of humankind's mental state after the fall. The creature — for now we are brutes — becomes subject to all the torments of the devil, he being the ruler within us. We become a servant to lust and 'self-ended things'; the devil captures our hearts with pride, covetousness, gluttony, excess in diet, foolery in clothing, vain toys, and foolish trifles and leads us away from the pure wisdom of our God until,

> [b]eing fallen under the earthly principle he [man] is covered with thick darkness, so that the mind of God he knows not, nor his own woeful state he sees not, the god of this world having blinded the eye which should show him his misery, and the ear being stopped which should hear the voice of the soul's shepherd . . . and whatsoever is spoken to man in this state . . . the serpent being above upon the earth, catcheth the thing into the imaginations, and the creature being led to consult with him there in the flesh, he beguiles the creature of the simplicity, and so keeps the creature in self, that he regards not the seed of God . . . ; he will lead his from one thing to another in things without, but never to see from whence he is fallen. (LL 3:51–52)

The serpent makes an appearance now, perhaps as a synonym for the devil. Humans are so utterly in thrall to the world that we consult the serpent about the occasional message we might receive from God through ministry. And the serpent sends us off on another chase or distraction. This happens constantly to me in meeting for worship. The imagination takes up the message and the meaning is lost because I look out in the vanity of giving a 'message' — as man first looked out at the other. Nayler reiterates the promise that an escape from this darkness is near at hand:

1. 'Concerning the Fall of Man'

As many as repents of their following this way of self-wisdom and knowledge, and come to stand still, to such he shows his salvation, and his kingdom near at hand. . . . And as the mind is stayed to wait for the kingdom of God in Spirit, the god of the world comes to be denied and resisted. (LL 3:52)

To resist the devil, we must look back to the Eden from which man was turned out.

[T]o that from which you are fallen must you look, and return into that from which you are gone out, that by the light that's in the midst of all this darkness and death you may be led in again by the blood of the cross, through the fire and sword, into the garden of God where he plants and feeds. (LL 3:53)

We must look back to the God-shaped seed within and travel back to Eden, braving the cherubim and flaming sword placed at the eastern entrance by God to keep us out (Genesis 3:24). The image of the garden is elaborated. It becomes a place of activity where God plants and feeds, and it is the refuge at the centre of the darkness. Nayler does not make it easy to reach. We have to follow the blood of the cross and go through the fire and the sword. George Fox describes it thus in his journal, probably in the year 1648:

Now was I come up in spirit through the flaming sword into the paradise of God. All things were new, and all the creation gave another smell unto me than before, beyond what words can utter. (CFP 1959, para. 9; QFP 26.03)

The 1959 *Christian Faith and Practice* does not include Fox's next sentence:

I knew nothing but pureness, and innocency, and righteousness, being renewed up into the image of God by Christ Jesus, so that I say I was come up into the state of Adam which he was in before he fell.'[3]

The rational and enlightened Quakers of 1959 would find that too close for comfort to perfectionism. To return to Nayler:

> So that which leads out into the knowledge is the fall; but that which leads into the simplicity of life, which is manifest in the Spirit, and not in the knowledge of the first man, that leads to the resurrection of life; for it is the hidden wisdom that God ordained before the world unto glory; so to the hidden man of the heart must you look to find it, which is not corruptible. (LL 3:53)

Knowledge led to the fall, so we must look back to how we were before the fall to find again a simplicity of life in the Spirit. The first man's knowledge, Adam's knowledge, has failed us. Instead, we must look into the hidden wisdom placed in us before we knew the world. 'The hidden man of the heart', a phrase a few early Quakers used for Jesus Christ, will show us the way.

The role of the Spirit within has always been important for Quakers, even when they have adopted a more orthodox view of Christian salvation. The London Yearly Meeting's epistle at the head of the 1834 revision of the book of discipline reads:

> But blessed be God, he has not only provided the means of reconciliation unto himself, through the sacrifice of Christ; he hath also, through the same compassionate Saviour, granted unto us the gift of the Holy Spirit. By this the patriarchs, and the holy men of old who lived under the law, walked acceptably before God. . . . To be guided by his Spirit is the practical application of the Christian religion. It is the light of Christ which enlightens the darkness of the heart of man; and by following this light, we are enabled to enjoy and maintain communion with him. The children of God are led by the Spirit of God: and this is the appointed means of bring us into that state of 'holiness, without which no man shall see the Lord'. (BoD 1834, pp. xiv–xv)

1. 'Concerning the Fall of Man'

The holy men of old appear to have been Christians before Christ, which is a typical Quaker understanding. The 1883 book of discipline is different in its emphasis:

> As a Christian Church we accept the immediate operations of the Spirit of God upon the heart, in their inseparable connection with our risen and exalted Saviour. We disavow all professed spirituality that is divorced from faith in Jesus Christ of Nazareth, crucified for us without the gates of Jerusalem. . . . To be guided by his Spirit is the practical application of the Christian religion. (BoD 1883, p. 20)

This passage can be read as if it were all written on the same date. In fact (as its heading says), it comes from three yearly meeting epistles: 1868, 1861, and 1830. By ignoring the historical context of each statement, the Yearly Meeting of 1883 produced a statement that appears timeless, as if this was what Quakers had always believed and would continue to believe. By the time of the 1922 revision, the connection between the Holy Spirit and Jesus was more tenuous. In its section on doctrine, the 1922 book contains ideas similar to Nayler's:

> Man is made to be the Temple of the Divine presence; but how is the building marred and broken; how often has it been the haunt not of the pure spirit of love but of base thoughts of pride, of lust, of selfishness. Yet let us be thankful that, though the sanctuary has been defiled, though it may be buried beneath earthen masses which the years have only made greater, in the depths of every human heart there is a temple still. . . . This life within our lives, which turns toward God, has been spoken of as the Seed. The Seed was an image which Jesus loved to use; and it carries within it the thought of silent growth, and of the mysterious birth of the living plant from within the dead husk of the corn. We must pass through this re-birth that we may enter into the heritage of the Kingdom; and we need not only the

birth but the growth, if the fruit is to ripen. (Britain Yearly Meeting's epistle of 1907, as quoted in CLFT 1922, p. 68)

A recent introduction to Quakerism by Rex Ambler adopts the psychological understanding of the Inner Light for the birth of a new self.

> What is needed therefore is that people find the truth again, accept it, and live their lives on the basis of it. This may seem a tall order, but we have to remember that 'the truth' as the Quakers understand it and pursue it is the reality of our own life, which we are already in some sense aware of, but have denied and repelled from our consciousness. What we have to do – and this is the Quaker advice – is stop this activity of telling stories about ourselves, stop defending ourselves and making up attractive ideas about ourselves and sit still with the silence – and with the reality of our life as we gradually become aware of it. This will be our first and formative experience of 'the truth.'[4]

I have three more points to make about Nayler's account of the fall. First, Nayler does not mention the concept of original sin. He does not say we are born sinful; rather, we are born with an opportunity to reconnect with God, expel the devil that has taken up residence in the seed left by God, and bring back God/Christ into the seed so that it germinates within us. This account applies universally; salvation is not limited to those born after Jesus was crucified, as later Quakers occasionally implied. Nayler's account of salvation depends on the hidden wisdom placed in the human heart by God when God made Adam and breathed spirit into him. Consequently, this salvation is available to those of any faith.

Second, a logical consequence of the fall as described by Nayler is that humanity should not exercise dominion over creation until they are once more in connection with God.

When we are not in unity with God and creation, we cannot know how to use creation. Nayler does not make this point, but it is one that, if the psychological explanation of the fall is adopted, helps to explain why humanity continues to destroy the earth. We no longer know how to use it.

Third, note the absence of the woman and the apple. Quakers did not blame the woman for humanity's fall. When Fox established women's meetings, it was

> [s]o that all the faithful men and women may in the Lord's Power be stirred up in their inheritances of the same Gospel, to labor in it, as help-meets in the Restoration as Man and Woman was before the Fall in the Garden of God.[5]

Men and women are equal in the new life and the new world that the risen Christ within us can build, although this has not always been the case in the Quakers' earthly world.

Finally, we see in early Friends a determination to refute the argument that we are all sinful, cannot be saved in this life, and must hope for forgiveness in the next. As time passed, however, this hopeful view declined. Thomas considers that although Fox (and Nayler) embraced 2 Corinthians 5:17 — *So if anyone is in the Christ there is a new creation: everything old has passed away* (NRSV) — Friends generally have not been immune to Calvinism. Despite this experience of Paul and of early Friends, we have inherited the other Pauline scenario of 'the Fall.'[6]

Why does humanity turn away from God and then some of us spend so much effort trying to remake the connection? We all have a range of 'intelligences', but we best learn using one or two of them, for example, by using verbal, visual, or kinaesthetic intelligence. I think there is in all humans a spiritual intelligence, and for some their spiritual intelligence is an important explanatory tool for understanding how the world works. *Christian Faith and Practice* contains a passage which gives some support to this idea:

> [I]t has therefore frequently been suggested that religion is a fantasy to satisfy subconscious cravings. Such a view assumes that religion is an unreal answer to a hunger for which the real satisfaction would be on the natural and material level. There is however no proof that this is true. Indeed the hunger may be capable of full satisfaction only on the spiritual level, material and natural answers being outward signs of a spiritual reality which surpasses them as the substance surpasses the shadow. . . . Belief in God is always an act of faith, but faith on the lines of the above argument is not contrary to reason, only to materialism. (CFP 1959, para. 143, written for the revision)

Nayler's account of the fall is an explanation of how we lost our spiritual intelligence and how we might find it again.

2. 'Concerning Light and Life'

> God is the life of every creature, though few there be
> that know it, for the darkness sees him not nor his life,
> though the children of darkness have got words in
> scripture (which were given forth from the light) to talk
> of; yet such know not God present. (LL 3:53–54)

God has created every creature, and therefore God is their
life. It seems Nayler is thinking only of humans here, not of
all of life on earth or in the universe, because it is humans
who have fallen and who know not God as they are in the
darkness. They do not know they are in darkness, for they
believe Scripture is the true Light. They read Scripture but
cannot understand it for God is not present in them. The
Light, essential to that understanding, comes next. As Nayler
writes,

> God said, "Let there be light," and it was so. And this
> light God saw that it was good. That is that which was
> in the beginning with God, the Word, by which all
> things were made and seen and without this was
> nothing made that was made, not anything seen to be
> good; and darkness was over the face of all the waters,
> till the light, which from the word came, who is the life,
> which life is the light of men. So none can see the life
> but with the light, which from the life comes, which to
> the life leads all that come. So this that was in the
> beginning is given to keep in order all creation. That is
> good, but the darkness comprehends it not, though it
> shine in it; so all that abide in the darkness are
> destroyed, not discerning the life, to order and govern
> the creation in the light. (LL 3:54)

Nayler here is mixing Genesis 1:3, *'Let there be light'*, God's
first command on the first day, with the opening of John's
gospel, *'In the beginning was the Word, and the Word was*

with God, and the Word was God' (John 1:1–2 NRSV). God spoke (using words) and created Light; it is the Light that enables us to see our darkness — it was divided from the darkness by God — and seeing our darkness enables us to find God as the Light draws us back to God. Those that live in darkness are not aware of the Word or the Light. They are destroyed because they cannot see the Light and so cannot order and govern the creation, and the creation, lacking order, destroys them. Nayler then writes about how bad the darkness is, with the creature being led into sects, opinions, and errors through using sensual wisdom, which takes the creature further into death and darkness.

> And here is the sole ground and cause why we have so many sorts of forms and opinions and ways to worship, but none that doth good, nor lives in what they say, because all have lost the life of God, which is only able to forth the righteousness of God. And self having got the form into the imagination above the life cannot receive the life that lies under. . . . And no other way there is appointed of the Father, to come out of this condition, but Christ Jesus, the light and life of men, who is the light that is in the world, though the world know him not. (LL 3:55)

> [B]ut when the light is minded, the creature comes to see. (LL 3:55)

There follows a description of the various stages a creature goes through from living in the darkness to living in the light, which can be summarised as follows:

1. The creature sees that death reigns and the self is polluted and defiled;

2. then the creature sees what has caused this bondage and hardness of heart;

3. then comes fear of God because the creature has lived out of the life of God;

4. then comes a troubled heart, and by waiting in the light in fear the cause of that trouble is seen;

5. wisdom from above is given to the creature to depart from the iniquity;

6. and there is a coming nearer to God.

Next comes a description of God's creation and the inner spiritual life as an abandoned vineyard covered with briars, sturdy oaks, and tall cedars, overgrown with weeds, thistles, and nettles: 'God walks not there because of the great abomination; and that is the cause of all your woe, even his absence' (LL 3:56).

Our hearts are envisaged as untamed nature, something that Nayler, a farmer, probably did not value as much as we (living on the other side of the romantic revolution) do. At the point of our recognition of the untamed and disastrous state of our spiritual health, Nayler moves from 'creature' to 'you'. More steps follow:

7. Then you will see it is only your own wills and ways that have separated you from the Holy One;

8. then you will remember all those times when the Spirit spoke to you and was ignored;

9. then you will acknowledge that the reasons you have lived so long in the fall are self-will and worldly pleasures;

10. then, when those are gone, you will see what it is that oppresses the just and hates that which God hates:

11. then you will see that that which destroys life is the Pharisee and hypocrite who makes a profession above the life but not in the life;

12. for, finally, you will know that those who are strangers to the Spirit cannot be of true judgment concerning the works of God.

Nayler's paragraph contains 12 steps. The experience may not happen in that precise order and some steps may be missed. We should note that step 5 requires help from above, that help has probably been repeatedly offered and rejected (step 7), and that it is only when fear and disquiet have prepared the heart for its reception that the call will be answered. Steps 10 and 11 require an element of social and political awareness. Unless we understand how worldly evil (with the devil running it) affects our own spiritual health, we cannot progress further. Nayler singles out professors and priests. In Nayler's time, one of the meanings of 'to profess' was 'to lay claim to a quality or feeling or knowledge and especially falsely or insincerely' (*Shorter Oxford English Dictionary*), and 'professors' were those who made such insincere claims. But also note that in the extract from his trial in Appleby on a following page, Nayler uses 'profess' entirely sincerely. To those who might lead us astray, we today could add advertisers and social media influencers.

How similar to Nayler's own search is this account? David Neelon's biography suggests the young Nayler was exposed early in life to principles of dissent from the state church because the local vicar at Woodkirk (also known as West Ardsley) was the Puritan and Presbyterian Andrew Nutter.[1] In the army, Nayler would have been exposed to Puritan preaching and books, and it is likely his spiritual search continued from there. He left the army in January 1651 in bad health after the winter campaign in Scotland. Soon after, he heard George Fox preach at Stanley, a village near Wakefield, and then again in March or May 1651. According to Fox himself, Nayler was 'convinced' at this time, along with William and Mary Dewsbury.

'Convincement' means, broadly, that a person becomes convinced of the truth of the Quaker message. It also contains overtones of the word 'conviction'. The person is convicted of their sinfulness or darkness and so seeks a new life. Early Quakers had no membership procedures – the disadvantages of being thought a Quaker by one's neighbours was enough to prove one's sincerity. Nayler, when convinced, would not have considered that he was joining an organised group — more that he was being led by God into certain behaviour and actions.

There is no specific account from Nayler of his own spiritual journey unless one assumes that everything he wrote is based on personal experience. In 1654, he wrote a letter, *'To them of the independent society'*, explaining why he had left the separated church at Woodkirk of which he had been a member before the civil wars. In fact, they had by that time excommunicated him for his alleged adultery. The first nine reasons are:

1. They have signed a joint covenant and are not gathered into 'unity of faith by one spirit' (an early Quaker argument against written creeds);
2. they worship in a church building;
3. they have 'a man to divine to you, always from a text of another man's words';
4. they baptise infants;
5. they sing the psalms 'in rhymes and meter, in the invention, and not in the spirit';
6. they use 'you' and not 'thou';
7. they persecute the innocent;
8. they enjoy hunting, coursing, shuffleboard, wanton jestings etc but those who know Christ 'know him to be a man of sorrows and acquainted with grief' and that is the proper demeanour for Christians; and
9. finally, they 'limit the holy one no more to speak to his people but by the letter'.[2]

All these outward behaviours were, for Nayler, an indication that the members of Woodkirk's independent church were still adhering to traditional social hierarchy by calling men masters and giving the elite the best places in assemblies, for Christ did not treat people differently according to their social status.

And here you are found out of Christ and his way, and according to your work you are judged, and not after your words; and by the light are you proved who say you are Christians and are not, but are such an assembly as the envious Jews were who acted these things against Christians. And though you may say that God is your Father, as they did, yet your works prove you to be of another generation.[3]

By comparing members of the independent churches to 'envious Jews' of another generation (or ancestry), Nayler, by implication, is comparing Quakers to the early Christians who split from synagogues and followed the teaching of the apostles. This is a self-description fundamental to early Quakers: Christ has come again to teach his people, and Quakers are the early Christians reborn.

Nayler's account of hearing the voice of God while ploughing and then leaving home to start a career as an itinerant Quaker minister is well known. It can be found in both the 1959 *Christian Faith and Practice* (para. 22) and the 2013 *Quaker faith and practice* (19.09). It was a sudden and probably unexpected culmination of years of searching. Here is how Nayler described it in 1652 to the magistrates at Appleby:

Colonel Briggs: What was the cause of thou coming into these parts?

James: If I may have liberty, I shall declare it. I was at the plough, meditating on the things of God, and suddenly I heard a voice saying to me, 'Get thee out from thy kindred, and from thy father's house' [Genesis 12:1]. And I had a promise given with it, whereupon I did exceedingly rejoice that I had heard the voice of God which I had professed from a child, but had never known him.

Colonel Briggs: Didst thou hear that voice?

James: Yea, I did hear it; and when I came home I gave up my estate, cast out my money; but not being obedient in going forth, the wrath of God was upon me, so that I was made a wonder to all, and none thought I would have lived. But after I was made willing, I began to make some preparations, as apparel and other necessaries, not knowing whither I should go. But shortly afterwards, going a gate-ward with a friend from my own house, having on an old suit, without any money, having neither taken leave of wife or children, not thinking then of any journey, I was commanded to go into the west, not knowing whither I should go, nor what I was to do there. But when I had been there a little while, I had given me what I was to declare. And ever since then I have remained not knowing today what I was to do tomorrow.

Colonel Briggs: What was the promise thou hadst given?

James: That God would be with me: which promise I find made good every day.[4]

This account conflates Nayler's years of searching and professing without hearing into one phrase: 'I was at the plough meditating on the things of God'. After hearing the voice of God, he starts on practical preparations (he told the magistrates he handed his estate over to his wife) but then hesitates, falls ill, recovers, and begins to pack a bag. Still no sign of leaving. And then he departs, without his bag or taking leave. Perhaps he was afraid to go back into the house in case the hesitations began again. This is not a confident prophet but a man struggling to do the will of God in the midst of providing for his family.

Similar experiences are recorded in London Yearly Meeting's books of discipline.

In the beginning of the year 1655, I was at the plough in the east parts of Yorkshire in Old England, near the place where my outward being was; and, as I walked after the plough, I was filled with the love and presence of the living God. (Marmaduke Stevenson, as quoted in CLFT 1922, p. 23)

This experience led Stevenson to his death on 27 October 1659 as one of the 'Boston martyrs'. Here is one that is not in a book of discipline. It comes from Martha Simmonds, who is regarded by some as the instigator of James Nayler's entry into Bristol. She wrote in 1655:

> And now in the tenderness of my heart longing for your soules good am I made open to you, having had a habitation in the City of London sometimes; for seven years together I wandered up and down the street enquiring of those that had the Image of honestie in their countenance, where I might finde an honest Minister, for I saw my soul in death, and that I was in the first nature, and wandering from one Idolls temple to another, and from one private meeting to another, I heard sound of words amongst them but no substance I could finde, and the more I sought after them the more trouble came on me, and finding none sensible of my condition I kept it in, and kept all close within me; and about the end of seven years hunting, and finding no rest, the Lord opening a little glimmerings light to me, and quieted my spirit; and then for about seven years more he kept me still from running after men, and all this time I durst not meddle with any thing of God, nor scarce take his name in my mouth, because I knew him not, it living wilde and wonton not knowing a cross to my will I spent this time; it something I found breathing in me groaning for deliverance, crying out, oh when shall I see the day of thy appearance; about the end of the last seven years the Lord opened my eyes to see a measure of himself in me, and which when I saw I waited diligently in it, and being faithful to it I found this Light more and more increase, which brought me into a day of trouble, and through it, and through a warfare and to the end of it, and now hath given me a resting place with him; and *this is my beloved and this*

is my friend O daughters of Jerusalem: And now all that have a desire to come this way must lay down your Crowns at the feet of Jesus, for now a profession of words will no longer cover, for the Lord is come to look for fruit, all types and shaddowes is flying away; and he that will come in may inherit substance and he that will not shall be left naked.[5]

This single sentence includes several of Nayler's steps. Simmonds sees her soul in death (1) and searches for a minister to help her but cannot find an honest one. The more she seeks, the more she is troubled (3), and then she has little glimmerings of light from above (4) but does nothing, although she sees that she is not allowing the Light to cross her own self-will (7). Then she realises there is a measure of God within her, and this grows and increases (5), and she finds a resting place in God. She then understands that none can travel her way without giving up their own will and that a profession of words is not sufficient (12). It is likely this journey did not literally take fourteen years; the two periods of seven years have some biblical reference. However, the books of discipline do suggest that it does take time before Friends are confident they have arrived.

John Wilhelm Rowntree's account of his spiritual journey is quoted from at length in *Christian Life, Faith and Thought* (1922). Rowntree (1868–1905) was a leading 'liberal' Friend and member of the Rowntree chocolate family. First, he describes himself as an average 'Christian' who reads the Bible, attends church, and leaves understanding of the Trinity or atonement to the clergy; Christ is his saviour, which means 'he will leave me alone in this world and save me in the next'. But then comes some external disaster, an illness, a business failure, 'the touch of satiety that is the scourge of the worldling', and 'suddenly I realise that my Christ was a lay figure. I made him and draped Him myself. I realise that at the heart of what I called my religion was but selfishness' (CLFT 1922, p. 55).

However, this dissatisfaction is not enough. Not even mortifications, penances, self-sacrifice, obeying conscience, and a sincere heart are quite enough; Rowntree seeks not only a clear conscience but Christ.

> There comes a time when the higher life of which I am always aware, and which I have tried to follow, becomes so merged in my thought of Christ and my devotion to Him, that I can hardly distinguish the two in my mind. There comes a time when suddenly I am on my knees, my whole soul flooded with light and love, tears in my heart and eyes, and unspeakable peace unfolding me. The pierced hands have reached through to me at last and draw me gently forth to him. . . . You say I have spoken in mystical language. . . . You say the experience is the result of mental suggestion practised over a term of years. I answer, No one believes that who has once been there and taken off his shoes on holy ground — the reality is too overpowering, the effect too profound. (CLFT 1922, pp. 56–57)

> But is this the experience of every one who has tried the experiment? . . . I think the true answer is this, that the measure of God's response is the urgency and strength of our appeal . . . that the character of the response is conditioned by individual needs, though in substance it must always be the same — the consciousness, more or less clear, of union with God in thought and action, of an eternal purpose and worth in human life, and of an all embracing love.[6]

> There are times when he cannot keep his eyes upon the cross, when the goal upon which he set his heart grows dim. . . . There is only one way . . . the prayer of the sinful man crying from the depths of his great need, "Create in me a clean heart, O God, and renew a right sprit within me"; the prayer of the longing soul seeking to escape from the clog of fleshy imperfection and to

breathe the free, pure air of the spiritual life. (CLFT 1922, p. 57)

In this account, the stages described by Nayler can also be discerned. It starts with the realisation that death and selfishness reign, then moves to a seeking that consists of form not content through increasingly sincere prayers and pleas and then to the final achievement of connection. The last sentences describe in poetic detail an overwhelming experience similar to many recorded by Friends. Another example is this description by Emilia Fogelkou of her own experience in 1902:

> But then one bright spring day — it was the 29th of May 1902 — while she sat preparing for her class under the trees in the backyard of Föreningsgatan 6, quietly, invisibly, there occurred the central event of her whole life. Without visions or the sound of speech or human mediation, in exceptionally wide-awake consciousness, she experienced the great releasing inward wonder. It was as if the 'empty shell' burst. All the weight and agony, all the feeling of unreality dropped away. She perceived living goodness, joy, light like a clear, irradiating, uplifting, enfolding, unequivocal reality from deep inside. The first words which came to her — although they took a long time to come — were, "This is the great Mercifulness. This is God. Nothing else is so *real* as this". The child who had cried out in anguish and been silenced had now come inside the gates of Light. She had been delivered by a love that is greater than any human love. (QFP 2013, 26.05)

Surely, Nayler would recognise in this the empty seed bursting and the seed of Christ replacing it as described in the earlier section on the fall of man. Contemporary Friends probably have equally compelling experiences, but they are recounted in a different language. In the 2013 *Quaker faith and practice*, in the chapter titled 'Leadings', there is frequent mention of being 'led by God' and 'waiting on and listening to the spirit'. As Val Ferguson wrote, 'Whenever we affirm that no one — priest, pastor, clerk elder — stands between us and the glorious and mystical experience of God in our lives, we are faithful Friends' (QFP 2013, 29.16).

One aspect is missing from the accounts I have extracted: the presence of other people. The solitary journey highlighted by Nayler is not, in fact, a common one. Other people help (and hinder) along the way. George Gorman reflected on his coming to Friends, sitting with others in worship in a dingy, ugly room on a rickety chair:

> It was in that uncomfortable room that I discovered the way to the interior side of my life, at the deep centre of which I knew that I was not alone, but was held by a love that passes all understanding. This was mediated to me, in the first place, by those with whom I worshipped. For my journey was not solitary, but one undertaken with my friends as we moved towards each other and together travelled inwards. Yet I knew that the love that held me could not be limited to the mutual love and care we had for each other. It was a signal of transcendence that pointed beyond itself to the source of all life and love. (QFP 2013, 2.03)

3. 'Concerning the Word'

> The word is that which was in the beginning, and was
> the beginning of all visible things, and that by which all
> things were made, but itself is invisible; which though it
> be the upholder of all visible things, yet can no visible
> thing reveal it; yet doth it reveal the ground and use and
> end of all visibles. And as without it "was nothing made
> that was made," so without it is nothing seen as it was
> made, nor anything can be guided nor used in its pure
> place; but whatever man meddles with, not having the
> word in him to guide, order, and sanctify, the same he
> defiles, and it is polluted as to him. (LL 3:60)

Nayler's section on the Word begins as does John's gospel: *In
the beginning was the Word, and the Word was with God,
and the Word was God. The same was in the beginning with
God. All things were made by him; and without him was not
any thing made that was made* (John 1:1–3 KJV).[1] Nayler's
interpretation of the gospel is to say that the Word made all
things that are visible and that unless one sees through the
eyes of the Word, nothing visible can be seen as it was made
by God. This is an important epistemological point for
Nayler; he divides his audiences into those who see the world
as God made it (and in its fallen state) and those who can
only see it with the five senses. And the world was made good,
but human ignorance of the Word means that human
meddling has spoilt and polluted the world. These are
powerful words at this time of environmental breakdown.
John's gospel continues: *In him was life; and the life was the
light of men. And the light shineth in darkness; and the
darkness comprehended it not* (John 1:4–5 KJV). Nayler
continues:

> Nor can this word be comprehended in heaven or earth;
> without this word can no holy Scripture be read with
> profit, for it opens the Scriptures, and the Scriptures

declare of it, yet cannot the Scriptures nor all the writings of the world comprehend it nor declare the depth and extent of it, which is beyond all generations; yet is it the teacher and guide of his own in all generations; and in all generations of saints hath been known in measure, more or less immediately, though it has no place in the world's profession. (LL 3:60)

The darkness comprehends not the light. Nayler extends the darkness to include all creation, all the generations of men and women through the ages and all their writings. Everything created is incomprehensible unless one has the Word with which to interpret it. Fortunately, there are always some of 'his own in all generations' who do have the Word and can guide and teach using it. Nayler says such knowledge 'has no place in the world's profession'; common-sense understanding does not recognise the Word and, if 'profession' is used in a modern sense, the few who might have the Word would not include any trained in theology at university.

Nayler continues, 'So hearing of a word, but not knowing it, men say the letter is the word' (LL 3:60). This is a natural mistake — we read the Scriptures, which talk of the Word, but fail to recognise it is within us and so mistake the Scriptures for the Word. This is a common Quaker argument. When faced with Scripture passages that could be turned against Quaker writings, Friends respond by saying: 'You have not the Word; therefore, you don't know the real meaning of Scripture.' A passage in a letter from Nayler to Fox dated April/May 1656 gives an account of a postponed debate. Nayler's adversaries refused to debate with him unless he denied that his call was from God, 'for if I was immediately called from God I would overturn the Scriptures & their faith also'.[2] The claim to have an immediate call from God is a theological trump card, and one can understand why others found it so infuriating.[3]

3. 'Concerning the Word'

Nayler goes on to say what possession of the Word will do for those who have it:

> But who hath the word hath that which comprehends death and hell and the grave; that which binds and chains Satan, overcomes the world, gives issues of life and light whereby the new creation is known, wherein dwells righteousness; and this everyone hath, so far as he hath the word abiding in him. (LL 3:60)

Again, this is a far-reaching and all-encompassing claim. But within the big claim are some words that reveal that Nayler had an understanding of human limitations. The Word gives 'issues', in the plural, which means revelation is gradual, not a single happening but many consecutive events as a person develops in understanding. The Light and life and righteousness that everyone has is limited 'so far as he hath the word abiding in him.' You shall see God according to the measure of Light with you. Everyone has the Word, but its revelations are limited by the extent to which a person recognises the Word within. Paul wrote, *Now he which stablisheth us with you in Christ, and hath anointed us, is God; Who hath also sealed us, and given the earnest of the Spirit in our hearts* (2 Corinthians 1:21–22 KJV). 'Earnest' is used, according to the *Shorter Oxford English Dictionary*, to mean 'money in part-payment, especially for the purpose of binding a bargain. Also, figuratively a foretaste, instalment, pledge, of what is to come.' Nayler says we are all given a foretaste, a pledge, an earnest of the Spirit: this will grow if we cultivate it.[4]

Nayler continues with a section contrasting what the Word gives with what the letter gives, which I summarise here:

> ➤ No person's will can change the Word 'for it is contrary to all men's wills' (by implication, the letter can be changed, translated, and reinterpreted);
> ➤ the Word hides from the wit, wisdom, and prudence of the wise but grows only amongst the babes

(whereas the letter grows only through the wit of humans);

➤ the Word sanctifies, but the letter does not;

➤ the Word is a 'fire and hammer' to all who have it — but the letter is not, being gentle and pliable;

➤ the Word will divide joints and marrow, the soul and the spirit — but not the letter;

➤ the Word 'is a reproach to every carnal mind' — and especially to those who profess the letter;

➤ those who have the Word are washed and cleansed and at one with God, but those who have the letter are in unclean fashions and customs and are not changed or reconciled to God;

➤ '[n]one can keep the word and his sins both', but those who profess the letter only are liars and polluters, and where 'sin stands the word is not known'; and

➤ the letter has no power to overcome the devil and break the bonds of wickedness, whereas the Word 'breaks down the seat of sin, and raises up and quickens the seed of God . . . and so quickens the mortal body to newness of life.' (LL 3:61)

Nayler describes people without the Word as wrestling with the Scriptures, adding symbols and parables but not being able to enter into the Word because humanity has gone out from the good, gone out from all that was created by the Word which God saw was good, and chosen evil. To help these struggling people,

> the light of the gospel is preached to turn man again to know the word, that coming to the knowledge thereof in his heart, and having his mind stayed thereto in the light, he may come to see the power of the word working in Spirit. . . . And this is not a self-taken-on performance from the letter, but is the eternal counsel and strength of God, commanded, moved, and performed in God's will and time, and contrary to the will of the flesh. . . . And with the living word is the living soul witnessed, and the life of Christ made

manifest in the mortal body, and the creature comes to have fellowship in the life, and is transformed thereinto and united in one; and this is the word of reconciliation, which unites God and the creature in Spirit. (LL 3:62)

It is paradoxical to tell people about the Word using the Scriptures because that will not help those without the Word. Nayler, though, preaches the *Light* of the gospel by which the Word can be understood. Scottish Quaker Robert Barclay's 1678 explanation of the Friends view of Scripture is quoted in all three of the recent books of discipline:

Nevertheless, because they [the Scriptures] are only a declaration of the fountain and not the fountain itself, therefore they are not to be esteemed the principal ground of all truth and knowledge, not yet the adequate, primary rule of faith and manners. Yet because they give a true and faithful testimony of the first foundation, they are and may be esteemed a secondary rule, subordinate to the Spirit, from which they have all their excellency and certainty: for as by the inward testimony of the Spirit we do alone truly know them, so they testify that the Spirit is the guide by which the saints are led into all truth. (CLFT 1922, p, 99; CFP 1959, para. 200; QFP 2013, 27.28)

The early Quakers were guided in their reading of the Scriptures by their experience of the divine Light. Fox learnt by direct revelation that everyone was enlightened by the divine Light without scriptural help, 'though afterwards, searching the scriptures, I found it' (QFP 2013, 29.04). They interpreted the Scriptures in the light of their own experiences in a very intimate way — the exodus was *their* exodus. This method of interpretation is now called 'new covenant' reading. As early Quaker preacher and author Richard Hubberthorne explained to Charles II in 1660,

I have believed the Scriptures from a child to be a declaration of truth, when I had but a literal knowledge, natural education and tradition; but now I know the Scriptures to be true by the manifestations and operation of God fulfilling them in me. (CFP 1959, para. 203)

Another early Quaker, Isaac Penington, wrote in 1667 about a similar experience he had:

We can truly say concerning the Scriptures, that now we believe, not so much because of the relation of things concerning Christ which we have found in them, but because we have seen and received the things which the Scriptures speak of. (CLFT 1922, p. 99)

And for twentieth-century British Friends, this was still the view:

We misunderstand the truth of the Inward Light if we imagine that it means a present inspiration independent of the past. Fox claimed that he had a word from the Lord as sure as any of the Apostles ever had. We join him in affirming our faith in the contemporary inspiration of the Holy Spirit. But Fox could never have made his claim if he had not recognized the word of the Lord which came to the Apostles. (H. G. Wood, 1951, as quoted in CFP 1959, para. 171,)

The same Spirit which inspired the writings of the Bible is the Spirit which gives us understanding of it: it is this which is important to us rather than the literal words of scripture. Hence, while quotations from the Bible may illuminate a truth for us, we would not use them to prove a truth. (London Yearly Meeting, 1986, as quoted in QFP 2013, 27.34)

My home contains some nine, or perhaps ten, different translations of the Bible. Christians have never had a single, uncontested set of Scriptures (either in content or translation), and literalist interpretations of scriptural meaning collapse very quickly. It used to be the case that Friends relied for consistency of belief on the inward Light, or Word, or Spirit, which was both individual, according the measure a person had and how it had grown within them, and constant because the Light is one and is available to all. The Word, by which the world was made and the true nature of the world was seen, was thought to be unchangeable. It united the person with God and united all persons in one understanding.

Is there still this consistency? I was at a Britain Yearly Meeting Agenda Committee meeting some time ago which decided it could not print in the *Yearly Meeting Proceedings* the epistle from an East African yearly meeting because it condemned homosexuality and those who practised it. The British Agenda Committee was certainly out of unity with some East African Friends. As a reading of the epistle showed, the African Friends thought British Friends had run out of the true way for we were no longer testifying to a truth that earlier Quaker missionaries had taught them and had believed themselves. The view of Quakers in Britain had changed. The British Friends on Agenda Committee claimed a later revelation, given to some and tested amongst all, concerning same-sex relationships. They found support for this in new interpretations of Scripture.

Because Quakerism had started in England, perhaps we subconsciously thought new revelations occurring in the same geographical area were the true word. Putting it like that makes me realise how silly it is to think that God might be geographically partial. Certainly, others could accuse us of having colonialist attitudes. Yet, Friends also recognise that individuals and communities receive continuing revelation. Revelation comes to individuals in specific places at specific times, so there are inevitably geographic and chronological differences around the world in humanity's deepening (or changing) understanding of God. Humans tend to think that 'later' is better, that the more recent the revelation the truer and more revealing of God's intentions it is. We believe we are traveling along a road of greater understanding so that as time passes we learn more about God. The image of the seed is one of growth, from two leaves to a tree. This might be true of individuals, but is it true of communities? Can entire communities find themselves in error? I should say that although I thought the Agenda Committee's decision not to print the Ugandan epistle was wrong, I embraced our new understanding about who God married.

> Creeds are milestones, doctrines are interpretations: Truth, as George Fox was continually asserting, a seed with the power of growth, not a fixed crystal, be its facets never so beautiful. (John Wilhelm Rowntree, 1904, as quoted in QFP 2013, 27.21)

Creeds may be milestones, not millstones, but do these milestones point towards somewhere, and how far have we to go? Nayler, in so far as he looked ahead, looked towards a world where all were converted, where all were Quakers, and where God's justice was effective in this world now. He certainly did not imagine or expect such a diversity of Quaker practice and understanding as we have today. He knew the Scripture/creeds could not unite us; he thought the Word would. But the Word or Spirit has brought us varied fruits. What we have left in common, as Val Ferguson described at the 1991 World Conference of Friends, is a unity of practice:

> Does anything unite this diverse group beyond our common love and humanity? Does anything make us distinctively Quaker? . . . [W]herever Friends are affirming each other's authentic experience of God, rather than demanding creedal statements, we are being God's faithful Quakers. Wherever we are seeking God's will rather than human wisdom, especially when conflict might arise, we are being faithful Quakers. Wherever we are affirming the total equality of men and women, we are being God's faithful Quakers.

3. 'Concerning the Word'

Wherever there is no division between our words and our actions, we are being faithful. Whenever we affirm that no one — priest, pastor, clerk, elder — stands between us and the glorious and mystical experience of God in our lives, we are faithful Friends. Whether we sing or whether we wait in silence, as long as we are listening with the whole of our being and seeking the baptism and communion of living water, we will be one in the Spirit. (QFP 2013, 29.16)

It would be churlish to criticise such moving words. Ferguson has described the thin membrane that both holds the world's Quakers together and keeps them apart from the world. Nayler would recognise some of the description: an immediate connection with God, or the Word, is possible provided we use our whole being to reach it; the Word is not of the human's will but God's; and it will demand actions from us. It is a thin membrane. Meanwhile, the destination becomes more contested.

4. 'Concerning Worship'

The worship of the true and living God stands out of man's will and knowledge, wisdom or prudence, as in the natural; for God is a Spirit, and in Spirit he is worshipped; not with men's hands nor with bodily exercise, farther than by the eternal Spirit the body is exercised, nor doth it stand in meats and drinks, nor divers washings, nor carnal ordinances taken on by tradition or imitation of others, but as every creature is moved by the Spirit of the living God. (LL 3:63)

So that before any can rightly worship God they must wait to know his Spirit that leads to know him and his worship. . . . So that all who would so worship him as to be accepted, you must know the light, and in it wait to know what God calls for at your hands: for it is not what men appoint you to do or not to do that will acquit you before the Lord. (LL 3:63)

Nayler says clearly that worship is not of this world — it is not of the 'natural', which means that humans cannot by reason or by following instinct learn how to worship the living God; nor should they follow the ways taught by others or the traditions of their people or nation. Every creature should worship as they are moved by the Spirit of the living God, and to do that they must first know the Spirit of God and from the Spirit learn how to worship. This might seem to lead to very disparate forms of worship, all being moved in different ways, until one remembers that the Spirit is from God who is one and that the Spirit's leadings will be the same for all.

So that the way to be well-pleasing to the Father is to wait in the light till you see something of the Spirit of life which is in Christ Jesus moving in you, and then to that join, in its power to worship; and that being of God, he cannot forget himself; and that is done in the name of Christ, which is done in his light and power and wisdom and strength; and whatever is done in his name is not denied of the Father; . . . nor did any ever worship in this nature but they found acceptance and the knowledge thereof. (LL 3:63)

It is very important to Nayler to know that his worship is accepted by God, that it is not despised like Cain's sacrifice, that God is well pleased by what God sees. If the worship is carried out correctly in the Light, then the person is acquitted by the Lord. Nayler uses the word 'Father' for God. Although all are equal before God, we are certainly not all equal with God.

For this know, that *God made man for himself and for his service*, and the living God is not as the dumb idols, that people should imagine a way to serve him as may best suit with the fashion and custom of a nation or a people: but he that made man hath given him a life from himself, to improve it in his service; and a light hath he given wherewith to see the moving of this Spirit of life, which ever moves after the will of God, because it is of him; and so where it is awakened it ever draws the creature towards God; the mind, and will, and affections, and love of God is in it, and who walks in the light sees this. (LL 3:63–64)

I come from a secular background, and the italicized assertion above is not something I am comfortable with. 'Service' is a word that has connotations of class, of servitude, of 'following orders without thinking' that does not sit comfortably with the modern European sensibility or with the modern liberal Quaker way of doing things. We have to take it either as a way of expressing a common religious apprehension (for example, of dependence, obedience, or 'letting go') or as an aspect of Nayler's theology that is challenging for modern Quakers. But before dismissing this sentence, consider the second half, where he says the Spirit draws the creature towards God, and how this might be expressed today. See the following from the 2013 *Quaker faith and practice*:

> Worship is the response of the human spirit to the presence of the divine and eternal, to the God who first seeks us. The sense of wonder and awe of the finite before the infinite leads naturally to thanksgiving and adoration. (QFP 2013, 2.01)

> The treasure I had found [in meeting for worship] seemed startlingly simple. . . . I and others were to start just where we were at the moment and proceed at our own pace from there. How blessed that there were no constraints of belief. The promptings of love and truth were the starting places and we could move at our own pace to recognise them as the leadings of God — the beyond drew me and others on from our limitations and despairs and smallnesses. (Ruth Fawell, 1987, as quoted in QFP 2013, 2.06)

Nayler continues:

> So you having received a light from Christ, in that wait, till therein you find the Spirit's leading, acting, and ordering; and here the least in the light is in God's service, when on him you are waiting in Spirit. And such as abide in the light, waiting upon God in the light, are kept from serving the prince of darkness; and having your loins girt and your light burning, you are always ready to know the voice and answer it with obedience; and then you serve God and not men, when you have a command from the living God, not taken on by tradition from men; for in vain do all worship, whose fear and service towards God is taught by the precepts of men; for all the children of the Lord are taught of the Lord. And they are the sons of God who are led by the Spirit of God. And such hearken to the Lord and know

his voice; and what they see and hear, that they do, and do not offer the sacrifice of fools. (LL 3:65)

'So you having received a light from Christ, in that wait'. The Quaker belief about worship has not changed since Nayler wrote these words. The direct contact between the Spirit of Christ, or God, and the human spirit is the basis of our individual and corporate life.

In these sentences, Nayler moves on from the time spent in worship on a Sunday — or another day — and, by implication, extends 'worship' to include any time when someone is acting in accordance with God's wishes; waiting in the Light leads not only to worship but also to action. With the light burning in our hearts, we must go forth! I try to imagine the feelings of those Quakers, like Nayler, who left their families, their occupations, and their security and went forth to do what they could see and hear had to be done. It feels altogether too much, if that is what being Quaker involves. But Nayler does allow for those without such courage, for 'the least in the light', he says, is in God's service. Possibly even holding the bags of others is service. And I am also reminded of Thomas Kelly's words written in 1941:

> How then shall we lay hold of that Life and Power, and live the life of prayer without ceasing? By quiet, persistent practice in turning all our being, day and night, in prayer and inward worship and surrender, towards Him who calls in the deeps of our souls. Mental habits of inward orientation must be established. . . . Begin now, as you read these words, as you sit in your chair, to offer your whole selves, utterly and in joyful abandon, in quiet, glad surrender to Him who is within. (QFP 2013, 2.22)

Nayler has not helped us much with forms of worship. He is very clear it should not be traditional, that anyone who does not wait in the Light but follows custom is not worshipping correctly. During the hundred years before Nayler wrote, religious practice had been changed frequently by legislation. Since the 1549 Book of the Common Prayer of Edward VI, Parliament had been telling the nation how to worship. The Scots had invaded England because of a disagreement over forms of worship. In 1655, Cromwell established a 'national' church accommodating the practices of Presbyterians, Independents, and Baptists whose ministers were appointed by county commissioners. The commissioners were instructed not to admit a man 'unless they could discern something of the grace of God in him'; knowledge of Latin and Greek and perhaps a university degree were no longer required. These changes had created in congregations a scepticism about all religious forms. Nayler is contemptuous of the changes in forms of worship and of those who constantly asked themselves

> if this be the right worship, & have it yet to dispute? (if not confident in a false way, which is much worse); and such are you who are fighting and contending for such a manner of worship as Christ never ordained, nor his own ever practised; as you may see if you compare your national worship with the saints' practice; which is changed in every particular, and that by men and councils, under pretense of decency and conformity, or something that stands in men's will, which God never commanded. But you may long worship here and call it God's worship, ere He own it by answering you. . . .
>
> And all you who are gone out in anything from Christ the true pattern and example, you are gone into the imaginations of men and so are become servants of men, and not of God, herein. For God is pure, and so is his way and worship, and without his command cannot be changed in the least jot . . . for it is not the name that makes it God's worship; but it is the nature of it, which must be in Spirit and will of God . . . for whatever your minds are in, that is your god you worship, and the pure God owns no such; for it's truth in the inward parts he seeks for, wherein none of you can worship who knows

not the living word in your hearts, to keep them up to God in your worship; and that worship which is not in the will of God is the worship of devils. (LL 3:65–67)

The only evidence Nayler, or others, have that Quaker practice is the only practice acceptable to God is that it works. Of course, other practices may also work: indeed, I suspect that it is the worshippers who are particular, not God. The finite and the infinite can make contact. We have to take on trust that what Nayler says will happen, does happen — and trust that it will happen to us. Over the years since Nayler wrote, Quaker forms of worship have changed, and now different yearly meetings manage their worship in different ways. It is important to remember that these splits were not begun over differences about forms of worship, even though they are now a defining feature.

For every Quaker, the meeting for worship is the centrepiece of their spiritual life, irrespective of how the meeting is conducted. And central to that meeting is the belief in direct contact with God. As London Yearly Meeting wrote in 1925,

In our life as a religious Society we have found it true that the spirit of man can come into direct contact with the Spirit of God and can thereby learn of God. (CP 1925, p. 2)

An Evangelical Quaker yearly meeting, Northwest Yearly Meeting of Friends Church, put it this way in 1987:

We believe that we may experience Christ directly and immediately without the necessity of priestly or ceremonial intervention and that this experience is available to every person. The spiritual life is nourished by the Holy Spirit, who teaches and guides us both individually and corporately according to His commandments.[1]

And in 1983, North Carolina Yearly Meeting (Conservative) published the following:

The silent worship of a Quaker meeting is communion insofar as it rises above silence as a symbol and allows the life of God into the souls of the waiting group. The worshipper becomes a part of the divine life, as it flows through, and transforms. Quaker experience supports the view that it is possible and practical to merge the values of individual and group worship. The unique worth of individual worship is in the fact that the worshipper need not adapt to any outward or traditional circumstances. A person aspiring to reach heights unattained need not be dragged down by others. However, care must be taken to avoid extreme individualism which might result in religious anarchy. The special role of group worship is found in the opportunity which it affords for the stronger to help the weaker. Those who know better the ascent can guide those who do not. But in this case an extreme of group control might create a type of uniformity out of which new life could not grow. The Quaker meeting for worship when it attains its ends avoids the two extremes and combines the power of each.[2]

Again, there is the belief that God and the individual can communicate directly. While advising on private worship, the above passage also praises communal worship as a way in which people can help each other to a greater understanding. This draws attention to one of the problems Quakers found with 'waiting in the Light'. Without care, a person's mind can wander, there can be an intrusion of secular ideas that may be inimical to faith, and a falling away from Quaker tradition may take place. We may start searching the Bible for intellectual support for favourite ideas or confuse the Inner Light with modern psychological theories about how the brain works. John Punshon, an advocate of programmed worship containing 'open worship', argues that silent worship became a dead form:

It was attended by a series of conventions and expectations that were experienced as quenching the spirit and that failed to express the range of emotions and convictions many people believed were essential to the religious life. Friends had got themselves into a curious bind here. On the one hand, there was the principle that ministry had to be spontaneous, on the other, the requirement that it had to be spirit-led. These principles were both taken with such seriousness that a kind of paralysis seemed to have occurred. At any rate, many Friends found their worship inhibited by excessive solemnity and the exuberance of the holiness movement must have felt like latter-day rain.[3]

He goes on to argue that one of the reasons for a lack of corporate commitment to Jesus Christ in unprogrammed liberal meetings such as Britain Yearly Meeting may be that without words, music, or other formal ways of anchoring worship to the Christian revelation there is no obstacle to the entry of ideas and concepts that are fundamentally inimical to the faith. Open worship within a programmed Christian service prevents this while preserving the theological significance (direct communication with God) of the silence. Interestingly, he absolves the American Conservative tradition from such strictures.[4]

Until 1924, Britain Yearly Meeting recorded the names of Friends particularly gifted in vocal ministry. Friends meetings relied on these people to keep the worship within a Quaker and Christian framework. This was a difficult task and one that Friends undertook with trepidation. The compilers of *Christian Practice* thought it wise to repeat advice from 1725 on this issue:

Although the labours of such as are called forth by the Spirit of Christ are highly serviceable in the Church, yet the aim of every true Gospel minister is to direct the minds of all to the Divine teachings of the Holy Spirit.

And as the religious strength both of preachers and hearers consists in their united dependence on Christ their Guide and Leader, so where any part of that dependence is broke off from Him, the holy Head, and placed on any instrument or member of that body, it hath sometime been experienced to become a burden on such instrument and a real impediment to its present service. (CP 1925, p. 5)

The visual image of the head of God upon the shoulders of a Friend in meeting is striking and brutal. Friends were clearly of two minds about recorded ministers. In 1698, Friends dissatisfied with the preaching of a minister were advised to first go to elders in the monthly meeting before publicly testifying against the minister. In 1723, they were asked not to keep their hats on while a minister preached as a 'token of disunion' (BoD 1834, pp. 162–63). In the nineteenth century, doubt continued. To give public ministry was both a blessing to the church and difficult to achieve:

Ministers, even those of large experience and gifts, may profitably be led into a review of their ministry in its varied relations. May all be preserved in the exercise of it in the life and power of the Spirit — dividing the word aright, — not falling short of the measure of the gift, and yet not exceeding it. Public prayer, thanksgiving, and praise ought ever to spring from a living sense of the wants and condition of the congregation. In this solemn service may all be impressed with the importance of their words being few and full. (BoD 1883, p. 55)

This advice for preachers and congregations is still relevant for Friends today.

Nayler had no advice about how worship should be managed. In London and Britain Yearly Meetings, over the years custom has suggested different forms to us. At first men and women were separated in worship — a seventeenth-century meeting house in my area meeting still has a gallery for the women to sit in, a raised bench for recorded ministers, and another bench at floor level for the elders — both facing the congregation. None of these are used now for their original purpose. All Friends attending meeting for worship now sit on chairs in concentric circles rather than on rows of benches. Conventionally, in most British meetings there is a table in the centre with flowers and on it copies of *Quaker faith and practice* and a Bible. The meetings usually end with everyone shaking hands with their neighbours after a signal from whoever is elder that week. When I started attending my present meeting, the clerk refused to shake hands, regarding it as an importation from the Anglicans. All these things are our customs and traditions, and Nayler, I suspect, would find all objectionable if we followed them only as custom. We may sit or stand in our meetings forever, but unless God owns it by answering our worship, it is in vain. If God does not answer, it matters not a jot whether we are in circles or rows.

One ingredient Nayler does not mention here is the presence of others in worship. *Love to the Lost* was written for the unconvinced, the nonattenders, so there would be little point in writing about the movement of the Spirit among converts. Some of Nayler's letters to meetings have survived, and in one dated 1 April 1656 — just after *Love to the Lost* was published — he writes:

> [I]n the eternal unity amongst yourselves meet often together, and suffer a word of exhortation one from another in the spirit of meekness. Love one another unfeignedly, and know one other in that which is pure, that therewith you may be gathered out of the world, up to God, from whom the gift comes.[5]

Quakers are clear that gathering together to seek the Light is more effective than doing so alone. The conservative yearly meetings give a very good reason for this. The power of a meeting for worship depends on the sincere dedication of the individuals who have gathered together, which will create a united communion in the presence of God wherein each one overpasses the bounds of his individual self and knows a union of spirit with spirit bringing him into a larger life than that which is known in spiritual separateness. (CP 1925 p. 4)

Finally, it would be wise to end on a positive note about worship, our most fundamental activity. Ben Pink Dandelion, at the end of the printed version of his 2014 Swarthmore Lecture, counted our strengths.

We have at our spiritual fingertips the continuing power and forever-possibility of Quaker worship; the 'magic' of what we so regularly find in the silence together, and of all we can achieve through that practice. As we move into the silence, we are moved through it. We find the spiritual at the heart of stillness, the garden of God's love and wisdom brought to life inwardly as a place to partake in the life of the Spirit. We find joy and wisdom and guidance and love all present, and can feel the binding of that encounter between us. In meeting for worship for business, we can still feel led by the Spirit into new and unimagined places. It is a wondrous gift, and we are changed by bringing our daily concerns into that space. We continue as the latest version of our tradition to have one foot in the here and now and one foot in heaven. Everything indeed can feel different, outwardly and inwardly. We achieve new insight, find a new place to stand in, and indeed know what to wait in. The experience of being gathered as in a net, in covenant with God, is ours if we are willing.[6]

5. On Women

Love to the Lost does not include a chapter on the topic of women, but I need to write about women in Quakerism in order to make sense of Nayler's relationship with Martha Simmonds. It is appropriate to put the chapter on women here, after the chapter on worship, because to Nayler's contemporaries one of the most extraordinary aspects of Quakerism was the ministry of women in worship.

Why were women allowed, encouraged, and empowered to minister in meetings, to appoint meetings, and to preach the message in public? Much has been written about early Quaker women, who are portrayed as early feminists, radical participants in the English revolution threatening to dismantle patriarchy. Literary critics, discovering that Quaker women produced about a quarter of English women's writings in the seventeenth century, have written about their spirituality and literary ambitions.[1] Present-day Quaker men can if they wish enjoy the reflected glory of being part of a movement that from the very first embraced gender equality. However, pleasing though this is for the men, I suspect they (and I) are taking advantage of a situation not of our creation. Kate Peters suggests:

> A very good reason for the acceptance by Quaker men of the participation of women in their movement is that they were already there. . . . The rapid growth of the Quaker movement was achieved essentially by the linking up from around 1652 of established groups of radical sectarians and Seekers, whose ideas already reflected more or less the newly publicised Quaker beliefs. Among these were groups of women sectaries. An early centre in London to which northern Quakers first travelled was a meeting at the house of Simon Dring, where there was 'none but two women' who were

69

preachers; and the link between them was probably the northern woman Isabel Buttery, a friend of James Nayler and other northern missionaries, and who distributed some of the first Quaker tracts in London.[2]

We know that Fox's first recorded convincement of another was the former Baptist Elizabeth Hooton, who held Quaker meetings in her own house. And this is another clue. Like Paul, the early Quaker men could not avoid women and their ministry because women found their audiences and offered their houses and barns as meeting places. Quakers used Paul's greetings to women helpers as evidence to support women speaking. The first Quaker publication to justify the presence of women was written by Richard Farnsworth in late 1653. Its title was *A woman forbidden to speak in the church.* His argument started from the premise that a church was not a building but a collection of people 'made all of living stones, elect and precious (1 Peter 2:5) and the Saints, their Bodies are made fit Temples for the Holy Ghost to dwell in (2 Cor 6:16)'. As Peters notes,

> By defining a church as the people comprising its congregation, it would become more acceptable that women should be allowed to speak 'in the church'; it established that women spoke as elect saints first and foremost. . . . Farnsworth went on to dismiss gender as a significant criterion in determining who should be allowed to speak in the 'church':

> 'That which is flesh is flesh, and that knoweth not the things of God, neither in male nor female, but is adulterated from God but that which is spirit is spirit, and is born of God, either in male or female, that knoweth him, and that is permitted to speak in the Temple'.[3]

It was, therefore, acceptable for women to speak in the church (and by implication do other things for the church and the movement), provided they did not speak as women. When she took on the role of minister, a woman was no longer female. Farnsworth later used this argument in Banbury court in defence of two Quaker women who were accused of assaulting the local minister and using blasphemous words to justify women speaking. Anne Audland, in her pamphlet about the trial (*The saints testimony*), reported,

> And when it was asked them on the bench, if the Spirit of God might not speak in the Temple, they were then put to a stand, or partly silent about the same; and RF [Richard Farnsworth] then and there said, if any of them would deny it, he would by plain scripture prove that the Spirit of God might speak in his Temple (meaning in the body of male or female).[4]

This argument was used by women themselves. They extended it to apply to men without the Word of God, those who were therefore considered 'spiritual females' and were thus forbidden to speak in church. Peters quotes a pamphlet from 1655 written by Priscilla Cotton and Margaret Cole:

> Indeed you your selves are the women, that are forbidden to speak in the Church, that are become women; for two of your Priests came to speak with us; and when they could not bear sound reproof and wholesome doctrine . . . they railed on us with filthy speeches . . . and so ran from us.[5]

In 1656, George Fox published a tract called *The women learning in silence*. The tract began by quoting Paul's statement that women should be silent in church (1 Corinthians 14:34) without contradiction to show that women should learn in silence but then reiterated Farnsworth's argument about spiritual equality.

Male Quakers were accommodating of women who had their own networks within the movement. Female Quakers received funds for travel; they published and preached; and in the 1670s women-only meetings were established with important functions (including permission to marry) within the Religious Society of Friends. This was very unusual for the time, and the presence of women in leadership roles needed explanation.

Women played a vital part in the national spread of Quakerism between 1654 and 1656. Peters, in a detailed examination of the spread of Quakerism in East Anglia, shows that Quaker women were often the first Quakers to arrive in a town, and their presence often created a disturbance forcing their arrest.

Peters describes events in Banbury during 1656.[6] Anne Audland, with Mabel Camm and the servant Jane Waugh, had gone to Banbury in late 1654 and deliberately courted arrest by allegedly assaulting the vicar. Audland then complained about her imprisonment in her first pamphlet, *A true declaration of the suffering of the innocent*. She quoted from Acts 2:18 on the front page: *And on my servants and on my handmaidens, I will poure out in those days of my Spirit and they shall prophesie*. This publicity brought more Quakers into town— Richard Farmworth, Robert Rich, Sarah Tims and Margaret Vivers—and each was imprisoned. Thus, by the time of Banbury quarter sessions in September 1655, there were six Quakers on trial, which generated more publicity and a second pamphlet from Anne Audland giving an account of their trials.

Quaker women raised disturbances in their parish churches. Phyllis Mack counts more than a hundred women who began their preaching career by breaking up a church service in their own town.[7] They were not easily prevented. Mack tells of Elizabeth Peacock, who

> walked into a London church, admonished the congregation to have contrite spirits, and was sentenced to hard labor for two months. She then returned to the same church, preached against hypocritical worship . . . and was removed from the building and released near her own house. The

following day she walked out of a Quaker meeting and into the chapel at Whitehall, where she announced that it was impossible to please God without faith; she was put in jail for six more weeks.[8]

These brave actions of Quaker women as preachers and missionaries were seen by Quaker men as work covered by the Spirit. However, for Quaker men, such displays (however helpful) did not empower women with increased worldly agency outside spiritual work. Christine Trevett points out

> the extra-ordinary ordinariness of many of these women. They wanted their mundane daily lives to be impregnated with the experience of the Spirit and its promise of love and peace and harmony. They went out into the street[,] faced physical abuse and cried this message over baying opposition, then they went home to check the household accounts and feed their children. They foresaw the millennium, wrote letters to the King and served beef and beer at supper.[9]

Mack argues this may have been a choice made by the women. Quaker women had no desire to live apart from the world as medieval religious women had done. They wished to 'imbue worldly concerns with the intensity and moral stature of an exalted spiritual life'.[10] Their actions may have been less about gender equality than the demand that in religious and spiritual matters male and female were irrelevant.

Rosemary Moore has discovered that when early meetings were set up in 1653 and 1654,

> [w]omen had only a limited part in these arrangements. Local women might have authority to "appoint meetings" but no women were regional overseers, and they were not normally signatories to official statements issued by Friends.[11]

Mack points out that women had only one claim to public authority, and that was as an instrument of God:

Whether she criticized the male ministers hysterically or rationally, her very attempt to dispute with them in public would probably have resulted in accusations of self-seeking and, ultimately, in personal disgrace.[12]

The distinction is clearly explained by a passage in *The Woman Preacher of Samaria* by George Keith, dated 1674:

It is permitted unto men, at times, to speak in the church. . . . An unlearned man may be permitted to ask a question in the church, which is not permitted unto a woman, nor is it needful, for She may ask her husband at home. But if the spirit of the Lord command or move a godly and spiritually learned woman to speak, in that case she is the Lord's more than her husband's, and she is to speak, yea, though the husband should forbid her.[13]

Peters believes that Quaker men found the presence of women potentially disturbing — they felt the women needed to be controlled — 'there was frequently a sense that their presence was fraught with difficulties'.[14] Women's natures were inherently unstable and were liable to 'run out', that is, to go beyond the guidance of the Spirit. Much early Quaker discipline concerned what to do about women who had run out. Edward Burrough sent a woman to George Fox with the note:

This little short maid that comes to thee, she has been this long while abroad, and in her there is little or no service as in the ministry. It were well to be laid on her to be servant somewhere. That is more her place . . . Friends where she has been are much burdened by her.[15]

Early Quaker men's private letters rarely mention spiritual equality. Before Farnsworth published *A woman forbidden to speak in the church*, he had published *An Easter Reckoning* (early 1653), part of which outlined the proper social relationships among God's own people in a godly commonwealth. He said,

> Wives be in subjection to your own husbands, and love them in the Lord, walking in obedience to his commands, and be not angry, nor proud, nor stubborn, nor cross, nor hasty, nor peevish, nor perverse do not scold, nor braul, nor lye, nor swear, for God doth forbid it. . . . Let not the woman usurpe authority over the man, but be in subjection.[16]

Men had only to be loving and gentle towards their wives. Like almost all other men in seventeenth-century Britain, Quaker men were patriarchal and (outside the worshipping group) held traditional beliefs about the roles of men and women. James Nayler did not feel the need to justify in writing the ministry of women despite their prominent role in Quakerism. Had he done so, it is probable that at the time of writing *Love to the Lost* he would have used the same arguments and biblical proofs as Farnsworth and Fox. In chapter 15, I argue that after his confrontation with Martha Simmonds, Nayler may have been more open to the true equality — both spiritual and temporal — of men and women.

Such a true equality has grown only slowly in the Religious Society of Friends. Mack writes in *Visionary Women* that to a historian of gender relations the period 1660–1700 seems initially to be a period in which prophetic Quaker women slowly disappear behind the edifice of a new structure, their voices muffled as feminine aspects of the movement become viewed as suspect. But as the new structure is built, she finds those who dissented from it were more likely to argue in favour of male-only delegates, that separatists were more likely to capitulate to the demands of the state and pay tithes, and that it was the 'bureaucrats' who advocated the protection of female ministry and the autonomous women's meeting.[17]

Through this bureaucracy, women appear in our books of discipline. Fox began setting up women's monthly meetings in 1667. They were intended both to increase women's confidence and to give women separate responsibility for their 'natural' spheres of activity — caring for the poor, the sick, and children and investigating and approving marriages. Progress on this was slow. An epistle from 1691 advised Friends to 'encourage faithful women's meetings and the setting of them where wanted' (Extracts 1822, p. 208), and such advice was repeated in 1707 and 1745. In those areas where they did have some authority, the women's meetings usually needed to refer decisions to the men or ask the men's meeting for money (Extracts 1822, pp. 210–11). When Fox established Six Weeks Meeting (so called because it met every six weeks), responsible for property and financial matters concerning all the monthly meetings in London, it began with 49 men and 35 women.[18] This large number was probably appointed to ensure there were always enough Friends available to make a quorum. The actual numbers were usually small, and twelve was a quorum. From 1728 only men attended, even though one of its responsibilities was the relief of the Quaker poor in London, usually an important concern of Quaker women.[19]

Women's ministry, especially travelling ministry, was usually accepted. At its height in the eighteenth century, it was common for women to travel to and from America and Europe without their husbands or children on preaching missions.

From the start of the (male-only) yearly meetings in London in 1668, a yearly meeting of Quaker women was held alongside. But it had no authority, nor could it record its decisions. It was not until 1784 that a women's yearly meeting was established, partly through the support of visiting American female Friends. Although it was valuable to the women to meet and to be able to circulate their minutes and epistles, they played no authoritative role in governing the

Society. [20] The minute establishing the women's yearly meeting made its subordination clear:

> This meeting agrees, that the meeting women friends held annually in this city, be at liberty to correspond, in writing, with the quarterly meetings of women friends; to receive accounts from them, and to issue such advice as in the wisdom of truth from time to time may appear necessary, and conducive to their mutual edification; and that the said meeting be denominated The Yearly Meeting of Women Friends held in London. Yet such meeting is not to be so far considered a meeting of discipline, as to make rules, or alter the present queries, without the concurrence of this meeting. (Extracts 1822, p. 209)

On some occasions, when it was felt the women had specific knowledge to bring to their deliberations, the men agreed to a joint meeting. During the nineteenth century, these became more frequent. In 1896, women could be members of Meeting for Sufferings (a committee of the Society that met between yearly meetings). Yet still, men found women's voices troublesome. A member wrote to the recording clerk (chief executive in modern terms):

> The women's voices are heard only in very small minority. . . . If Woman Friends would give us their opinions in equal numbers with men, either the time occupied would be doubled, or the self-restraint would have to be two-fold on the part of the men. [21]

From 1897, most sessions of yearly meeting were open to both men and women. In 1907, the logical step was taken and the separate women's meeting was laid down. Separate women's monthly and quarterly meetings around the country continued to meet; the last known one was laid down in 1944.

The nineteenth century saw the growing acceptance of women's voices in Quaker debates about the movement, such as at Richmond, Indiana (1887), and Manchester, England (1895). At Richmond one of the clerks was a woman, as were thirty-two of the eighty-six delegates, but the 'women's question', as it was known, was not debated and the role of women was not mentioned in the decision minutes. At Manchester the opening and closing addresses were given by women, seven other women gave addresses, and sixteen women responded to papers by men. However, women continued to be excluded from leadership roles even though (as several pointed out) they were in the majority in their local meetings. Many men and some women felt that separate bodies for women violated the Quaker commitment to male-female partnership, whereas for others separate bodies were necessary because it was clear that joint bodies resulted in male-only leadership. Nevertheless, women-only bodies were founded and thrived. The United Society of Friends Women founded in the U.S. Midwest became an international organisation, building links between Quaker women across continents and theological differences.[22]

The women's liberation movement of the 1960s and 1970s revived the 'women's question' within Quaker circles. In Britain, the Quaker Women's Group was established, and in 1986 it gave the Swarthmore Lecture. This was ground-breaking not only in its topic — Quaker feminists speaking of their experience — but in its presentation by a group of anonymous women who used music and other 'theatrical' devices to put their message across. This was followed up with an international conference of Quaker women at Woodbrooke, Birmingham, England, attended by seventy-six women from twenty-one countries. The conference revived the sense of Quaker sisterhood, and its epistle and video clips were widely publicised. By this time, the vast majority of British Quakers were accepting of women in leadership roles. Still, it was not until 2015 that three women sat at the table in a yearly meeting.

6. 'Concerning Faith'

He that hath living faith which is in Christ lives by it; and the life that he lives is above all the world and the powers of darkness; and the least measure of that faith is perfect, and is present power against all the assaults of Satan, if in it the creature abide faithful, and run not to other helps, and so lay himself open to distrust; for it is the gift of God [Ephesians 2:8], whereof whosoever receives a measure, he hath a measure of the Son, above which the Father will not suffer any temptation . . . (LL 3:69)

These are the opening words of this section of *Love to the Lost*, and the sentence continues for more than three hundred words to form the first paragraph. Nayler writes of the faith that keeps a believer pure and above the world; we are to wait in faith, armed against the temptations of the devil,

alive to God's righteousness, waiting in faith to see it revealed through obedience thereto, from faith to faith, as it is written, "The just shall live by faith"; and this is the living faith, which purifieth the heart until the life of godliness and so reveals the righteousness of faith for an inheritance. (LL 3:69)

Here, Nayler is paraphrasing the words of Habakkuk (2:4): *Look at the proud! Their spirit is not right in them, but the righteous live by their faith* (NRSV). Paul quotes this in Romans 1:16, where he says, *I am not ashamed of the gospel; it is the power of God for salvation to everyone who has faith* (NRSV). In Galatians 3:11, the same quotation is used to prove that no one is justified before God by the law. It is worth remembering that by 'gospel' Paul does not mean the written gospels but the 'good news' — the message that Christ's resurrection has the power to transform us. Paul is referring to an inner power, just as Nayler is.

And so God's righteousness is received in the heart by faith, and by obedience thereto brought forth into the world, a witness against all the unrighteousness of the world; and so the righteousness of God is preached through faith, in all whose faith stands in Christ Jesus: but that is a dead faith which brings not forth the life of Christ into the world; and that's the reprobate faith which is to the good work reprobate. (LL 3:71)

There is another sort of faith, that preached by ministers and priests for those

who hear a thing with the outward ear, and so set themselves to believe or not to believe it, in their wills or outward persuasion, from others, or in their own imagination; and as their imaginations, thoughts, and conceiving changes, so their faith changes also; and so it cannot be steadfast, because it stands not in the measure of God known in the heart. . . . And so not standing in that which is contrary to the will of man and power of sin, it lies under the wills of men, and power of the prince of this world; and as the world and times changes, so doth that faith, but can never lead out of the world and all time, up to the redeemer of the soul. (LL 3:70)

Nayler characterises those who have this deficient faith as those who believed the words of Scripture and the prophets that God was their Father but were without the word of faith in their hearts. They are like those who

not having the word of faith in their hearts . . . slew the Son of God and set the murderer free: and as that faith which is dead works death, so that faith which is living worketh life. And a profession of faith without righteousness is like a body without life; and like as a living man is known by his actions, so the living faith by its fruits. . . . [T]hat is a dead faith which brings not forth the life of Christ into the world; . . . he that errs from the righteousness errs from the faith also which is held in a pure conscience; and he that makes shipwreck of a good conscience, and puts that away, makes shipwreck of faith also. (LL 3:71)

Good, or pure, conscience is different from faith but does help achieve faith. Nayler contrasts the faith of the world, with its 'outward' ear and which changes with the world and is in time, with the living faith

that stands in that which is of God in a pure conscience . . . a mystery , not known nor received, and so cannot be improved, which is the true faith, which is the gift of God, which none can receive but in the Spirit. (LL 3:70)

I am interested in the phrase 'not known nor received', which might mean he thinks of faith as being innate and as a gift given before birth — something within that acts as a yeast strengthening the person's search for God.

Nayler does not use the definition of faith given in Hebrews 11:1, *the substance of things hoped for, the evidence of things not seen* (KJV). Robert Barclay, the first systematic Quaker theologian, used this for his definition of faith half a generation later. For Nayler, that definition might not have provided faith with the active principle of impelling a person towards righteousness or holding them on the right track. The definition in Hebrews is more intellectual than heartfelt. Nayler argued that his opponents had only a paper or outward faith, so to agree that faith was a theological construct would not allow him to claim its transformative power.

Nayler explains how those without faith are judged by the Light:

And in the eternal light is all your faith seen and judged to be without Christ, and without foundation, who are out of the light and out of the life. And your faith is seen to be the same with the scribes and Pharisees, who believed the Scriptures and thought to find life therein, but did not believe in the light, and so would not come to Christ that they might have life. (LL 3:71)

In traditional theology, the Pharisees could not have come to Christ before his death. Nayler here must be thinking of Christ as an eternal spirit, coeval with God, who enlightens humanity inwardly. Possibly he is thinking of Christ as another word for the Light.

> So all your faith which is out of the light, which from the letter you have formed, is a faith set up in your own wills, and not that which is given of God: for that faith that is the gift of God believes in the light and follows it, and so leads to the life. (LL 3:71)

Faith is a gift from God. Faith is given to us to enable us to recognise the Light within. And faith is the determination of the self to help that faith grow and spread across our personality and earthly life until transformation is effective. Nayler enumerates the fruits of the living faith:

> [F]or that faith that is the gift of God believes in the light and follows it, and so leads to the life; and this faith that stands in the light and life is the living faith and never without works, which works are love, meekness, patience, mortification, sanctification, justification, &c. — the works of God in Christ Jesus, in which God's workmanship is seen in the new creation, received in the faith and in the obedience to which the soul is purified, and victory witnessed over the world, sin and death. (LL 3:71–72)

Nayler's list of virtues reminds me of Paul in Galatians 5:22–23: *But the fruit of the Spirit is love, joy, peace, longsuffering, gentleness, goodness, faith, meekness, temperance: against such there is no law* (KJV). The works that Nayler wants to see are not only works of outward charity but the fruits of an inner change which has led to real outward change.

6. 'Concerning Faith'

Friends continue to use the term 'faith' in this active sense. The two long reflections on faith in *Christian Faith and Practice* from well-known Friends Rufus Jones (CFP 1959, pp. 91–93) and John Wilhelm Rowntree (CFP 1959, pp. 94–95) both use it in this way. So do writers in *Quaker faith and practice*, Pierre Ceresole (QFP 2013, 26.26) and Charles F. Carter (QFP 2013, 26.39). My favourite modern quotation is this:

> My experience came after many years of doubting and uncertainty. . . . God, who through many people and events over a period of several months had been pursuing me, put his hand on my shoulder. I had to respond — yes or no. It was unequivocal, inescapable and unconditional . . . a gift of faith for me to reject or accept. (Roy Farrant, 1974, as quoted in QFP 2013, 26.13)

Nayler would have recognised the suddenness, the gift, and the absoluteness of the decision.

7. On Ann Nayler

We know very little about Ann(e) Nayler, maiden name unknown, spelling of first name varied. James married her in 1639 and moved to Wakefield in Yorkshire. We do not know what he did there or how he supported his family; perhaps she came from Wakefield or he had connections there from his school days. Three daughters were born: Mary (1640), Jane (1641), and Sarah (1643), and a son John was born sometime during the civil war. When John executed his father's will in 1663, he listed five siblings, including himself, and a brother of James called William.[1] At an unknown date, James, Ann, and the three daughters moved back to James's father's house and farmed. We know this because he described himself to the court in Appleby as a 'husbandman', which means he worked the land but did not necessarily own it, and as having left his father's house after a call from God. His father may have died before they moved back from Wakefield. Scholars believe that Ann managed the holding while he was away. It would not have been very profitable, but it must have provided a living of sorts. Neelon describes the soil, terrain, and weather of this area as unsuitable for crops or grazing.[2] There was no monetary incentive for landowners to amalgamate or improve the small farms. Tenants were left to fend for themselves whilst the landlords invested in industry in the towns.

The civil war then interrupted the marriage. Some historians think James Nayler was not home at all during the war, and Hill describes Nayler's marriage as 'de facto divorce by removal'.[3] But, as Neelon points out, all of Nayler's military service (except for his time in Scotland, Cheshire, and perhaps Westmoreland) took place no more than one or two days' ride from home. Pontefract, where he spent a lot of time, is only twelve miles from his home, and it appears his son was conceived during the civil war.[4] Some of his later preaching tours also took place near to home.

Nayler returned from the war seemingly for good in 1651. He was at first an invalid but seems to have recovered enough to plough and work the farm. But then he heard his call and hesitated. The emotional and spiritual turmoil made him very ill, and it was thought he would die. He recovered and suddenly walked out, continuing on down the road in an old suit after seeing a visitor to the gate. His act looks callous and uncaring, but there seems to have been forgiveness. Ann came to see him when he was imprisoned in Appleby and nursed him in Bridewell after his whipping. Finally, if the marriage had ended, why would Fox encourage him to return home in 1660?

What is interesting about Ann is that she was not a Quaker; she is not mentioned in early Quaker letters preserved at Swarthmore. Any letters between her and James have not survived. She appears in Quaker history as 'the wife who visits him in prison'.

At Appleby, Nayler was accused of adultery with a Mrs. Roper of West Ardsley. She owned the house in which meetings of the independent church and those with Fox were held. There seems to have been no truth in the accusation. Ann Nayler made the journey to Appleby, and her presence meant the gossip stopped. Nayler wrote to Fox:

> The coming over of my wife was very serviceable & hath stopped many mouths & half [sic] convinced them of many lies they had raised & was believed in the country. And I myself had great refreshment by her coming, for she came & returned with much freedom & great joy, beyond what I in reason could expect, but I see she was sent of my Father & fitted not to be hinderer, but a furtherer of his work, blessed be our God forevermore.[5]

The phrase 'beyond what I in reason could expect' suggests James did acknowledge the difficulties the manner of his leaving had caused Ann. The world would have understood had she not come to Appleby. But she did come, and he was greatly refreshed by it. The last clause suggests he thanked God for such a willing support.

Nayler's sudden abandonment of his family, though not unusual for early Friends, was the subject of public comment and derision. A pamphlet published in 1654 by five Newcastle ministers reported that, when asked what he did about his farm, Nayler said he gave it to his wife. 'A pretty shift' was the comment, expressing derision that a man could not keep his own family.[6] Peters glosses Nayler's remark as showing that his primary concern was the public rebuttal of his discredited household and patriarchal authority and that he expected from his wife only that she should not hinder God's work.[7] However, the context also suggests the authors are accusing Nayler of hypocrisy by appearing to rid himself of world goods while in fact keeping them 'in the family'.

The magistrates at Bristol asked Nayler if he had a wife.

Answer: There is a woman whom the world calleth my wife, and there are children that were mine according to the flesh.[8]

Ann visited James in Bridewell after his punishments. Her arrival certainly improved his prison conditions. She petitioned Parliament twice in her own handwriting to get them improved and succeeded. Had she not hurried to London, he would probably have died in Bridewell. Rather than think the marriage had failed, it might be more reasonable to describe their long separation as caused by his unavoidable service — in the army and to God.

That is about all that is known concerning Ann Nayler. She outlived James, but it is not known for how long. Nayler or Naylor is a common name in that area, and it is not possible to trace her descendants. Some historians think that one of her daughters had a Quaker wedding. Gaps can be filled by imagination, and in Dorothy Nimmo's cycle of poems *A Testimony to the Grace of God as Shown in the Life of James Nayler 1618–1660*, Ann is shown caring for the farm and her children in a rather dour and silent manner:

> James off Northward Monday, left plough out
> and field half done. Set Tom to finish,
> did well but slowly. Headlands rough.
> Trace broke where it was cobbled,
> will have to be replaced
>
> Good year for apples. Set pigs to windfalls
> And dung the orchard. Calves looking grand.
> Wethers to market, prices only middling.
> Ten pounds of apple cheese. Cleaned ditches
> Rain. Sarah still poorly.

Then she travels to Appleby:

> Appleby for James. Two days there and back
> over by Stainmore. High poor country.
> Black-faced sheep. A bitter wind.
> James off his food, says the Lord keeps him.
> Two trees down round the back when I got home.
> I set Tom to them, firing for winter.
> Finished the ham. All the girls poorly.

And she appears one more time:

> Snow over Christmas but it didn't lie.
> London for James. His tongue's nigh healed
> but his brow's badly yet. He was very low.
> I saw that Martha. I could have told him.
> He'd not have heeded. Parted kindly.

Ann's final comment on James in the poem is:

> Better he stayed at home and died in bed

I would have mourned him then.[9]

Had Nayler done that, we would never have heard of him. At least they parted kindly (in the poet's view) — and he did try to get back home. 'That Martha' was the other woman, Martha Simmonds, the woman with whom James was most closely associated and whom contemporaries accused of causing all the trouble.

8. 'Concerning Hope'

Hope is a gift of God and is pure, and stands in that which is pure, showing that purity of God, and his righteousness in Christ Jesus, the beholding whereof stays the soul from joining to the wicked one, when he tempteth, because he sees in the light a better work to serve; so that until the time of that being manifest, the hope is as an anchor to stay from following the unclean one, and so keeps out of the sin, and so makes not ashamed, even then in the time of want it hopes against hope. When that life of Christ is not yet seen in its full power, yet it is evidenced in the hope, which is wrought in the patience and experience, whereby the love appears and the faith works. . . . And this is that hope that enters within the veil into the holy place, where the life and immortality is brought to light, which the mortal eye nor carnal senses cannot approach to. (LL 3:72)

Nayler had in mind when writing this passage a verse from Hebrews: *Which hope we have as an anchor of the soul, both sure and stedfast, and which entereth into that within the veil* (Hebrews 6:19 KJV). Paul refers to hope in his letters: *Hope makes not ashamed* (Romans 5:5 KJV) and *For we are saved by hope: but hope that is seen is not hope: for what a man seeth, why doth he yet hope for?* (Romans 8:24 KJV). But, in addition to paraphrasing Paul, Nayler is here suggesting that hope is a lifeline, something to hold on to while expectantly waiting for a new life. The hope of a new life will enable the soul to break down the barriers of this world and enter into the next.

But the devil hath begotten another hope, as like this as may be, in his servants who believe him and are acted

> by his spirit, which stands in another ground and brings forth another fruit, and that is although they be servants to sin . . . yet there is hopes of salvation; and such hope as may not be judged false nor questioned, although the witness of God in the conscience doth testify to the contrary, yet it must not be heeded, lest they be deluded. . . . [T]o wait for the testimony or witness within is to deny Christ at Jerusalem, and the greatest blasphemy that can be spoken of; and to wait for that mystery that hath been hid from ages (to wit), Christ within the hope of glory, is to deny the person of Christ and his blood and sufferings. (LL 3:73)

Nayler here mocks the orthodox Christian Calvinist predestination theology that Christ died for the sins of those who were saved, those whose salvation was decided before they were born. There is, therefore, no need for them (or anyone else) to question their salvation, even though their consciences might suggest they have done wrong. The Puritans argued that waiting for the revelation of Christ within, as the Quakers did, was to deny the efficacy of Christ's death, which was an outward payment for the salvation of those who were predestined to be saved.

> So he [the devil] sets them to look for the kingdom of Christ without them, and a Spirit without, and a light without, and a word without, and righteousness without, and in that to hope; while he [the devil] dwells in the heart, and there in darkness upholds his kingdom of sin and seat of unrighteousness all their life. (LL 3:73)

These poor people, deluded by priests, live in a false hope, expecting to be saved while not looking for the salvation that is offered in their own hearts. Furthermore, this hope is the hope of avoiding hell, a negative hope rather than a positive hope of freedom from sin. The devil's hope casts God as partial, saving some and casting others into hell, whereas 'the end of the lively hope is no less than God's righteousness to attain and live in, as it is received' (LL 3:74).

Nayler again references Paul, this time the letter to the Colossians: *Even the mystery which hath been hid from ages and from generations, but now is made manifest to his saints: To whom God would make known what is the riches of the glory of this mystery among the Gentiles; which is Christ in you, the hope of glory* (Colossians 1:26–27 KJV). Nayler continues by questioning why anyone would believe in this outward hope, 'that unreasonable hope in unreasonable men'. How could they expect to be saved at the end of their lives if they continued to live in sin, yielding their minds and bodies to the devil and feeding their vanity by talk of personal salvation? All the while they are lost, for they are not born (begotten) into that lively hope,

> whereunto they are kept by the power, in hope through faith, unto salvation from sin, that thing that he that's begotten of God longs and hopes for, which hope shall not fail. (LL 3:74)

Hope, then, may not only be a psychological aid that keeps the soul strong in its endeavours to break through from this world into a transformed life. It may also be a spiritual or theological requirement. This is a true hope that rejects the outward, taught message of waiting in this world in sin for salvation in an afterlife but instead continues to hope that Christ, the image of the invisible God, is here and able to transform our lives. The inner faith given us (see chapter 6) may also give us strength to do this. As Paul wrote to the Colossians, *As ye have therefore received Christ Jesus the Lord, so walk ye in him: Rooted and built up in him, and stablished in the faith, as ye have been taught, abounding therein with thanksgiving* (Colossians 2:6–7 KJV).

Hope does not appear in the indexes of any of the London Yearly Meeting's books of discipline. Looking into *Quaker faith and practice*, I found this from Pierre Ceresole (1935):

[I]f you want to believe in him [God], if you feel something great behind it all and not just words, well, work for God and you will see not only that it comes to the same thing, as believing in him, but something infinitely more alive, more real, more powerful which fills you and satisfies you more than anything you might vaguely imagine under the name of 'real and living faith'. (QFP 2013, 26.26)

Here, one needs the hope that God exists before embarking, in hope, on a journey, initially of make-believe, that may eventually become reality. This is a course of action that I find is recommended quite frequently to those without faith. When I first attended the Quaker meeting in Rochester, Kent, I promised myself to go as regularly as possible for six months and see what happened. At the end of six months, I could not find any reason to stop going. It was another four years before I applied for membership. I now wonder if, in Nayler's theology, my inner faith, unknown to me, was using hope to bring me into Quakerism.

There is another sort of hope, the hope that God will come again and punish the wrongdoers or the hope that all will be better in the life to come. One of the books I read when in Rochester was Janet Scott's *What Canst Thou Say?* that expressed Quaker theology of the 1980s.[1] Scott has a chapter on hope. She outlines the growth of eschatological expectations of the end of the days in the years before the birth of Jesus. This expectation that the 'end is nigh' was used to interpret Jesus' actions. His healings were a part of the battle between Good and Evil, and 'his death is interpreted as the first fruits of the final resurrection — it is not that he has come back to life but that he has gone through and beyond death into the life of the world to come'.[2]

Eschatological thought is the belief that Christ will come again, physically, into this world to rule for a thousand years. Millennial ideas were very common in seventeenth-century Britain. During the civil wars, the idea developed that the

New Model Army and its leaders were the saints who would bring Christ's rule to pass. The execution of the king was thought of as a necessary political act to clear the way for Christ. Quakers were not immune from this line of thinking. Rosemary Moore quotes Farnsworth as writing in 1653:

> The great day of the Lord is coming. . . . We look for new heaven and new earth . . . and the nations that are saved shall wake in the glorious light and liberty of the sons of God. . . . Light is rising in Parliament [the Nominated or Barebones Parliament, full of dissenters] and people, to see the deceits of the priests. . . . Now the kingdom of Jesus Christ is setting up in the spirits of his people'.[3]

Moore argues that the typical Quaker belief was that the kingdom of the Lord was already beginning to be present in the hearts of the believers and that a final consummation of the arrival of Christ's rule was also possible.[4] Quakers ceased expecting Christ's arrival on earth as the second half of the century went on and political events turned against them. Nayler certainly believed that Christ was risen again in the hearts of believers. I think he was too pragmatic a politician to assent to Christ's physical arrival, although he does use rhetorical language associated with this idea.

There is a danger (into which Quakers did not fall) that such millennial expectations create a divine discontent with the believers' present circumstances through comparison with the new values and community that will come. They can also lead believers to delay doing anything about present evils on the grounds that all will be remedied 'in the end'. Scott uses a close reading of Mark's account of the crucifixion to argue that Mark believes Jesus' suffering and death is both 'the day of the Lord' expected by the prophets and a demonstration that

> no experience of pain or degradation or despair can alienate God's love from us; and that it is precisely here,

in the willed bearing of suffering, and the setting aside of self that God's rule is made manifest and effective. The kingdom is present in every loving heart and selfless act. . . . [W]e see that God is our hope. Further, this hope is not only for the future but for the present for God has already acted, is present with us in all the circumstances of our lives, calling us to be open to the spirit of love.[5]

9. 'Concerning Love'

The love of God is but one, and in one, nor can any
receive it but who receive that one, the Son of God; and
this cannot stand with self, or any changeable thing; for
God is that love, and none can dwell in it but as he
dwells in God: so it's pure and perfect. As the creature
comes to live in God, as he is, into his image and
likeness; so with the pure light his love is seen and shed
abroad in the heart, whereby the power of faith works,
to the overcoming of all that is contrary to God. (LL
3:74)

The love of God is eternal, pure, and perfect; it is not to be
found in changeable things such as humans. It is experienced
only by people living in God. Then, the love is shed abroad
through the person's changed heart, a heart changed through
the power of faith. I think by this Nayler means it is the heart
that spills the love abroad, both within the person's spiritual
heart and also externally through their actions and words.

So the love of God abounds, and who dwells in it
worketh no ill; but the work of love fulfils the law of
God, which is upon all that's gone out from him into the
world and self-ends. (LL 3:74)

What has gone out from the person who lives in God are the
carnal and worldly motivations, which because they are
thrust out are now enemies of God's love.

[F]or whosoever will be a friend to the world is the
enemy of God; for the world's love arises from the spirit
of the world; but the love of God is a fruit of God's
Spirit, and none hath the love of God but who hath that
Spirit from which it springs, which is eternal,
unchangeable and above all carnal things, nor can time
or carnal things quench it, for it endures forever. (LL
3:75)

The felt love of God in one's heart sweeps away all previous life judgments and beliefs. It overturns one's perception of 'right' behaviour and leads one into what appears from the outside to be acts of selfishness and betrayal of the ties of love found in marriage or a long-term partnership. Quaker ministers (as others) could find themselves breaking this love for one lone person in favour of God's love for the world. The English Quaker Katherine Evans was imprisoned with her companion Sarah Chevers by the Inquisition in Malta from 1659 to 1662 after a single day of preaching on the island. She wrote to her husband from prison:

> Oh, how may I do to set forth the fullness of God's love to our souls. . . . O the ravishment, the raptures, the glorious, bright-shining countenance of the Lord our God; which is our fullness in emptiness, our strength in weakness, our health in sickness, our life in death, our joy in sorrow, our peace in disquietness, our praise in heaviness, our power in all needs and necessities. He alone is a full God unto us, and to all that can trust in Him. He has emptied us of ourselves, and hath unbottomed us of ourselves; and hath wholly built us upon the sure foundation,, the Rock of Ages, Christ Jesus the Light of the world, where neither the swelling seas nor raging foaming waves, nor stormy winds, though they beat vehemently, can be able to remove us. (CLFT 1922, pp. 25–26)

And, after perhaps reflecting on the seas that separated them, she told her husband and children,

> I have been very sensible, dear husband, . . . of your sorrowful souls for us. As being members of one body, Jesus Christ being our Head, we must need suffer together that we may rejoice together . . . the heavier the cross the weightier the crown. (CLFT 1922, p. 26)

I hope her husband understood her motivation. The Quakers certainly went to a lot of trouble to get her and Priscilla home.

Their solution was to use court connections and persuade the Queen Mother's Lord Almoner to use his influence and persuade the pope to ask the Knights of St John in Malta to release them. They came home in 1662.

A person full of God's love would not countenance worldly pleasures such as customs, fashions, sports, respect of persons (giving preferential treatment to those of higher social status), and vain pleasures. God's love is active in the world through the reproofs and actions of those full of that love. Those full of God's love may pass judgment on the habits of the world. To return to Nayler:

> So that this love of God consists of reproofs, judgment and condemnation against all that defiles the creation, and against the creature who yields to that pollution; and this is pure love to the soul, that deals faithfully therewith in declaring its condition; and that was the great love Christ showed the Jews, when he told them they were hypocrites, blind guides, liars and said, "Woe to you, ye serpents, ye generations of vipers, how can you escape the damnation of hell?" [Matthew 23:33]. And many such plain true words he spoke in love to them. And that was the love of God in Paul, which said to Elymas, "O full of subtlety and all mischief, thou child of the devil, thou enemy of all righteousness, wilt thou not cease to pervert the right ways of the Lord?" [Acts 13:10]. For all the love that can be showed to any creature is to deal faithfully and truly with them as they are seen in the light. (LL 3:75–76)

> So that love is seen to be filthy which spares filthiness, which defiles the temple of God; but that is pure, which purges away the filth and condemns the unclean, and all that loves it. . . . Therefore, says God, "let love be without dissimulation; abhor that which is evil, cleave to that which is good" [Romans 12:9]; and that love is it which uncovers sin, which condemns sin to death, and covers it with righteousness. (LL 3:76)

This is what we might today call 'tough love'. The section after 'Concerning Love' in *Love to the Lost* is titled 'Concerning Judgment', and Nayler's description of judgment is similar to love. It comes from God and is rightfully used to give God's judgment on the world

> to purge away the filth of the daughter of Zion with the Spirit of judgment and the Spirit of burning [Isaiah 4:4]. (LL 3:77)

God used the Old Testament prophets such as Ezekiel, Jeremiah, and Micah as well as the New Testament apostles to give God's judgment upon the world. Nayler uses these examples to argue that all God's servants can give God's judgment on 'such as know not God'. Indeed, the ability to pass correct judgment upon others is a sign that a person is a servant of God.

> And so in all ages he placed his judgements in his servants, who are to judge the heathen and such as know not God therewith; and so many as did believe it and receive it did repent and found mercy, and the rest were hardened. (LL 3:78)

Thomas Weld and others wrote of the Quakers' 'undeniable conformity' (similarity) to the Pharisees (a strict sect that kept to the letter of the Jewish law) in their pamphlet *The Perfect Pharisee*. The Quakers' 'railings' revealed their spiritual arrogance (and hence similarity to the Pharisees).

> In one paper of theirs, which one of us hath, you have all these horrid railings against the ministers, calling them priests, conjurers, thieves, robbers, antichrists, witches, devils, sir-simons, serpents, bloody Herodians, scarlet colored beasts, Babylon's merchants, wolves, dogs, swine, sodomites, &. Readers, we are not ashamed of the gospel of Christ nor of the reproach of men, because of it. But consider how fully they make good that of Jude 13, "raging waves of the sea, foaming out their own shame," &c, though Michael the

Archangel "when disputing with the devil, durst bring no railing accusation against him."[1]

Nayler replies to this accusation in his pamphlet answering Weld:

> Was it railing in Christ to call them "the children of the devil, who brought forth the works of the devil"; or to call them "serpents and vipers," who sought by their subtlety to devour the simple? Or to call Herod a "fox," who was a king; or for the apostles and saints to call them "dogs, and swine"?[2]

I cannot find a convincing biblical reference that correlates with Nayler's passage. Early Quakers were known to use especially vituperative language, and I think Weld and his co-authors have a legitimate complaint. I think this is better interpreted as Nayler using broad biblical paraphrases to justify his own condemnation of rulers and society in general. He was a prophet; he had been given (as had many Quakers) the gift of discerning God's judgments, and it was his duty to use his gift. His judgment was God's love acting upon the world to change it.

Such condemnations can be made to a crowd of 'unbelievers' without much danger, though it may not help in their convincement. This is not the sort of behaviour one associates with present-day Friends. The British books of discipline soon advised against it. Until 1925, every printed discipline contained a section called 'Love and Unity'. In 1925 and 1959, this became 'Christian Unity' – which is something different.

> Advised, that friends be tender to the principle of God in all, and shun the occasion of vain disputes and janglings, both among themselves and others: for this many times it is like a blustering wind, that hurts and bruises the tender buds of plants. (London Yearly

Meeting epistle of 1676, as quoted in Extracts 1822, p. 59)

Among the gospel precepts, we find not any thing more strongly and frequently recommended by our Lord Jesus Christ and his apostles to the primitive believers, than that they should love one another; and as we are sensible, that nothing will more contribute to the peace and prosperity of the church, than a due regard to this advice, so we earnestly desire that it may be the care and concern of all friends to dwell therein; and, in the unity of the Holy Spirit, to maintain love, concord, and peace in and among all the churches of Christ. (London Yearly Meeting epistle of 1730, as quoted in Extracts 1822, p. 60)

The next extract comes from the 1883 book of discipline in a section titled 'Love and Unity in the Church'. 'Church' here can be read as meaning the Quaker church or the broader Christian churches. I think it is talking to both. The language is much more prosaic than Nayler's, almost legal in its account of who belongs with whom, yet it does to me echo the earlier words of Nayler that 'the love of God is but one'.

The Church is the body of which Christ is the Head. In union with Him the various members are brought into fellowship with each other. Collectively they are one body; individually they are members one of another in Him. . . . They that are truly his are in the Spirit of the Lamb. He gives them of his patience, his meekness and gentleness. He teaches them how to bear and forbear; how to "be subject one to another"; and when and how, in faithfulness to Him, their lowly and long-suffering Lord, they must make concessions to one another, and give up, if need be, something of their own individual freedom for the general good. (London Yearly Meeting epistle of 1878, as quoted in BoD 1883, p. 72)

The 1922 *Christian Life, Faith and Thought* included an extract from the 1915 London Yearly Meeting epistle:

9. 'Concerning Love'

We have met this year in the midst of the tragedy of war. . . . It seems to many that a God of Love could not permit such terrible happenings. "They continually say unto me: Where is thy God" (Ps xlii.3). We cannot give an answer of strength and consolation to such a cry in terms of any traditional faith. It is only as our faith is rediscovered and resettled on a rock foundation that we can help a bewildered world. We thank God that a new and living experience of His power and purpose has come to us. Our hope is in this word: — God is Love; the power of God is the power of undying and persistent love. It is through the hearts and minds and wills of men and women that He works, and He waits for them to open their hearts to Love and to follow with unwavering courage. (CLFT 1922, p. 82)

Quakers kept hope alive during the devastation of the First World War with the belief that God is love and that in the long term only love can change the world.

Neither 'love' nor 'God's love' appears in the indexes of the books of discipline of 1959 or 2013. However, the same understanding of love is there.

To find religion itself you must look inside people and inside yourself. And there, if you find even the tiniest grain of true love, you may be on the right scent. Millions of people have it and don't know what it is that they have. God is their guest, but they haven't the faintest idea that he is in the house. (Bernard Canter, 1962, as quoted in QFP 2013, 26.37)

All my life I've heard 'God is love', without understanding what was meant. Recently I've come to feel that in a very real way G-d/ess is the love that loves in and between and among us. The ebb and flow of my commitment to love, to peace, to harmony makes G-d/ess stronger or weaker in my heart. (Rose Ketterer, 1987, as quoted in QFP 2013, 26.35)

British Quakers have rather lost sight of Nayler's judgmental love. We should remember that *Love to the Lost* is a public account of his theology addressed to non-Quakers; to write or speak of the love that flows between Friends in their communities might not be useful in such circumstances. It is also possible that, after his imprisonment, Nayler changed his mind about judgment and love. Geoffrey Nuttall, in his 1953 address to the Friends' Historical Society, observes that after 1656 Nayler seemed more understanding of 'backsliding'. Nayler understood then, if he did not before, that a convinced man can unintentionally fall again into sin.

> Finally Nayler's perception, all too painfully, how the genuinely committed Christian may still, "not willingly," fall in the struggle with sin, misled and temporarily worsted, prompts him to plead that such backsliders shall receive not condemnation from their fellow-Christians but pity, forgiveness and love. "They are . . . more to be pittyed," he writes, "because of the simplicity that is deceived." After all, this is the attitude God adopts towards the sinner, as Nayler had learned in the midst of his own error [his ride into Bristol].[3]

In *A message from the Spirit of Truth unto the Holy Seed Who are chosen out of the world and are lovers and followers of the Light*, printed for Thomas Simmonds in 1658 with a preface by Rebecca Travers, Nayler addresses London Quakers who are called to God and urges them to throw off all worldly things 'that the holy name of Christ may be glorified in you'. He urges them to put on God's love,

> as he is the Son of God's love, and so hold him forth towards all men that especially towards the brethren, so much the more as this being that which the enemy hath cast long upon the children of light (to wit) want of love.[4]

It is interesting that Nayler says Quakers generally were accused of a want of love. He might have meant this was how the public perceived them after nearly a decade of 'railing', or he might have meant this was how Friends had treated him and his followers. He goes on to urge Quakers to clothe themselves in God's Love

> and that you be clothed therewith, from heaven, so plentifully, that you may have to cast over a brother's nakedness a garment of the same love, who came from above to lay down his life for his enemies, and of the same power, who can forgive sins and offences above seven times a day, beholding each other's with that good eye which waits for the soul and not for the sin, which covers and overcomes the evil with the good, that with him you may be perfect in love, judging, and receiving one another in the increase of God, and not in that which is for destruction; giving more abundant honor to him that lacketh, that in the body be no schism, nor defile one another, nor keep alive a brother's iniquity, nor blot out the name and appearing of the Holy Seed in the least.[5]

There is a remembrance in this passage of 2 Corinthians 5:4 where Paul says *we wish not to be unclothed but to be further clothed, so that what is mortal may be swallowed up by life* [NRSV]. This is an image of the immortal life being put on over the top of our mortal life (crudely, as one might 'put on' wet-weather gear). For me, this is more evidence that Nayler (and perhaps Paul) thought our resurrection was in this life. Ashworth discusses 2 Corinthians 5:4 and its use of 'clothed'. He concludes that Paul uses the same image as Nayler of 'immortal life' being put on over the top of 'mortal life', with the sense that 'we do not wish to lose our mortal life' but rather wish that the mortal life be further clothed with immortal life.[6] I like the idea that some Friends may have enough love to be able to clothe another with their spare love.

I conclude this chapter with a long quotation from a non-Quaker author, the early-eighteenth-century Anglican priest William Law (1686–1761). His writings were much loved by Friends in the eighteenth century, and what he has to say about the Spirit of Love is worth reading:

But the Spirit of Love is not in you till it is the spirit of your life, till you live freely, willingly, and universally according to it. For every spirit acts with freedom and universality according to what it is. It needs no command to live its own life, or be what it is, no more than you need bid wrath be wrathful. And therefore when love is the spirit of your life, it will have the freedom and universality of a spirit; it will always live and work in love, not because of this or that, here or there, but because the Spirit of Love can only love, wherever it goes or whatever is done to it. As the sparks know no motion but that of flying upwards, whether it be in the darkness of the night or in the light of the day, so the Spirit of Love is always in the same course; it knows no difference of time, place, or persons; but whether it gives or forgives, bears of forbears, it is equally doing its own delightful work equally blessed from itself. For the Spirit of Love, wherever it is, is its own blessing and happiness because it is the truth and reality of God in the soul, and therefore is in the same joy of life and is the same good to itself everywhere and on every occasion.[7]

10. 'Concerning Perfection'

> God is perfect, and so are all his works and all his gifts; and whoever receives his gifts, receives that which is perfect. And by receiving and joining to that which is perfect is the creature made perfect. (LL 3:79)

Friends held that through Christ the original goodness of creation was restored; Fox (1648) described passing through the flaming swords that guarded Eden and into a new creation where everything was as new.[1] The disobedience of Adam had brought sin into the world: the obedience of Jesus, the incarnate word full of grace and truth (John 1:14), brought justification and redemption to all people (Romans 5:18). Nayler writes,

> And no further than the creature is in this perfection, can any be united to God, nor appear in his sight, nor be blessed, but . . . is in the fall, unredeemed, and hath no more of Christ, than what he hath of perfection; for perfection is of Christ, and imperfection is of the devil; and these are two contraries, and comes from contrary grounds, and brings forth contrary fruits, for he that is of God is of perfection and believes perfection, but who is of the serpent cannot own it nor believe it, being blinded by the god of this world. (LL 3:79–80)

Already, we moderns are plunged into difficulty understanding this unless we grasp some of the theological background. An examination of conversion narratives shows that most of Nayler's neighbours would have had a pessimistic view of human nature. For them, perfection would be achieved by only a few of the elect. It was a three-stage process.

Puritan doctrine dictated a two-fold experience of Law and Gospel, in which the Christian must learn, through experience, that justification cannot be earned. [Puritan conversion narratives] describe an initial legalistic stage . . . followed by an experience of grace which reveals that as one of the elect, the person is freed and justified in spite of sin.[2]

Finally, they spent the rest of their lives in a continuous war between flesh and Spirit which, for a few, would end in 'sanctification' and ascent into heaven. Very few, if any, of them would become perfect, and none dared think they were already.

Early Quakers preached a more dramatic two-stage process: conviction of sin following by a winnowing or spiritual purification through fire or something similar which culminated in an experience of regeneration, an unshakable unity with the indwelling Christ. This was sometimes called the 'day of visitation'.[3]

God sent his Son into the world to preach perfection, even the perfection of the Father, that all who will believe may inherit it; and all that believed him, believed perfection. And when he had left a perfect example in all things, he ascended, and gave gifts to men . . . all for the perfecting of the saints, that all might come up to one faith, to a perfect man to the measure, and stature, and fullness of Christ [Ephesians 4:13], so that he may be an everlasting redeemer, perfecting the work of God in every generation of them that believe in his work and follow him. And this all his ministers improved to the same end, and preached and prayed that they might present every man perfect in Christ Jesus, from whom they had received the gift [Ephesians 4:11–12]. (LL 3:80)

Being perfect is about being in unity with Christ and God:

10. 'Concerning Perfection'

> And all that know this perfect will and acceptable work of God knows it begotten and brought forth in self-denial in all things; and not of us, but of him that is perfect. (LL 3:80)

So, it is not by our own efforts that we are perfect (elsewhere in this section, Nayler describes righteousness as a 'gift put into the believer'). Nayler uses the example of the apostles after the resurrection; they did not go about copying Jesus's works but were commanded to wait for the Holy Spirit.

> Therefore were they commanded to wait at Jerusalem till therewith they was endued [with the Spirit]; and then they was made able ministers, not of the letter but of the Spirit; and their testament in the Spirit, and not old in the letter, for that of the letter kills, but the Spirit perfects. (LL 3:83)

However, after the work of the apostles, the church fell away and 'the mystery of iniquity entered'. Then, another ministry came into the world which had

> begotten another kind of faith in the world, wholly reprobate as to perfection, preaching against it with all the power that may be, holding it for blasphemy, and calling it a doctrine of devils and the like. . . . The work of Christ is and ever was to renew man again to his perfect estate; but the work of antichrist is to withstand it, and each hath his ministers suitable to their ends intended. Christ's end is to perfect, the devil's is to keep unperfect. (LL 3:80)

Opponents of Friends targeted the doctrine of perfection as a particularly odious Quaker doctrine; it had radical political and social implications, and it took away the need for priests. Very early in his ministry, in 1647, George Fox preached in Manchester. Some of his listeners were convinced, but

> [t]he professors were in a rage, all pleading for sin and imperfection, and could not endure to hear talk of perfection, and of an holy and sinless life.[4]

Nayler is clear that to imitate perfection is not beneficial — there is no possibility of 'justification by works'. Those who are not perfect cannot know Christ or God. Our faith must stand in what God can do, not in what we can do. However, there is an ambivalence in Nayler, for he is clear that even if righteousness comes to the believer as a free gift, it has to be nourished and maintained through denial of the self in all things. Nayler's 'conversion' experience seems to have lasted over a number of years, starting with the probably 'legalistic' approach of the independent church in Woodkirk, moving on to army debates and personal reflection, and concluding with his conviction after meeting George Fox. The struggle to deny 'self' in all things meant a Friend's outward behaviour appeared similar to one of the elect struggling to achieve sanctification. The elect, however, were in a very different position to Quakers because of their attachment to the written word:

> In your vain imaginations and comprehensions [you] are judging you know not what, and limiting the spiritual covenant of God to the literal; and because you who are in the letter (searching with your wit) can find no perfection, therefore you will judge the spiritual covenant also: that so the devil may forever keep people from the coming in of the better hope. For if the first covenant made nothing perfect, not the second neither, what hope is there for people, seeing no imperfection can enter into the kingdom of heaven? (LL 3:83)

Perfection was not a specifically Quaker doctrine; it was also claimed by Ranters, who did not believe it was necessary to continue to deny the self to nourish the spirit, and consequently they acquired a reputation for bad behaviour which was frequently in the popular mind passed on to Quakers as well. Later Friends, even as early as Barclay and Penn, modified perfectionism. They did not themselves expect to be perfect but felt they were moving towards it through right behaviour. Tousley argues that

10. 'Concerning Perfection'

[t]he doctrine of perfection formed the basis of Quaker identity, as Friends saw themselves as a community called out of the world to corporate holiness.[5]

The Quaker distinctives of simplicity, peace, waiting, truthfulness, and refusing oaths were all upheld 'by the experience of sanctification within the community and desire for perfect obedience to God's will'.[6] Tousley notes,

> Oversight of discipline became the work of elders, and the spiritual struggle of second-generation Friends was often over acceptance of the stringent ethical demands or testimonies which set Quakers apart.[7]

This is about the outward habits of perfection in the individual and the concern that those outward habits are maintained so that the perfection of the entire community is not thrown into doubt. For this reason, Friends could be 'read out' of their meeting for continued bad behaviour such as drunkenness, debt, or overly adopting the manners and customs of the world. It is very difficult, especially when young and attempting to make a living amongst one's peer group, to avoid such adoption. Advices 37, 39, and 40 in *Quaker faith and practice* are there to remind us to at least try for a modicum of perfection.

> Are you honest and truthful in all you say and do? Do you maintain strict integrity in business transactions and in your dealings with individuals and organisations? Do you use money and information entrusted to you with discretion and responsibility? Taking oaths implies a double standard of truth; in choosing to affirm instead, be aware of the claim to integrity that you are making. (QFP 2013, 1.37)

> Consider which of the ways to happiness offered by society are truly fulfilling and which are potentially corrupting and destructive. Be discriminating when choosing means of entertainment and information. Resist the desire to acquire possessions or income

through unethical investment, speculation or games of chance. (QFP 2013, 1.39)

In view of the harm done by the use of alcohol, tobacco and other habit-forming drugs, consider whether you should limit your use of them or refrain from using them altogether. Remember that any use of alcohol or drugs may impair judgment and put both the user and others in danger. (QFP 2013, 1.40)

The advice here is about outward behaviour, supporting Tousley's argument that the Society became more interested in the appearance of corporate holiness. Elias Hicks (1748–1830), a Quaker from Long Island, New York, in 1806 wrote in his journal that he found himself while travelling in a meeting that was stupid, ignorant, and full of unbelief. He waited and found this darkness came 'from a want of due attention to and right belief in the inward manifestation of Divine Light' that shows what is right. The relevance of this observation to perfection is in the words that follow, which the first editors of his journal (New York Yearly Meeting) deleted as embarrassing or as likely to support the arguments of their orthodox opponents.[8]

And that it is only owing to this want of attention and belief in this divine principle [inward manifestation of Divine Light] by the children of men that makes the atheist, the deist, the predestinarian, and universalian — with every other profession or denomination of Christians which do not believe in the sufficiency of that divine principle to procure for us a state of freedom from sin in this life. And without which, no salvation can be witnessed either here or hereafter by any accountable being. And the reason of this ignorance and unbelief is founded in their unwillingness and refusal of making use of the means appointed by our gracious Creator as the only medium by which that knowledge is to be obtained — on which the belief of his necessary and very essential doctrine of perfection from sin is founded.[9]

Hicks is saying, Do not underestimate the power of the inward Light. It can change you completely. It must be able to do that because it comes from the All-Powerful. And if you are unable to accept that possibility you will remain in ignorance and darkness, even though you may sit for hours in corporate holiness. Hicks is arguing that perfectability, or its possiblity, is a logical extension of the Quaker belief in the Divine Light.

One of the sections written for the 1925 *Christian Practice* is titled 'Personal Character'. To my mind, it sets out an impossible standard of behaviour. It is indeed a counsel of perfection, but it should not be dismissed just because it may seem impossible to achieve.

> The patient Master Builder of the City of God builds with the hearts of men. . . . As we respond to the drawings of the heart of God, we are filled with a spirit which restrains the animal and sets free the true man, charging us with a power from beyond ourselves for self-discipline and service and enabling us to love. . . . If we would indeed take a place in God's larger work, more is required of us than the ordinary virtues of respectability. . . . [The people around us] recognise if our conduct is commonly distinguished by strength and firmness. . . . [I]f we are possessed, too, of a considerate and helpful kindliness, and by a gentleness and graciousness which reflects the Christ life, our neighbours are at once made happier and stronger and more able to bear their burdens. These are the signs of a life that is filled with the spirit and is in line with the purposes of God.

> Paul writes, "It is my prayer that your love may be more and more accompanied by clear knowledge and keen perception" (Philippians 1:9). Wilful ignorance and the ignorance due to laziness are the cause of irreparable

damage to our fellow men and to the cause of God. . . .
The true scientist's longing for the facts, the power of
appreciation and judgment, often acquired through
familiarity with the best in art and literature, the
capacity of expression that comes with careful writing
and thoughtful conversation, the sensitiveness that is
made keener by the study of economics and politics —
these are qualities we must work and pray for. It is
important also, if we are to have any share in
influencing the thinking of those around us, that we
should be able to contribute something more
convincing than general exhortation, to be really
helpful we should be familiar with the lines of accurate
thinking and argument and with the main schools of
thought. . . . Our service to God is incomplete without
the contribution of the intellect.

It is the special gift of the Christian to be able to put
away bitterness and loneliness, to destroy pessimism
and hardness, to inspire kindliness and courtesy and
unselfishness. The real love which is immediately
recognisable by any man, is based on deep knowledge
of both man and God, and of the right relation of man
to God. It is the overflow of the grace of God through
human personality. It is that which brings men back to
God. (CP 1925, pp. 98–101)

This does seem a very hard ideal to live up to. Is it helpful to
set such a model before us? Chapter 18 of *Quaker faith and
practice*, titled 'Faithful Lives', sets many lives before us. I
have read and reread the memoir of William Dent (1778–
1861), and he seems to have had many of the virtues
mentioned in the passage above. He was a plain tenant
farmer, and when he moved into his farm, the houses in the
village were unsanitary, the labourers had no allotments to
grow additional food, and the children no school to attend,
although there was a pub. Joshua Rowntree wrote the
following about Dent in 1913:

10. 'Concerning Perfection'

When at four score years his [Dent's] call came to go up higher he left a village where every cottage was a healthy home, where all able-bodied labourers wishing for an allotment could have one. The public house had gone and a good village school had been established. For many years the school mistress had lived in his house. A Bible Society anniversary in his big barn was the annual festival and Eirenicon of the district. It may fairly be said that the whole neighbourhood was slowly uplifted by the coming of one quiet life into its midst. (QFP 2013, 18.11)[10]

11. 'Concerning Government or Magistracy'

> There is no just government but what is of God, and in whomsoever he (having called them) placeth his power and authority. (LL 3:83)

Nayler makes no mention here of voting for governors; they are chosen by God, something that Charles I would have agreed with. However, Nayler goes on to explain that these governors must themselves receive the authority of Jesus and do as Jesus would do.

> Therefore saith the apostle, 'Let every soul be subject to the higher power' [Romans 13:1]. And he that will rule for God must first see that his own soul be subject to the higher power and must know one higher than he; and so himself coming under that power, then with that power and authority upon him, he goes forth to rule with God, for God; and having set up his [Jesus's] kingdom in his heart, he goes to make way that his kingdom may be set up in others. . . . And so his government, being according to that in every conscience, . . . shall witness him and his government to be of God, and so he that resists shall receive to himself damnation [Romans 13:2]. (LL 3:83–84)

This is similar to the idea of the rule of the saints, which is that only 'godly men' should be appointed rulers, something Cromwell attempted in the appointed Barebones Parliament only to find that godly men quarrelled about what should be done. Nayler continues by giving three examples of rulers who have been recognised as carrying out God's will.

> ➢ Cyrus (accounted a heathen), recognised by Isaiah as God's appointed and a shepherd to his people [Isaiah 44:28 and 45:1];

> ➢ Moses, dreadful in his authority ruler but the meekest man in the world, and
> ➢ Samuel, a poor man whose authority made the elders of Bethlehem tremble at his coming [1 Samuel 16:4].

Nayler then says it is too much to give more particulars.

> But if it be said, Must not men own wicked magistrates? I say, they are to be owned and obeyed in all things, as they are appointed by God; for God limits them and hath set bounds to them, though they know it not; and so far as they command the will of God they are to be obeyed for conscience sake. (LL 3:84–85)

Presumably, Cyrus had no idea that he was following the will of the Israelite God. And Nayler, later in the chapter, says he could have no reward for his just actions because he did not know Christ was guiding and leading him (LL 3:86–87).

But should rulers command what God forbids or forbid what God commands, then none should be obeyed for conscience's sake. And many in all ages have suffered violence to keep their consciences clear.

> And here is the ground of all persecution that ever was, when governors are out of the fear of God and stand in their wills, and walk after the flesh. . . . And from this ground have the lambs been devoured always as evildoers, but ever innocent. . . . And in the time of such governors hath the Lamb borne testimony in much patience, meekness and longsuffering, bearing all the venom and envy that the serpent could cast out upon him where he was manifest in the creature [meaning that the governors were led by the serpent to condemn the servants of the Lamb] for a witness against all such rulers; that his longsuffering might lead them to repentance and leave them without excuse in the day of his wrath; and against such is he finishing his testimony at this day. (LL 3:85)

This could be seen as a foreshadowing of Nayler's own behaviour when he was tried and punished by Parliament. He suffered in silence to shame his accusers into repentance and to give them no excuse for the violence done towards him when they stood before St Peter. He also describes the politics of the day as an example of God destroying those who ruled outside his authority. He then goes on to say that the rulers of today (1656) are worse oppressors than before, for each generation learns from the last and is

> (to the things of Christ) more blind and deaf. So that it's rare to find one who hath an ear to hear oppression; but not one, whose heart is perfect to deny the world's favor, to bear witness against the ground of oppression: so the just man perisheth. (LL 3:85–86)

The chapter continues by explaining the differences between the ruler without God in his heart and those who channel God's will into the world. The first should be challenged:

> And to such as these who mind not that of God to govern withal, hath God sent his servants to testify to their faces of their departure from the just principle, and so cannot please God with his government (yet did they never plot against them, nor murmur), which if they did hear, they rejoiced to see them established as a blessing to the place and people. (LL 3:87)

If they do not hear, then God's servants are made to mourn

> that God should be grieved and his creature lost, especially in such a place by which God may be so dishonored and a nation or town plagued from the Lord for his sake who hath the sword of God in his hand, and suffers sin but punishes the innocent, both which the Lord will revenge. . . . So when the righteous reigns, God is honored and good men rejoice; but when wickedness gets up in the king, then the Lord is dishonored and the glory departs. (LL 3:87)

Finally, Nayler mentions the king and perhaps gives his own reason for voting for his impeachment — the king was a wicked man. Interestingly, the 1665 edition of this pamphlet and George Whitehead's 1716 edition change 'king' to 'magistrate'. One can guess why.

In the generations after 1660, 'circumspection' became the Religious Society of Friend's watchword. In 1688 came the 'Glorious Revolution', but for Quakers the result was far from clear.[1] A written epistle of 1690 laments that:

> [A]lthough we gave plain and Christian advice and admonishment last year, for friends to beware of all airy discourses, disputes, and controversies, about the kingdoms of this world; that all might walk circumspectly and wisely, . . . yet contrarywise, to our grief, we have heard too much complaint and reflections, occasioned by some who have not observed a true bridle to their tongues, but have been too busy, loose, and airy, in discourses of this nature [concerning the outward powers]; and therefore we do exhort and admonish all such in the fear of God . . . to be watchful, careful, and circumspect for the time to come. (BoD 1834, p. 31)

The 1692 epistle of London Yearly Meeting recorded its satisfaction at the peaceableness of Friends in general towards the civil government. In 1719 came the first of many reminders that Friends should not defraud the king of his customs, duties, or excise. In 1769 and 1775, Friends were reminded to avoid being ensnared by the animosities of contending parties and were also reminded of the text *Thou shalt not speak evil of the ruler of thy people* (Acts 23:5 KJV; BoD 1834, p. 33). Throughout the eighteenth century, Friends maintained a mixed approach towards the law and the authorities. Nayler had not protested to Parliament about the illegality of its proceedings against him. But during the Commonwealth and after 1660 Quakers did use the courts to establish their innocence. The chapter called 'Sufferings' in the 1822 Extracts begins with a minute from 1675:

> As this meeting doth not enjoin or advise any friends, in sufferings for our Christian testimonies, to take a court at law for remedy, neither can we impose upon them, not to use law in any case; but a freedom is left to the sufferers, to use such means as consist[ent] with the unity of friends, and their own peace and satisfaction in the truth, and bearing a faithful testimony in righteousness. (Extracts 1822, p. 181)

Instead, the advice as given in 1682 was:

> Upon consideration of sufferings in general, it is advised, that in cases of difficulty, and where friends who are sufferers stand in need of advice in any particular case, they send up their respective cases to the meeting for sufferings in London. (Extracts 1822, p. 182)

This was repeated in different words in 1746 and in 1789. The most likely cause of 'suffering' for propertied Friends during these years was the nonpayment of tithes. Tithes were a tax in kind levied locally for the upkeep of the church and support of the priest. Nayler had written extensively against them, and nonpayment was a distinctive Quaker practice.

> Advised, that our ancient testimony against tithes, which we have borne from the beginning, and for which may have deeply suffered, some not only the spoiling of their goods, but imprisonment even unto death, be carefully and punctually upheld and countenanced, in the power of God; and that all those who oppose, slight, or neglect that testimony, be looked upon as unfaithful to the ancient testimony of truth, and dealt with according to the gospel order established among us. (Extracts 1822, p. 184, written in 1675)

In 1706, the yearly meeting clarified that the last clause in the above passage here meant disownment — that is, publicly saying someone was not a member of the Society (they could still attend meetings for worship). Friends went on paying tithes, and some priests, or local authorities, made it easier for Friends to hide this from their coreligionists by mixing the tithe payment in with the poor rates levied for the maintenance of the local poor, which Friends had no objection to paying. In 1756, the yearly meeting advised that this was illegal and that such rates could be refused (Extracts 1822, p, 190). In 1796, the yearly meeting was obliged to remind Friends that their 1706 advice about disownment still stood, suggesting that payment of tithes was not uncommon amongst Friends (Extracts 1822, p. 194). Tithes were turned into a money payment in 1839 and abolished entirely in 1936, although they seem to have ceased to worry Friends long before that. As well as tithes, other practices could lead to Friends 'suffering' in some way:

> This meeting having weightily considered the propriety of receiving and recording the sufferings of friends, for not illuminating their houses, and not shutting up their shops, on public occasions, is of the judgement that friends should send up an account of such sufferings, from time to time, to this meeting. (Extracts 1822, p, 183)

From early on in their history, Quakers were accustomed to collecting information about social problems, collating it and presenting it to a central authority with arguments as to how it could be ameliorated. As well as their own sufferings, Quakers are well known for lobbying governments on a variety of issues such as slavery, tithes, oaths, and marriage regulations. The radicalism shown by early Friends continued but in a more pragmatic form. The books of discipline contain epistles and minutes about these and other issues, but there is no space to discuss them here. One point perhaps should be made: the Quaker reliance on the role of God to influence the course of events. In 1833, as Parliament was legislating for the final abolition of slavery, London Yearly Meeting minuted:

> It is with reverent thanksgiving to our Almighty Father in heaven, that we now look forward to the termination of this cruel and disgraceful system as an event not far distant. . . . the House of Commons [is] engaged in legislating upon this deeply-interesting question. We humbly commend these proceedings to the blessing of the Most High. (BoD 1834, p. 251)

Quakers could take part in public life and hold public office after the abolition of the Test Acts in 1829. The Test Acts had required office holders appointed by the Crown to take communion and an oath of loyalty, neither of which Quakers could do. For the next hundred years, the books of discipline express a muted enthusiasm for public office. The advice below was first written in 1836 and was repeated in 1883 and 1925:

> And let those who enter on any public office be concerned in the first place, to fulfil its duties in the fear of the Lord, seeking for his help, and diligently and faithfully performing the trust reposed in them, as those who have to render an account not to man only, but to God. We desire that our dear friends may, on these occasions support in simplicity and fidelity all those testimonies which distinguish us from others. . . . Fulfil the law of immutable righteousness; uphold the standard of truth-speaking and inflexible integrity in all things; watch over your spirits that you be not leavened into the spirit of the world, if so be you have known what it is to be raised above it; shun all party combinations and pursue in humility the course of Christian independence. (BoD 1836, supplement of 1844, p. 343; reprinted in BoD 1883, pp. 133–34 and CP 1925, p. 114–15, with minor revisions to the language)

These concerns did not prevent Quakers from standing for Parliament. In 1698, John Archdale was elected to Parliament but would not take the oath of allegiance and so was never admitted. In 1832, the prominent and rich industrialist Joseph Pease (1799–1872) was elected for South Durham. Parliament found a way around the difficulty of oath-taking by including a provision for affirmation of allegiance rather than an oath in the 1832 Reform Act. Pease retired from Parliament in 1841. He spoke in the House on the three planks of his programme: anti-slavery, the desirability of agricultural protection (mainly tariffs on wheat which kept up the price of food), and his opposition to any statutory restrictions on the hours of work for factory children. Joseph Pease was followed in Parliament by many members of his family. A Pease could be returned to Parliament at any time he chose because he combined 'the politics of influence with the politics of individualism', meaning the Peases had a strong political machine to get out those who had the vote but always presented themselves as political 'outsiders'.[2]

In the nineteenth century, a total of thirty-three Quakers were elected to Parliament, mostly Liberals.[3] Of these, about a third were from the Pease family and its immediate connections. They fell out amongst themselves over home rule for Ireland and rarely voted as a block. The influence of Quaker members of Parliament on parliamentary and ministerial matters was small. This contrasts with their influence on business and banking, which was large. The next century saw a fall in the number of Quaker members of Parliament.

By the start of the twentieth century, members of the Religious Society of Friends were more used to the idea of 'public service', and many were motivated by the ideal of service to work in teaching, social work with the poor in 'settlements', as civil servants, as elected councillors, and, occasionally, as members of Parliament. The First World War profoundly changed the social attitudes and concerns of

British Quakers. In 1918, London Yearly Meeting adopted the following eight 'foundations of a true social order', a radical programme of social progress based on the teachings of the New Testament.

i.   The Fatherhood of God, as revealed by Jesus Christ, should lead us toward a brotherhood which knows no restriction of race, sex or social class.

ii.   This brotherhood should express itself in a social order which is directed, beyond all material ends, to the growth of personality truly related to God and man.

iii.   The opportunity of full development, physical, moral and spiritual, should be assured to every member of the community, man, woman and child. The development of man's full personality should not be hampered by unjust conditions nor crushed by economic pressure.

iv.   We should seek for a way of living that will free us from the bondage of material things and mere conventions, that will raise no barrier between man and man, and will put no excessive burden of labour upon any by reason of our superfluous demands.

v.   The spiritual force of righteousness, loving-kindness and trust is mighty because of the appeal it makes to the best in every man, and when applied to industrial relations achieves great things.

vi.   Our rejection of the methods of outward domination, and of the appeal to force, applies not only to international affairs, but to the whole problem of industrial control. Not through antagonism but through co-operation and goodwill can the best be obtained for each and all.

vii.   Mutual service should be the principle upon which life is organised. Service, not private gain, should be the motive of all work.

viii.   The ownership of material things, such as land and capital, should be so regulated as best to minister to the need and development of man. (QFP 2013, 23.16)

11. 'Concerning Government or Magistracy'

The above 'foundations of a true social order' are the closest the Religious Society of Friends in Britain has ever come to adopting a political programme. Friends were encouraged by London Yearly Meeting to take some responsibility for public affairs and, by implication, to use these principles in their own public and commercial lives.

> The free institutions under which we live give many of our members a direct share in the responsibilities of government and in forming the healthy public opinion that will lead to purity of administration and righteousness of policy. This responsibility belongs to them by virtue of their citizenship, and our members can no more rightly remain indifferent to it, than to the duties which they owe to their parents and near relatives. Men and women of alertness, intelligence and high principle are needed today, to combat the indifference, ignorance and self-interest which are continually impeding the wise solution of great national questions. (CP 1925, p. 115, drafted for the 1911 edition; repeated in CFP 1959, para. 582)

These sentiments were particularly apt after the end of World War I. Legislation in 1918 and 1928 had had the effect of widening the electorate in Britain from seven to twenty-two million and including women. According to the 1928 general advices:

> In your daily work, and in your social and other activities, be concerned for the establishment of the Kingdom of Heaven upon earth. Live not for yourselves but for others. Remember your responsibilities as citizens for the government of your own town and country. Study the causes of social evils. Work for an order of society based on mutual service and directed beyond all material ends to the true enrichment of human lives. (CFP 1959, para. 541)

The present *Advices and Queries* contains very similar sentiments (QFP 2013 1.01).

The 1959 *Christian Faith and Practice* showed a widening sense of Quaker social responsibility and of its origins. In 1958, Friends held a conference on the industrial and social order which reconsidered the eight foundations of 1918 and asked what 'this inheritance required of us in our everyday living'.[4] The extracts from the minutes suggest Friends were struggling with finding a voice and a message.

> This country is not predominately Christian and it is in this setting that our Christian witness is called for. For this we need the insights, but not the practical solutions of our forebears, for the world we know has changed beyond all recognition in comparison with theirs. (CFP 1959, para. 547)

> The extremity of our sense of difficulty and difference, however, has brought us not to a feeling of despair of accomplishing anything at all, but to a new sense of dependence on and challenge from God to use our individual aptitudes and versatilities in situations that now as in the past are subject to change as a result of dedicated human lives. Indeed, our consciousness of the extremity of our plight serves to underline our affirmation that with God all things are possible. (CFP 1959, para. 549)

By 1994, Friends in Britain were uncomfortably aware of their middle-class, resource-intensive lifestyles. The 1994 *Quaker faith and practice* placed two quotes about this at the start of chapter 23 on social responsibility:

> We know that Jesus identified himself with the suffering and the sinful, the poor and the oppressed. We know that he went out of his way to befriend social outcasts. . . . The worship of middle-class comfort is surely a side-chapel in the temple of Mammon. It attracts large congregations, and Friends have been

known to frequent it. (H. G. Wood, 1958, as quoted in QFP 2013, 23.03)

The duty of the Society of Friends is to be the voice of the oppressed but [also] to be conscious that we ourselves are part of that oppression. Uncomfortably we stand with one foot in the kingdom of this world and with the other in the Eternal Kingdom. (Eva I. Pinthus, 1987, as quoted in QFP 2013, 23.04)

The Society has moved from keeping a separation, a hedge, between itself and the world to urging upon its members a fuller involvement in the world. We are urged by the Society to do our bit to ameliorate, or even rid, the world of its evils: substance abuse, gambling, poverty, poor housing, discrimination, torture, conscription, factory farming, and so on. Chapter 23 of *Quaker faith and practice,* 'Social Responsibility', contains 103 paragraphs. The 'hedge' is no longer very high and is not one behind which the Society can cultivate its corporate holiness or individual perfectionism in solitude. Friends may do better than many at treading lightly on the world and its people, but our feet can still be heavy. Is it possible to challenge the entire system within which we find ourselves without first showing in our lives a greater difference from the majority than many of us would be comfortable with? The last paragraph of Chris Alton's 2018 Swarthmore Lecture returns to a familiar Quaker exhortation concerning the kingdom of God on this earth — behave as if it were already present:

May we go forth and reshape the world. May our exploits be worthy of the first blockbuster film to tell the tale of a civilization that averted climate change, of a people who dismantled entrenched social inequalities of class, race, gender, sexuality, and more; a people who learnt to live in peace with the needs of all catered for within the limits of our planet. Let it tell a story not of heroes, but of communities that forged our future anew.

We must imagine this future, for, if we cannot imagine it, we cannot speak it into existence.[5]

Are we able to turn the system upside down while still being 'watchful, careful and circumspect'? Is speaking enough?

12. On Nayler's Politics

This chapter examines Nayler's writings which are implicitly or explicitly political. All his writings come from his faith, and some 'political' stands are unmistakably Quaker; these include objections to paid ministers ('hirelings') and the payment of tithes. It was difficult to be a Quaker, especially in the early years, without adopting these policies.

The first political act of James Nayler that we know of was his decision to take up arms against the king. Not many men did that, even in 1642, and many were probably forced into it by circumstances. It's not possible to be sure, but it is probable that fighting was Nayler's choice. His second known political act was to vote with the majority of General Lambert's war cabinet on 12 December 1648 for the trial of Charles I as a criminal; as the charge was treason, this meant he was voting for the execution of Charles I.

These events occurred before Nayler became a Quaker. The first statement we have from Nayler of his views after conversion was during his imprisonment at Appleby in January 1653. Most of the questions were about theology, and then at the end Justice Pearson asked about tithes:

> Justice Pearson: *Why dost thou speak against tithes, which are allowed by the states?*
>
> James: I meddle not with the states; I speak against them that are hirelings, as they are hirelings: those that were sent of Christ never took tithes, nor ever sued any for wages.

Justice Pearson: *Dost thou think we are so beggarly as the heathens, that we cannot afford our minister maintenance? We give them it freely.*

James: They are the ministers of Christ who abide in the doctrine of Christ.

Justice Pearson: *But who shall judge? How shall we know them?*

James: By their fruits you shall know them; they that abide not in the doctrine of Christ make it appear they are not the ministers of Christ.

Justice Pearson: *That is true.*[1]

It is worth mentioning that Justice Pearson subsequently converted to Quakerism and wrote a book against the payment of tithes. This exchange, as reported by Nayler, shows Nayler was anxious not to offend against the state's laws. In Orton, before his arrest, he was careful not to preach illegally in the church or create a riot in the open field adjacent to the village. He takes the 'nonpolitical' line that he judges not the actions of the state but of individual priests. If their behaviour is not Christ-like, they do not deserve payment; if it is Christ-like, they cannot accept payment. Quakers were able to support their ministers. Nayler ignores the financial difficulty of those ministering to poor congregations and the social and financial questions raised by a national ministry. Christ's demand for a free ministry is superior to human arrangements, hence the argument against tithes. This echoes a section on magistrates in *Love to the Lost*:

I say, they are to be owned and obeyed in all things, as they are appointed by God; for God limits them and hath set bounds to then, though they know it not; and so far as they command the will of God they are to be obeyed for conscience sake; but when they are contrary to God ... then God is to obeyed.[2]

12. On Nayler's Politics

In 1658, writing from prison after his trial by Parliament, Nayler argued that Quakers' discovery of the truth made them separate from the laws of the Gentiles, separate from the pride and vainglory of lordship. Although Quakers act in accordance with the scriptural verse *'Submit yourselves to every ordinance of man for the Lord's sake'* (1 Peter 2:13 KJV), Nayler writes,

> [I]n humility we find a power above pride, higher than oppression, higher than men's wills . . . so we deny the lower, that we may subject ourselves to that which excelleth, which is ordained of God. And to every ordinance of man are we subject for the Lord's sake; but should we bow to the spirit of pride, we should betray the Lord, and give his honour to another.[3]

Rulers should seek honour by first seeking the will of God. Nayler here is arguing against the forms of honour and respect that were customary in his time. He refuses to recognise the social hierarchy that the forms of respect upheld.

The exchange in Appleby in January 1653 was taken down in Nayler's handwriting at the time. When published in March 1653, the paper included a letter 'To the Christian reader' in which Nayler complained that men who may have fought for the king were now using weapons to disperse Quaker meetings and leaving people bound tightly overnight in open fields. The implication was that these men were untrustworthy, having fought for the other side. The pamphlet also reproduced a petition against himself and Fox that was sent up to the Barebones Parliament in Whitehall.[4] Nayler asks, why is their valuable time being wasted in reading such trivia?

> How is it that such men should dare to divide the people of England, to trouble the Council of State (in the throng of business concerning the management and improvement of all the might series of glorious

providence made out to this infant Commonwealth)? . . . However, reader, we need not fear; we hope the Lord will never suffer that monster persecution again to enter within the gates of England's Whitehall.[5]

Nayler here expresses some hope that the Barebones (the Parliament nominated by Cromwell and the army to establish a new order of government and religion) would ensure the principles Nayler had fought for were implemented. A pamphlet published soon after his release from Appleby contains a section on the rising gentry:

> God is against you, you covetous cruel oppressors who grind the faces of the poor and needy [Isaiah 3:15], taking your advantage of the necessities of the poor, falsifying the measures and using deceitful weights [Proverbs 11:1], speaking that by your commodities which is not true and so deceiving the simple, and hereby getting great estates in the world, laying house to house and land to land till there be no place for the poor [Isaiah 5:8]; and when they become poor through your deceits then you despise them and exalt yourselves above them, and forget that you are all made of one mould and one blood.[6]

Nayler and Fox — 'Ministers of the Eternal Word' — published a joint paper in 1653 in which Nayler wrote:

> Woe, woe, woe unto thee, thou that art exalted as high as heaven, yea, into God's throne; but thou shalt be cast down to hell; the Lamb is risen to rule the nations [Revelation 5:12–13]. Woe unto the covetous cruel oppressors who live upon dust, you grind the faces of the poor and oppress them that are fallen. . . . The fire of the Almighty is kindled, and it shall never be quenched till it hath devoured and burnt up you and your heaps and made you a curse to the generations that shall come after. . . . Who could have believed that England would have brought forth no better fruits than

these, now after such deliverance as no nation else can witness. Oh tell it not amongst the heathen.[7]

One of Nayler's first pamphlets (published on 17 March 1653) contained a 'Call to Magistrates, Ministers, Lawyers and People to Repentance' in which he wrote:

And is not the Lord "overturning, overturning, overturning"? . . . And you lofty ones of the earth who have gotten much of the creation into your hands and have thereby set your nests on high and are become lords over your brethren. And was the creatures made for that end . . . and he who can get the greatest share should become the greatest man and all that have little shall bow down and worship him? . . . [F]or he who made all things good [Genesis 1:31], made all men of one mold and one blood to dwell on the face of the earth . . . not to heap them together to set your hearts upon them.[8]

And are not those laws which ought to be used to preserve people from oppression, by abusing, made the undoing of whole families, impoverishing towns and countries? The law, as it is now used, is scarce serviceable for any other end but for the envious man who hath much money to revenge himself of his poor neighbours, which maybe never did him wrong.[9]

These extracts taken from Nayler's early work show a man enraged by the injustice of inequality as experienced by the poor and those without land who are harmed by those who use the law contrary to its true purpose and by those who oppress people who want only the freedom to meet and worship. Such oppression had come about with the growth of a market in land the century before. Above all, there comes through the angry words a great sadness and bewilderment about how, after nearly a decade of war and bloodshed, England could still contain such practices. Meanwhile, what was Nayler's response to such oppression? In 1653, he published with George Fox at York *A Lamentation (By one of England's Prophets) Over the Ruins of This Oppressed Nation*. England was 'oppressed' because the new rulers were as disciplinarian as the old ones when it came to the unlicensed preaching of God's word. Nayler begins:

> Oh England! how is thy expectation fled now after all thy travails? . . . Hast thou looked for reformation but all in vain! for as power hath come into the hands of men it hath been turned into violence, and the will of men is brought forth instead of equity . . . and the rich are exalted above the poor and look to be worshipped as God . . . but it is done by those who pretend to be against oppression; and for whom under that pretense thou hast adventured all that is dear unto thee to put power into their hands.[10]

There is much denunciation of the present rulers and the laws that allow innocent preachers to be thrown into prison. Towards the end, Nayler advocates not more violence but resistance in the name of God:

> And now look no more to the arm of flesh for freedom, for therein hath been your woe; but wait for the deliverer out of Zion the Ancient of Days [see Daniel 7], and God of Israel's seed who hath letten you see the emptiness of all created helps to which your eyes have been looking, that you might return, and complain to him only, who is the fountain from whom all his find pity. . . . I say arise and deliver yourselves from the guilt of oppression and cruelty of these men, and humble yourselves before the Lord that you may receive wisdom from him and boldness to declare against all violence and injustice, and set yourselves to deliver the oppressed to the utmost, that you may be hid . . . and have a sure house and be established.[11]

I am struck by the phrase 'deliver *yourselves* from the guilt of oppression'. This suggests that unless we act, we are complicit; unless we behave as free people and risk the legal consequences, we acquiesce in the oppression of others as well as ourselves. Nayler had no desire for more violence. But, he was compelled to stand up and follow Christ's leadings and speak against the 'monster persecution'.

In 1655, Nayler published *To Thee Oliver Cromwell, in whose hands God hath committed the sword of justice* calling for liberty of conscience.

> It being a matter of the greatest concernment to every man's conscience that loves Christ, not to uphold any ministry . . . which is not sent by Christ, therefore take heed . . . to give liberty herein, that there be no forcing to uphold any one soul that say they are ministers. . . . And you magistrates shall not need to meddle in this thing   . . . to force a maintenance.[12]

He then refutes arguments against such liberty, the first being that it would make men heathens. But, if Cromwell first enacted a law to punish sin without exception and then allowed all to worship as they wished, outward actions would soon reveal those 'who hath not a principle of God to guide his worship with constraint'. Those who had no constraint (Ranters?) would be punished. Next, heathens would be found out, and their guilty consciences, without being forced, would bring them to the word of God:

> And such being declared to be heathen would be ashamed, and being convinced in their own consciences might come to be saved, which now pass under the name of professors.[13]

Nayler clearly thinks many Puritans and Calvinists are heathens. Similarly, ministers of the Antichrist would be discovered, for those whose first interest was money would soon stop preaching if they were not paid. Nayler argues that ministers of God will always be supported by the faithful and by God:

I bear witness who was sent out without bag, or scrip, or money, into the most brutish parts of the nation, where none knew me, yet want I nothing. In prisons, in wanderings, in beatings, in stonings, in mocking, my joy I would not change for all the parsonages in the world.[14]

Neither should others be forced to pay for the maintenance of churches or cathedrals. Why should some be forced to repair the houses of others, especially of those who meet in private houses and/or hire meeting places? To those who complain the houses of God would fall down,

I answer, houses of God they are not; conveniency is the best you can plead for them; and of all men, you who stay in those houses have least cause to find fault with such as go out, seeing they leave you the houses you so much esteem of.[15]

Finally, he argues against requiring people to take oaths, 'seeing the plain commands of Christ and his apostles doth so often forbid it', which was why Quakers did not do it. Nayler argues that swearing on oath does not prevent lying and that prosecuting liars for perjury would be more effective.

I answer such will not matter what they swear neither, were it not for fear of an outward law; but if you make an equal punishment of false witness [perjury] . . . you shall soon have them more afraid to lie than ever they were to forswear [break their oath], and hereby come to cleanse the land of all false accusers and accusations.[16]

This address to Cromwell shows a pragmatic approach, based on an understanding of men's motivations without recourse to biblical examples or theological argument. The pamphlet came in a year (1655) during which Cromwell issued several proclamations requiring everyone to attend an approved place of worship, forbidding the disturbance of ministers, and extending 'vagrancy' to include travelling on a Sunday without good reason. All of this made it harder for Quakers to meet legally.[17] Nayler's testimony about his ministry shows that he was someone who tried to act according to the leadings of God in his heart. The tract ends with a description of Nayler's politics:

> Thus in faithfulness to God, and in love to you, with whom I have served for the good of these nations betwixt eight and nine years, counting nothing too dear to bring the government into your hands in whom it is, as many can witness with me herein. And now my prayer to God for you is that you may lay down all your crowns at his feet, who hath given you the victory, that so the Lord being set up as king in every conscience, all may be subject to your government for conscience sake.[18]

Cromwell has the victory. Let there be liberty of conscience, and all will find the word of God in their souls and turn Quaker, supporting a godly government. Nayler had been willing to fight for liberty of conscience, but he was not necessarily eager to fight for a more comprehensive political programme. His experience in the war appears to have left him a pacifist. He seems willing to leave the political struggle for a more just society to others in the army or supported by it. Hill makes the point that it was only through the power of the army that religious radicals could hope to implement any of their reforms. Outside London, the army's protection was important to Diggers and to Quakers.[19] Nayler was not, in our terms, a democrat. He was probably too poor to have voted in the elections of 1640. Liberty was about freedom to preach and worship. His social programme for helping the poor and oppressed was the redistribution of land by the rulers, not the Digger solution of common ownership. Nayler always denied being a Leveller. Neelon argues that Nayler 'may not have been friendly with the officers Fox found worthwhile in his efforts, and that Nayler was not in accord with the Leveller agenda that apparently attracted Fox'. [20] He probably supported to the very end his old General Lambert and the military governments of the Commonwealth despite their failure to realise the kingdom of God.

Why was religious freedom so important to early Quakers (apart from the immediate benefit of avoiding prison)? Quaker scholar Douglas Gwyn's reading leads him to the conclusion that

> [t]he Lamb's War did not risk and lose lives simply to allow private opinions or consumer preference to rule in religious life. Religious freedom was a crucial means by which Friends believed their concern for social transformation, a covenantal re-ordering of society, would take place. Most of all, religious freedom meant allowing *God* the freedom to build a new social whole from the grassroots upward, working through the consciences of each man, woman, and child.[21]

The revolution would be accomplished by God working through a transformed humanity, not by top-down political changes or a social war against the rich. Consequently, for Nayler and other Quakers the defeat of 1660 was not only a personal defeat or a military defeat, it was also the defeat of God by the Antichrist. The fight to break the carapace of traditional society and allow God's Spirit to flow unconstrained, bringing in its wake social change, had failed.

The rapid turn of events in 1659 and 1660 are explained by Hutton and Morrill as a desire for order and certainty in government that trumped principle — better a single person ruling than continual argument. Hutton says that despite the horror of war, the terrible climate, and the social dislocation,

> [t]he radicals of seventeenth-century England worked within the context of a very successful society. Secular reform was directed to improving the system in detail rather than altering it in essentials: when a Quaker could complain of a magistrate that he had arrested him under a defective warrant, an October revolution was not very likely. The government . . . was not, for its

age, that bad, and the same instinct kept many Englishmen paying taxes, and turning for justice to even an unpopular regime [whether republican or monarchical].[22]

Quakers were thought to threaten that underlying stability and reasonableness by challenging, through their behaviour and beliefs, the fundamental social understandings upon which social cohesion depended. To survive, British Friends soon retreated into a 'hedged community' interested only in theological discourse, not in social change. Nayler did not live to see that.

13. 'Concerning Good Works'

As there is but one good, so there is but one worker of good in heaven and in earth, who by the word of his power made all good in the beginning; and in this good work and will was man wrought in the will of God; in his image and goodness he stood, but falling from this steadfastness that was in God, and betaking himself to self thereby to become wise, he became subtle and proud in himself, seeking to be as God, was cast out from God, his power, love, and goodness; and being fallen into the dark imaginary of his own heart; and finding himself under the curse (whereof the light of Christ in the conscience is a witness) he hath set himself to make a likeness of God and Christ and God's worship, and good works, faith, hope, patience, love, &c., but being under the powers of darkness neither knows God nor his work; but is deceived by the prince of darkness and so doth please himself with an imitation of God and his works, but without power; and so, as he imagines, is doing good. But the testimony of God in his heart bears witness against him, that his work is not perfect, not accepted. He also imagines that he is redeemed, but is still under the commanding power of Satan, led captive at his will; who that he may the more strongly bind him, he leads him sometimes into a seeming worship, that so he may not so much suspect his way, not be too much troubled at his other unrighteous practices; so that the worst of men in this state have a worship; and each sort thinks they are right, though there be but one way, and they all without it; and each in their thoughts are not so bad as others, but have their several good works, though there be but one good work, and they all out of it in their own works. (LL 3:90–91)

Only God's work can be good. Many people do 'good works', but how can we be effective, how can we model, or mirror, the intricate web of goodness that is creation? Much so-called good work results in greater evil. Joseph Rowntree wrote in 1865:

> Charity as ordinarily practised, the charity of endowment, the charity of emotion, the charity which takes the place of justice, creates much of the misery which it relieves, but does not relieve all the misery it creates. (QFP 2013, 23.17)

Nayler answers the question about good works by setting the bar very high and asserting that the only good works we know are the works of God. First there was the goodness of creation, when all was good, including humankind, who, living within God's own works, did good without prompting or consideration. Then humans ate from the tree of good and evil to become like God. But God threw them out of Eden for fear they might go on to eat from the tree of life and live forever (Genesis 3:22).

It is worth examining further the psychological portrait that Nayler draws and why this prevents unregenerate humans from performing good works. Nayler's account does not have humans thrown out of a physical location; instead, we are 'cast out of God' — we no longer have a connection with God. We have taken ourselves into our selves, into our own minds, into our own ego, and away from God. Perversely, by seeking to become like God, we have ceased to be with God. We no longer live with God, doing good without prompting or consideration. Now, in compensation for our loss, which in our hearts we feel as an unfathomable loss, we struggle to make for ourselves a likeness of God and God's good works. And, Nayler says, we are bound to fail in our attempts to rebuild Eden. In our hearts, we know this. In our hearts, we know that our good works will not be accepted, just as Cain's sacrifice was not accepted. Most good works are failed attempts to rebuild Eden.

Nayler draws a psychological picture of those who believe they are doing good but are actually doing the work of Satan. 'Good people' believe their good works will, eventually, bring them back into Eden, bring them back into God's heart as redeemed people, saved from Satan and hell. And Satan cleverly provides them with religious experiences and a worship that reinforces this belief. We are hoodwinked by our own desire to be with God. And, having this primary desire met, we are not too worried by our other backslidings or 'unrighteous practices', nor by the evidence that our charity does not relieve all the misery it creates. 'Good people' see that others have different charities and different forms of worship, but this diversity does not cause them to question the validity of their own ways. No — they continue to think they are right and not as bad as the others; some may 'charitably' believe that others do perform good works, though not as good as their own. But, Nayler says, they are all wrong, all children of Satan, for there is only one way and *none of them have it.*

The quotation earlier from Joseph Rowntree gives a brief typography of charity: some establish foundations for education or health, impartially helping those who meet set criteria; some are emotionally led to help individuals; and some campaign to relieve wrongs but do not address the root cause. And then, if I may add to Rowntree, there are great movements that seek to do good: governments hope to exterminate, by war or genocide, those whose actions create evil in the world; politicians persuade parliaments to seek vengeance for violent deaths by killing those who have killed so they cannot kill again; religious leaders persuade their followers to rebuild Eden on earth through forcible conversion to their faith; and sects withdraw from the world to practice good in seclusion, terrifying their members into an unholy routine of 'goodness'.

Nayler says these 'good people' are led by Satan. They are, inevitably, doing Satan's work in the world, for charities and individual charity need evil to justify their own existence and therefore prolong evil to keep themselves in work. But at no point does Nayler say these people are themselves evil; indeed, he says they know the work they do is useless for 'the testimony of God in his heart bears witness against him' (LL 3:90). And it is this Light, this tiny piece of God that remains in us after God has cast us out of God's work, which enables us to know what good works we can do.

At this point, one might honestly despair. What good works could one possibly do that would not turn out to be the work of Satan? And is Nayler's own prescription for good works any more certain to be of God?

Nayler begins by saying it is very hard to persuade those who believe they are not as bad as others that they are wrong. In fact, it is impossible; one has to rely on the little bit of God in one's own heart:

> Only such who mind the light of Christ in their dark hearts, which manifests to them the evil deeds and reproves them for them, and can believe it to be the light of Christ, . . . only such come into the good work and will of God. For without the word was nothing made, nor without it can any be redeemed. For it is the word of the Lord, heard and received, that quickens the dead and raises to life that which is dead in the trespasses and sins: and the spiritual man being quickened, the power of the word brings forth in him the work of God's righteousness, which was from everlasting; which, in the measure thereof, confirms the creature unto God in righteousness, who lost the image in unrighteousness; and so is the creature renewed in the spirit of the mind and inward parts to receive wisdom and power in the hidden man, how to escape the evil and resist it, and to bring to light what God begets in the heart, and so the new creature is seen

created in Christ Jesus unto good work, to walk therein, as was foreordained.

And as the believer is found diligent in the light waiting, and in the Spirit obedient to this work, in this work he comes still more to learn God's power and teaching and Christ's obedience, and God's wisdom and care over him, in leading into the sufferings and tribulations, trials and temptations, and the faith and fellowship with Christ therein; in which, if the creature stand, not a hair can fall, but he is sure to come out more pure than gold; and so in all this work he grows in the knowledge of Christ and his sonship, toward the measure and stature and fullness of the perfect man, into the likeness of God.

And this is no self-work, nor can it be wrought in any but where self is denied and a cross to self taken up; so boasting is excluded, the creature having nothing but what he hath received, neither by his own will nor deed, but by believing in the light, and in obedience of faith. And with this faith and work are all the world judged, who are in their own works, and all that are without works, whose faith is dead, . . . whose works are their own, their prayers are abomination, where the works come not from this everlasting work and workings. For though there be many works, as to the creature's obedience and measure, yet they all complete but this one work of the creature's redemption, and God's praise therein, the beginning and end of all. (LL 3:91–92)

It appears that before we can do good in the world, we must be remade, or partially remade, in the image of Christ *unto the likeness of God*. It is no good to use charity money and hire another builder to rebuild Eden; you have to find the original builder within you. How can this be done? 'For without the word was nothing made, nor without it can any be redeemed.' When Nayler uses the term 'the word', he does not mean the words of the Bible but the Word as used at the start of the Gospel of John. It is (as he says in 'Concerning the Word') the beginning of all visible things but is itself invisible,

> yet doth it reveal the ground and use and end of all visibles. . . . [B]ut whatever man meddles with, not having the word in him to guide, order and sanctify, the same he defiles, and it is polluted as to him. (LL 3:60)

For a reader who stands on the other side of the Enlightenment and who has been brought up, if only by osmosis, to look for 'scientific evidence', this description is no description. In the seventeenth century, demanding someone turn to God was an understandable social activity, and if, in the twenty-first century, we are to go further with Nayler, we need to find a secular activity that is similar. Perhaps the closest we might see around us today is the psychological change required of individuals in 12 step programmes, or any situation in which a person is asked to look at themselves and at what they have done to others. Our society, through our therapists and psychologists and even prison educators, makes a demand similar to Nayler's upon those whose ways lead them towards an early grave or prison. Often thought of as 'patients' or 'transgressors', they are asked to summon up a desire for change coupled with the deliberate exercise of willpower to remodel themselves.

We may be willing to start from where Nayler asks us to (because we have seen others start from that line, albeit on other journeys), but where Nayler asks us to go is very different. Whereas a reformed alcoholic can continue in adultery, oppression of their colleagues, etc., provided they do not drink, Nayler requires us to reach further into our personality and soul. He asks for nothing less than a complete re-formation, 'and so is the creature renewed in the spirit of the mind and inward parts to receive wisdom and power . . . and to bring to light what God begets in the heart'.

Yet, there is hope here for the faint. Nayler is not an impossibilist; he understands that this sort of change rarely comes overnight, that the change may work silently, hidden in the inward parts, only to be suddenly revealed by a change in outer circumstances. And it is never complete. We move *towards* the ideal typology of the perfect human (Jesus Christ) according to the 'measure' of God we have within our creaturely or physical person. And there are many works, many manifestations of the change, which I take to mean that our good works may not be the same as our neighbours' and also may evolve as we change. But the end goal is the same for all; our redemption. Nayler tells us to start from within and work outwards; he does not make the more usual prescription, which is to start outwardly 'doing' and hope that the external good will move within. Good works will not redeem us; only good lives can do that.

How do we recognise God's works?

And of this work of God is all the world ignorant, who are preaching, pressing, and acting their good works (as they call them), but all their works do not manifest a power that brings them out of sin and the world's conformity, and service thereof in his ways and worship; but every good work of God in his saints, who become obedient to his working, as they subject to bring forth the good work and will of God; every work begets the creature nearer to God and into his likeness and nature. . . .

. . . God's works are those which are from everlasting, before the will of man or the world's customs, and therefore must conform to neither; but everyone who into this work will come must deny the world and their own wills, and all that is in them must bow and conform to the motion of the Spirit and to its workings (which is seen to such as in the light dwells), and in its way and time must bring forth the fruits of the Spirit in due season; not the works of the flesh, nor to the flesh, but the working of the Spirit to God, in the sight of God; and the praise of such is not of the world, who bring not

> forth to the world; but of God who bring forth to God,
> and the world praises its own. (LL 3:92–93)

Nayler gives several criteria here by which good works can be recognised. First is the effect on those doing it. Does it make them more like God? Are they less sinful? Second, are the good works in some way 'everlasting', not of this world? Third, does the good work bring forth the Spirit, not the flesh? Finally, is the reaction of the world to these works one of suspicion and condemnation? Good works can also be described as embodying a vision of God's work in the world. It is in some way preordained, decided on by God who is looking for hands to do it; it is 'everlasting' because it has needed to be done since the fall and is a building block of the new world. Because this world has fallen, the work will be transformative, not of this world but at a tangent to it. And lastly, the result of the good work will be 'of God who brings forth to God', so those doing the good work cannot expect any praise from those who are still in the world.

Nayler's generation did many marvellous things in the world, but the object of Quaker preaching was not to establish orphanages or schools — it was to change people. The transformation by God of creatures into spirits who could do the good work of God was what the early Quakers wanted. It seems, then, that good works start with, and are part of, the remodelling of ourselves.

14. 'Concerning the Lord's Supper'

This is the thing that all the world's professors are contending about; and indeed, is of great use and profit to the weak believers, who have not yet seen the Lord, for bringing them into one body and blood, mind and heart, and soul and spirit. But since the mystery of iniquity began to work, the world's teachers and professors having lost their indwelling in the body of Christ . . . are so far from being thereby made one in the blood of Christ, that they are shedding one another's blood about the form, which they are all out of, and have lost, and the power also. (LL 3:108)

I like the way in which Nayler mentions the community-building effect of taking Communion; it is something he builds on later. The blood lost over the form of the Lord's Supper or Eucharist has been immense. Within Nayler's memory and life, there were the wars of religion in France, the Peasants' War and the Thirty Years' War in Germany, and, most recently, massacres in Ireland.

Nayler describes the diversity of belief amongst those who took Communion in his time,

who have a day to go into the idols' temple, and there to eat bread and drink wine in a self-solemnity, once a month, or three times a year, or as they imagine, some affirming the body and blood of Christ to be in the creature after consecration (as they call it), some saying, Nay, but it is spiritual after consecration; others saying, It is still carnal and not changed because of words; and one imagines the body of Christ real in it, another not real, but by faith (as they say). But in this they all agree, that they return back into the pleasures of the flesh and fashions of the world, there to eat and drink the rest of God's creatures, to spend on their lusts. (LL 3:110)

The contempt in this passage is as physical as the host it dismisses.

There is scriptural support for a commemoration involving food, but there is no need to illustrate that here. From these passages, over many centuries, was elaborated the medieval belief, which is described by Margery Kempe in these words: 'I believe in the sacrament of the altar in this way, that whatever man has taken the order of priesthood, be he ever so vicious a man in his living, if he say duly those words over the bread that our Lord Jesus Christ said . . . it is his very flesh and his blood and no material bread'. Stories were told of laypersons and clerics who saw flesh and dripping blood instead of bread and wine and were promptly convinced of their errors.[1]

The Protestant Reformation in Europe challenged this belief, and Protestant leaders variously described the presence of Jesus in the bread and wine. Luther thought the body and blood of Christ could be everywhere the Mass was celebrated; Zwingli viewed it as a sign of the reality behind the Mass; and Calvin argued that sign and reality were one but that God did not come down to sit on the altar — instead, the celebrants were drawn up into heaven.[2]

Doubts about the efficacy of the Eucharist had been present in England since Wyclif(fe) and the Lollards, from the 1370s onwards.[3] Hill and others say that the Lollard influence was particularly strong in the same areas (including West Yorkshire) as early Quakerism, and it seems likely to me that Nayler's hostility to any established church and its sacraments was learnt from his neighbours as much as from Fox. The fourth conclusion of the Lollards presented to Parliament in 1395 began:

The Fourth Conclusion that most harms the innocent people is this: That the sacrament of bread induces all men but a few to idolatry, for they ween [believe] that Christ's body, that never shall out of heaven, by virtue of the priest's word should be essentially enclosed in a little bread, that they show to the people.[4]

Such anti-transubstantiation ideas continued to be expressed in popular radicalism down to Nayler's time. Nayler's account of the Eucharist is this:

And this was that the apostle received of the Lord, and was so practiced in the purity of the church, before they ran into confusion, which did continue steadfastly in the apostles' doctrine and fellowship, breaking bread and prayer, daily breaking bread from house to house, did eat their meat with gladness and singleness of heart, in the fear and favour of God. And this was to be done at all seasons, when they eat and drank: in their eating and drinking they were to do it to the Lord, and therein to have communion with his body and his blood [1 Corinthians 10:14–22]. (LL 3:108)

If you intend to sup with the Lord . . . be in remembrance of him, and in his fear, that a death you may witness to the lust and excess, which is that which slew him since the foundation of the world, . . . and so come to die to that which slew him, then you do show the Lord's death till he come; and when he comes he shall not find you eating and drinking with the drunken, nor beating your fellow-servants. (LL 3:111)

Nayler says that Jesus left this communion as a sign to his apostles, knowing that their nature would draw them earthwards as the Holy Spirit had not yet come to them.

Man that lives upon the creatures is soon drawn into them, and so to forget his coming who is the maker thereof. . . . And so orders the outward food as unto

God and not to carnal things, the mind grows thereby, and so to the pure all things are pure. (LL 3:111)

Jesus instituted his communion and commemoration at a meal because he could be sure in the future all his disciples would eat and while eating would remember their meals with him. However, Nayler comments:

> [H]ow soon were they returned into the carnals, and to their fishings, and the like, having forgot the promise of his coming, till he renewed the remembrance of it, making himself known in breaking of bread again after his resurrection? (LL 3:112)

Nayler's point was that it was not until Jesus returned from the dead and again broke bread with two apostles on the way to Emmaus that their eyes were opened and they remembered to eat in memory of him (Luke 24:30–31). If we today eat in memory of Jesus, we are showing a truer commemoration of the Lord's death than the priestly elaboration of the Eucharist. Indeed, if taking the Eucharist is all you do, Nayler warns,

> you who do this for just an hour and then feed without fear, not showing the Lord's death in all your other eating, so oft as you eat and drink till he come, you are they who eat judgment to yourselves herein [1 Corinthians 11:28–32]. (LL 3:113)

Rejection of the sacraments is a visible difference between Quakers and other denominations. The 1847 supplement to the 1834 book of discipline quotes the 1840 epistle of London Yearly Meeting:

> Our sense of the spiritual character of the reign of Christ, and of the inadequacy of outward forms to satisfy the soul, remains the same; and we continue to feel ourselves conscientiously restrained from uniting in any of the modes of worship which others think it right to adopt. (BoD 1834, supplement of 1847, p. 366)

In its rejection of 'outward forms', the epistle echoes Nayler's attack on differing forms of worship. In the general epistle of 1866, Friends used a different argument, one based on Hebrews 8:

> It is a simple *spiritual* service. That which was represented in the sacrifices of the law was fulfilled and ended in the Lord Jesus Christ, and in the exercise of faith in Him the reality is now to be enjoyed. "He is the propitiation for our sins," the High Priest who hath passed into the heavens, now to appear our Mediator and Advocate in the presence of God. (BoD 1883, p. 21, emphasis in original)

The epistle goes on to say that in these days, after the coming of the Christ, there is no reason for worship to be dependent on the presence of one person or for a form of words to interfere with the workings of the Lord's free Spirit.

In the new discipline of the 1920s, the argument against sacraments returned to the 1840s view:

> We feel we must maintain our practice in these things as a vital part of our belief — as our testimony to the reality of the Spirit's presence with and guidance of our individual and corporate life. We do not make use of the outward rites of Baptism and the Lord's Supper, but we do believe in the inward experiences they symbolise. (CLFT 1922, p. 77)

In the 1959 discipline is an extract that warns of the complacency that can result from this theology, words that echo, more tenderly, the warning from Nayler:

> It is easy to make a form of our very rejection of forms. . . . It is a bold and colossal claim that we put forward — that the whole of life is sacramental, that there are innumerable 'means of grace' by which God is revealed and communicated — through nature and through human fellowship and through a thousand things that may become the 'outward and visible sign' of an 'inward

and spiritual grace'. (A. Barratt Brown, 1932, as quoted in CFP 1959, para. 215)

There is no value in 'pretending' communion for an hour of silence on Sunday and treating the rest of the week as secular time.

In liberal, or post-liberal, Quaker thinking, 'communion' has moved from a unique ritual with a universal significance to the idea of the 'universe as revelation'[5] in which the universe and the history of evolution are seen as both providing spiritual revelation and as requiring salvation through our actions. As sinners (because we are destroying the earth), we beg forgiveness from creation and seek to make amends for our (humanity's) past actions. In this, Quakers have joined in practical work with people of other faiths and with members of secular organisations.

> Our adoption of the [World Council of Churches'] concern for Justice, Peace and the Integrity of Creation grows from our faith and cannot be separated from it. It challenges us to look again at our lifestyles and reassess our priorities and makes us realise the truth of Gandhi's words: 'Those who say religion has nothing to do with politics do not know what religion means.' The earth's resources must be conserved and shared more equitably and, as we are an integral part of creation, this is our responsibility. (London Yearly Meeting, 1989, as quoted in QFP 2013, 25.10)

Some Friends see these times as new times. The waiting and remembering, the 'meantimes', are over. The terrible environmental condition in which the Earth (Gaia) finds herself demands our immediate action. This is a matter of physical survival and of spiritual salvation.

> And now at this critical point in time, when our outdated world view no longer satisfies, comes this breakthrough: science and mysticism speaking with one voice, the rediscovery of our own (Christian) creation-

centred and mystical tradition, and the recognition of the spiritual wisdoms of the native traditions. . . .

Are we willing to open ourselves to this wider vision, to cease our urge to control and dominate, to listen instead to our hearts, to recognise again the integrity and sacredness of this planet which we have so abused? This means entering into a new relationship with 'our Mother the Earth', it means seeing ourselves again in a cosmic context, a larger perspective. . . .

If we can move from our 'human-sized' viewpoint and look instead from the cosmic viewpoint, there is a sudden and dramatic widening of the lens through which we look. Redemption is seen to be for all creation, and our human story, far from being diminished, is incorporated in the whole drama of an emerging universe. (Grace Blindell, 1992, as quoted in QFP 2013, 29.18)

15. On James Nayler and Martha Simmonds

Martha Simmonds was born on 10 January 1624 in the parish of Meare, three miles from Glastonbury. Her father, George Calvert, was the vicar there. Her mother was Ann Collier, and this was her father's second marriage. Vicars received £20 a year at that time, and life was difficult. From George's first marriage, only one of five children, a boy called Sampson, survived to adulthood. Ann Collier had seven children, of whom four survived to adulthood: Elizabeth, Giles, George, and Martha. Martha was named after a child from the first marriage who died the year before she was born. Her father died in August 1628, when she was four and a half. There are no further parish records for the family after August 1636. Sampson had gone to Cambridge and become a priest, and in 1639 he was established in London, as was Giles, who had completed an apprenticeship to a bookseller. It is probable that Martha and her mother Ann moved to London in 1639 and that Martha lived with Giles in his premises at the Black-Spread Eagle, St Paul's churchyard.[1] However we know nothing for certain about Martha's life between 1639 and 1655.

Giles Calvert finished his apprenticeship in 1639 and became a prolific publisher, especially of Continental mystics, writers who may have influenced early Quakerism. He was well known to radical religious sects, and it was natural for early Quakers to turn to him as a publisher. Between 1653 and 1656, Calvert published over half of all Quaker texts.[2] Martha seems to have been well placed to read early Quaker tracts and was soon converted to Quakerism. In 1655, at the age of thirty-one, she married Thomas Simmonds (he seems to have used the 'd' more than she did), a bookseller and printer from Birmingham. Giles helped establish Thomas at the Bull and

Mouth in Aldersgate, where he sold and published Quaker tracts. Neither Thomas Simmonds nor Giles Calvert were themselves Quakers. Martha Simmonds's first appearance in Quaker records was in December 1655 in a letter written by James Parnell from Colchester. He wrote that she had been put in jail for speaking in church to the priest. She had also walked through the town in sackcloth and ashes. This is typical of the disruptive behaviour of Quaker women publicising their faith and seeking imprisonment to bring in better-known Quaker preachers, in this case James Parnell.

James Nayler came to London in June 1655 to support the ministry of Edward Burrough and Francis Howgill. Clearly, Simmonds heard him speak, and she probably met him at her brother's home. After a month or so, Burrough and Howgill left for Ireland, and Nayler was expected to carry the burden of preaching and directing the mission in London. Quakerism did best in rural areas. London was a different challenge, with a large number of competing sects and preachers. Popular opinion made every utterance a political or social critique. The Fifth Monarchists and Ranters were both active in London. The Fifth Monarchists believed in the imminent physical arrival of Christ on Earth, where he would rule for a thousand years. The Ranters' message was that people had complete liberty to do as they were led. The Quakers took converts from both these sects. The Quakers' message of the inner Christ and the need for spiritual and social transformation was similar to both. It was a confused and confusing mix. And remember also that in 1656–1657, more died in London than were born.

Simmonds's single-page tract *When the Lord Jesus came to Jerusalem*, published by her brother in 1655, is an example of the sort of Quaker message current at the time. The title uses the motif of Christ entering Jerusalem, common amongst millenarian sects, and Simmonds draws on millenarians' worries about how Christ would judge them to persuade them towards the Quaker inner Light.

What will become of thee, thou murderest the just in thee, there is a Talent to be improved in thee [Matthew 25:15], how wilt thou give an accompt [account] of it; the Steward is now come. . . . If thou wilt turn in thy mind to the light of Christ in thee, the light will discover to thee thy fallen state.[3]

But to say in response to the coming that Christ has saved me and I have only to believe is not enough. This is a common refrain in Nayler's writing. Simmonds continues:

But it will be said unto thee, when thou thinkest to sit downe with thy Lord; Friend how camest thou hither without a wedding-garment [Matthew 22:12]? . . . Faith is another thing than thou takest it to be. . . . Adam when he disobeyed the minde and will of God, then he entred into his own will, and so was turned out into the Devils Kingdome. . . . [S]o that Scripture comes to be fulfilled in thee, which are the words of Christ; Loe I come, in the volume of thy booke it is written of me to doe thy will O God [Hebrews 10:7], which is the book of conscience in thee, there the will of God is to be done. . . . [T]herefore take heed what thou dost; for when the booke of conscience is opened, thou shalt witnesse thou hast been warned in thy life-time.[4]

There is nothing here that Quakers could object to. Licia Kuenning (who has read enough Quaker tracts to know) comments:

Nothing in the brief but lucid and thoroughly Quaker wording of Martha Simmonds prior to this controversy prepares us for the heat of the denunciations levelled at her.[5]

James Parnell thought well of Simmonds. She may have attracted followers who possibly helped her act out with public 'signs' such as her walk through Colchester.

By March 1656, Nayler was overwhelmed with work and asked Howgill and Burrough to return to London. Burrough was back in London by 22 April 1656. When Howgill returned, sometime later than that, he wrote to Margaret Fell:

> We have about twenty meetings in a week in this city, and ten or twenty mile about, great desires; and if we can we go out; but we cannot stay; great is our care . . . E.B salutes thee — he is almost spent: few know our condition.[6]

The Quaker leaders (Nayler, Dewsbury, Howgill, Burrough) in London were clearly exhausted.

We come now to Nayler's 'fall', as contemporary Quakers and some historians have described it (see the chronology of mid-1656 on pp. 174–175). Martha Simmonds came into conflict with senior Quaker ministers in London. In the divisions this created, Nayler (after some hesitation) took her side against other senior Quakers. Nayler then experienced a physical and mental breakdown that lasted at least a couple of months, from early July to September. During this time, Nayler did not preach or write. During his illness, Simmonds was accused of (in modern terms) manipulating him and persuading him to carry out the ride into Bristol which culminated in his trial for blasphemy by Parliament and his imprisonment. His trial had important theological and administrative outcomes for Quakers because it led to a more disciplined and centralised Society.

At this time (early 1656), Nayler was engaged in frequent verbal disputes with a Baptist, Jeremiah Ives, who persistently demanded evidence from Nayler of the validity of his calling and a sign from God giving him the authority to preach the gospel. Nayler's tract attacking Ives was published in July; I assume it was written at least one month earlier. Ives replied in August 1656.[7] Apart from mentioning exhaustion and 'witchcraft' as reasons for Nayler's collapse, William G. Bittle interprets subsequent events as growing out of Nayler's momentary doubts about his own calling and the demands of millenarians in Quaker meetings for a leader.[8]

Simmonds, Hannah Stranger, and perhaps others, came into conflict with the London Quaker leadership during spring 1656. If we believe Bristol priest Ralph Farmer's account of Simmonds's words to the Bristol magistrates, it may have been because of her desire to minister outside London and their belief that 'I was too forward to run before I was sent . . . but I was moved by the power, I could not stay though sometimes they denied me'.[9] But Parnell thought well of Simmonds. Burrough's letter of reproval dated to May does not give many clues. He said she was:

> out of the truth, out of the power, out of the wisdom & out of the life of God; for you are turned from the light of Christ Jesus within you & doth disobey it, & it lends your ear to another, & follows a lying spirit of divination which is put into your mouth, . . . and you are turned from the life into the power of death, which worketh in the mystery of iniquity . . . & the man of sin exalts himself in the temple of God. . . . You worship the image & sets up altars to another than the living God, who is light; & you in the feigned hypocrisy & worships the works of a man's hand & man & not the works of God, is shut up in the grave, & & a thickness of earth & filth is above it.[10]

William Dewsbury followed up with another letter, which began,

> Martha Simmonds, thou hast departed from the counsel of God, & in the evil imaginations of thy heart thou is run forth to utter words without knowledge. . . . [Simmonds has] in thy deceitful practice opened the mouth of the enemies of God to blaspheme his name.[11]

What Simmonds and others were now saying was *not* acceptable. If they had a 'spirit of divination', were they showing signs of 'witchcraft'? Possibly her 'deceits' were political prophesies for the future, which were embarrassing for Quakers. The term 'practice' could imply some sort of regular 'sign' or demonstration. Were Nayler's works 'the works of a man's hand' she worshipped? Her only publication at this time was directed at millenarians, but she also seems to have had tendencies in that direction, and this could have been a problem. The rift was widely known, and it seems that Nayler, at this point, supported Burrough and Dewsbury in their condemnation of Simmonds.

In early June 1656, Nayler took a brief trip to Yorkshire to settle a dispute and called at Lincoln on the way back for the same purpose. During his time in Yorkshire, Nayler wrote a letter *To All Friends at London* which Neelon describes as modelled on 2 Thessalonians. In that letter, Paul was concerned to damp down expectations of the second coming. Nayler cautioned Friends against such expectations:

> . . . which is all done in that nature which is impatient, and stands not in the counsel of God; but that you all stand in that which is not flesh, armed against self . . . and keep your dominion in the life of Christ; and therein feel your authority over all that would shake off the yoke, and cannot joy in the cross: harken not to unprofitable things, neither lend an ear to the wicked; stand you still armed in the covenant of promise, till the mystery of iniquity be revealed against the workers thereof.[12]

In 2 Thessalonians 2:7–8, Paul calls for restraint until the wicked man or lawless one is revealed by God and consumed by Christ:

> *For the mystery of iniquity doth already work: only he who now letteth will let, until he be taken out of the way. And then shall that Wicked be revealed, whom the Lord shall consume with the spirit of his mouth,*

and shall destroy with the brightness of his coming.
(KJV)

Both Burrough and Nayler refer to 'iniquity'. Is it possible that Simmonds was saying that some senior Quakers were an 'iniquity' at work and suggesting to Nayler that he should reveal and destroy them prior to the second coming? Was a less apocalyptic ministry from other preachers thought to be delaying the second coming? When Nayler returned from Yorkshire, Simmonds complained to him, possibly for the second time, about her treatment. And it was Nayler's reaction to this complaint that caused the breach between Nayler and other senior Quakers in London. There are three accounts of what happened: a letter from Burrough and Howgill to Margaret Fell dated 13 August; a letter from Richard Hubberthorne to Margaret Fell dated 26 August 1656; and the account Simmonds gave to magistrates in Bristol on 25 or 26 October 1656.

Burrough and Howgill explain that around the first week in July 1656 they left London for a short tour, taking separate routes, intending to meet each other again in Bristol for the large St James's Fair which started on 25 July. Howgill wrote Nayler a most loving letter from Oxford dated 12 July.[13] His letter to Margaret Fell explains:

> [B]ut soon after my departure [it seems to be Howgill writing] two women of this city [London] who were in the openings and prophecies run out into the imaginations and lying wonders, and James [Nayler] let them in and harkened unto them, and was quite overthrown, and lost all taste & savor, and was brought totally under the powers of deceit; and set these women upon the top of all, although they manifested both him and them; yet he went out of this city and left all under the power of darkness & the enemies to rejoice, . . . but we know little of all this.[14]

For Howgill to say he knows 'little of this' is strange because he must have known of the original division. The reference to 'manifested' might mean they considered Nayler as behaving like Christ in his actions, but the sense is not clear to me. Burrough and Howgill write that Nayler left London in 'darkness' with the enemies of Quakers rejoicing, suggesting the division among Friends was widely known.

Hubberthorne's letter of 26 August attempts to explain to Margaret Fell what had happened in London while Howgill and Burrough were away. It reads as if he had not been there himself.

> I went to Martha Simmonds, which was the woman that F.H. [Francis Howgill] mentioned in his letter. And I asked her the ground of these things which had made the differences, . . . and she . . . having nothing in her mind against me as against others, she told me something plainly how he come under judgment: she being at one time in a meeting, she spoke and was judged by F. H. [Francis Howgill] to speak in her will, and she being troubled in her mind went to James [Nayler] & told him that she was moved to speak and then was judged, and he also judged her. And told her that she sought to have the dominion & charged her to go home and follow her calling, & that with the other things wrought in her mind. And the other woman, Hannah Stranger, she also went to James and said that he had judged the innocent, and not judged righteously, and something to that effect did she & Martha speak to him, which word he received to be the word of the Lord. And coming under the power of their words, judgment came upon him, and much trembling night and day, while he was in London, for some nights lying upon a table, and then they reigned & deceit got up especially in Martha to glory and boast over all . . . and with it labors to break and destroy the meetings if it was possible.[15]

Nayler had at first agreed with the discernment of Howgill, Burrough, and Hubberthorne that Simmonds was 'run out' into her own will and told her to go home and follow her calling (as a housewife?). But, subsequently, Nayler changed his mind, and this reversal caused a mental breakdown in Nayler so severe that other Friends thought Simmonds had 'bewitched' him. Later in the same letter, Hubberthorne describes how Simmonds interrupted his meeting on the day he wrote by

> singing with an unclean spirit, and the substance of that which she said in her singing was "innocency, innocency," many times over, for the space of an hour or more. But in the power of the Lord I was moved to speak soon after she begun. . . . And she continued singing.   . . . [T]hen the word of life in others rose against her. . . . [T]hen she was tormented against me and tried on deep subtlety for a long time together, turning it into a song, and that we were all the beast, and I the head of the beast.[16]

Clearly, the interview with Simmonds had gone badly, and Hubberthorne was no longer in Simmonds's favour. By the time Hubberthorne wrote (26 August 1656), Nayler was in prison in Exeter. After his collapse friends had spirited him away from Simmonds's kitchen table and taken him to the St James's Fair at Bristol. There, Nayler made a dramatic entrance into a large (five thousand people) Quaker meeting with two women and a man (probably Thomas Wedlock from Ely). Howgill's letter of 13 August describes the event:

> I was speaking, and when I saw that man [Wedlock] coming before him bareheaded and saw the other [Nayler] I was almost struck dead; and E.B. [Edward Burrough] seeing stood up and spoke, and so we quieted the meeting gallantly, and went to him & bid him come with us, but they held him, and he would not go, and many friends who knew him expected him to speak; but he was as a dead lion. At last the woman

came away, and he followed, and Friends got him into a Friend's house; but he would not speak a word to neither John Audland, nor to Edw. Burrough, nor I nor none of the precious Friends of London; we stood lamenting over him and crying, but he resisted us, and the women cried like bears when we desired to part them.[17]

Howgill was shocked at Nayler's appearance because he was being given reverence and respect as a person and in particular was being honoured by the removal of Wedlock's hat. This was unprecedented in Quaker circles.

Nayler and Simmonds were parted eventually, and Howgill sent Nayler, with some trusted Friends, to visit Fox in Launceston prison. However, the authorities were arresting all suspicious travellers for vagrancy, and Nayler and his companions were arrested at Oakhampton and sent to jail in Exeter. Meanwhile, Simmonds and Hannah Stranger appear to have reached Fox at Launceston, evading the watchers on the road. Fox wrote to Nayler, probably after seeing him in Exeter:

> Martha Simmonds, which is called your mother, she bid me bow down, & said I was lord, & king, & that my heart was rotten, & she said, she denied that which was head in me, & one of them said, she had stopped Francis Howgill's mouth, & silenced him, & turned my word into a lie, & into a temptation, & she came singing in my face, inventing words, & Hannah boasted, & said, if they was devils make them tremble, & she boasted what she would do, & cry against.[18]

After this visit, Simmonds went to Oliver Cromwell's sister, the wife of Major-General Desborough, who was very ill, and offered to nurse her without payment provided Desborough would sign Nayler's release. The release arrived around 20 October, brought to the Exeter jail by Thomas Simmonds. Simmonds had secured from Desborough the release of Friends in Dorchester, Colchester, Ipswich, and Bury St

Edmunds on the same date. Once released, Naylor began the walk back to London with Simmonds, a woman named Dorcas Erbury, and Hannah Stranger. The men included Hannah's husband Thomas, Timothy Wedlock, and Robert Crab. This journey ended at Bristol on 24 October with the infamous 'sign' of the travellers who re-enacted the entrance of Jesus into Jerusalem.

What was it that Simmonds and Stranger had found to say to Nayler in July in London that was so powerful? How was he persuaded to 'let in the adversary'? Simmonds gave her account under questioning to magistrates in Bristol following the re-enactment of the 'sign' of Christ's entry into Jerusalem. This was taken down and subsequently printed in an anti-Quaker tract by Richard Farmer titled *Satan Enthroned in his chair of Pestilence*:

> She being demanded by the magistrates, why she was accounted a witch? made this answer. "Being among the people called Quakers in London, I was moved to declare to the world, and often they would judge me exceedingly, that I was too forward to run before I was sent, . . . but I was moved by the power, I could not stay though they sometimes denied me, yet I was forced to go, and my word did prosper; . . . and then was I moved of the Lord to go to James Nayler, and tell him I wanted justice, and he being harsh to me, at length these words came to me to speak to him, which I did, and struck him down: 'How are the mighty men fallen; I came to Jerusalem and behold a cry, and behold an oppression,' which pierced and struck him down with tears from that day; and he lay from that day in exceeding sorrow for about three days, and all that while the power rose in me, which I did not expect, seeing I knew he was in that condition: But after three days he came to me and confessed I had been clear in service to the Lord, and that he had wronged me, and should have done justice,

but did not do it. And then he lay at my house three days".[19]

The magistrates had been told — presumably by Quakers — that Simmonds was a witch, but they did not take this seriously. Simmonds's statement expresses clearly the strength of her leadings and her frequent rejections. In places, her account conflicts with Hubberthorne's. Were there two meetings between Simmonds and Nayler or one; was Stranger present when he was 'struck down'; in whose house did he lie for three days in sorrow; why the repetition of three days? I suspect Simmonds had at least two meetings with Nayler, and perhaps Stranger lobbied Nayler in between. Possibly there were public meetings at which Simmonds again 'misbehaved'. The mention of three days is, I think, a biblical reference to the resurrection and not a true chronology. The most interesting evidence is the words she was given to say, which are a paraphrase of Isaiah 5:7: 'How are the mighty men fallen; I came to Jerusalem and behold a cry, and behold an oppression'.

God tells Isaiah of a man with a fertile vineyard and wine vat on a hillside, guarded by a watchtower. The man expected it to yield grapes for wine-making, but it yielded only wild grapes. What more could the man do? What more could God do with the vineyard (Jerusalem) and its people, who were wild and rebellious? All the vineyard (and Jerusalem) can hope for now is to have its hedges removed so it becomes a waste of briars and thorns. The vineyard had yielded rebellious men (vain in their personal glory and enjoying the praise of the community), and God was coming to destroy them. In the words of the King James version:

> *For the vineyard of the Lord of hosts is the house of Israel, and the men of Judah his pleasant plant: and he looked for judgment, but behold oppression; for righteousness, but behold a cry.* (Isaiah 5:7 KJV)

The following two verses, if Nayler remembered them, would have also struck home:

15. On James Nayler and Martha Simmonds

Woe unto them that join house to house, that lay field to field, till there be no place, that they may be placed alone in the midst of the earth! In mine ears said the Lord of hosts, Of a truth many houses shall be desolate, even great and fair, without inhabitant. (Isaiah 5:8–9 KJV)

Simmonds was saying that the Quaker community, the planting of the Lord in the darkness of Britain, had failed her. The community from which she had expected justice had proved itself false, not only to her but to God's expectations. God would come and punish the community by destroying it. The last two verses quoted above are a cry against enclosure, aggrandisement, and wealth. These are corruptions which Nayler had often written about. Simmonds was saying he and the other men were doing the same to the Quaker community: aggrandising themselves and building their own house of words and destroying their neighbour's speech. Nayler took these words as being from God. Hubberthorne took them as being used by the devil to sow division and judged Nayler for mistaking their origin. Simmonds appears to have been amazed at the effect of her words, 'which I did not expect'.

It is significant, to my mind, that this dispute is about control of ministry and who is authorised by God to speak. In effect, Simmonds claims that anyone led by God should speak and that no one but the speaker can know whether or not they are truly led. She may also have produced more dramatic 'performances' with singing and 'signs' than Friends thought suitable. Howgill and Dewsbury were claiming an authority of discernment, beyond the meeting's, to determine who could speak. They were claiming a priestly role to control and direct the London open meetings. They would have been anxious to keep those who came under control. The crowds at these open meetings could have mixed expectations; they were comprised of some soldiers, some Baptists, some Ranters, and some Millenarians (Fifth Monarchists) as well some serious, interested seekers. Some were looking for strong leadership, and Nayler's charisma was an obvious attraction to them and an implicit challenge to Fox. Howgill and Dewsbury might have been fearful that factionalism would develop and lead to rival meetings led by different preachers.

Simmonds's words may have reminded Nayler of what he preached on worship — that all who would rightly worship God must wait to know God's Spirit and that should the creature run before the Spirit, 'there comes all the dead works and worships'.[20] 'How the mighty are fallen', said Simmonds. Nayler may have convicted himself of developing a contempt for 'ordinary' people who did not have his ability to express God's truth, and, when hard-pressed in open meetings, he may have himself 'run out' from the truth. Later, Nayler wrote that this spirit of what we could call spiritual elitism was so subtle that

> [w]heresoever it enters by consent it is hardly got out again; and if it be it is not without much sorrow. . . . [T]he rest of the people of God everywhere may be saved from this devourer who goeth daily about to deceive, and whosoever he takes he casts into the earth or into the sea, for wickedness is with him wheresoever he goeth.[21]

After hearing Simmonds's words, Nayler might have seen himself as contaminated and infectious to the people of God, a source of temptation, so that others would be fixated on him and not on the Light. Was it then impossible for him to preach again and be sure that what he said was the word of God? Nayler published only the tract against Ives between June and December 1656, and he did not or could not speak at the fair in Bristol.

There is no overt mention of women's rights by any of the players in this episode. I do wonder whether, coupled with his spiritual condemnation, Nayler did not feel some accusation of what we would now call gender bias. It was, after all, women who had accused him and a woman whom he had judged. Some historians have seen this a dispute about the role of women in Quakerism. Nayler placed particular emphasis on both the uselessness of intellectual achievements and the capacity of all men and women to be totally inhabited by Christ. Such principles must have been especially meaningful to women and men who perceived their own convincement as, above all, a rejection of social status and (in worship) all gender distinctions.[22]

There is no avoiding the fact that Nayler did attract both men and women to his side in a way that was more about his personality than his preaching. Thomas Welbeck appears to be one; Dorcas Ebury and John and Hannah Stranger were others. They were seen behaving as if Nayler were divine and addressing him as 'Son of God' and 'Prince of Peace'. As Neelon says: '[A]ll played on semantics in their testimonies to avoid proving blasphemy; for example, Hannah Stranger said she worshipped Nayler because Nayler would be Jesus when a new life was born in him.'[23]

Quakers soon had their poor opinion of Simmonds and her malign influence on Nayler confirmed. Richard Hubberthorne visited Nayler in Exeter jail and found him somewhat well disposed towards him and other Friends. However, Simmonds arrived, and Hubberthorne wrote that Nayler 'was much subjected to her' and that she remained 'in her filthiness still'._Hubberthorne's view was confirmed by a visit to Nayler in Westminster prison. He wrote on 25 November to Margaret Fell about the women around Nayler:

> The women are exceeding filthy in Acting in Imitations & singing. And that power of darkenesse in them rules over him as I wrote to thee at the first . . . they will kneel before him &. James speakes pretty much to Friends as in justifieing all their actings to be in innocency.[24]

Hubberthorne left with great pity for Nayler but sure that at the end, once the cloud of darkness over him had faded, 'the sun would shine over it'. In February 1657, in another letter written after Nayler's physical punishments at the hands of the authorities, Hubberthorne said the women were continuing in this way and had also interrupted meetings at the Bull and Mouth by singing psalms and reading from the Bible. At one meeting, Simmonds broke bread and drank drink and gave the remains to the multitude in imitation of the Eucharist.[25] As a vicar's daughter, she would have been very familiar with the ritual. If she had been doing this the year before, that would account for Howgill's description of her as worshipping an image and setting up an altar. Simmonds was blamed by almost all Friends for the 'fall' of Nayler. Later historians have agreed with this. William Braithwaite is uncomplimentary about Simmonds, and Carroll, in his very detailed account of the affair, thinks it 'very likely' that Simmonds engineered the whole episode:

> Her almost hypnotic influence on Nayler and the apocalyptic expectations with which she and her small circle were filled . . . made it possible for her to use Nayler as a 'sign' of Christ's coming.[26]

This may explain events in October 1656, but it does not explain the rift in June 1656, and it was that division which created Nayler's temporary breakdown and his subsequent willingness to be a 'sign'. Leo Damrosch quotes from *To the Life of God in All* (1659) to suggest that Simmonds was the cause of Nayler's spiritual 'fall':

> But not minding in all things to stand single and low to the motions of that endless life, by it to be led in all things within and without, but giving way to the reasoning part as to some things which in themselves had no seeming evil, by little and little drew out my mind after trifles, vanities, and persons which took the affectionate part, by which my mind was drawn out from the constant watch and pure fear, into which I was once begotten, and spiritual adultery was committed

against that precious pure life which had purchased me unto himself alone.[27]

This is not a physical adultery but a drawing towards human affection and perhaps a certain glorification in Nayler's status as a minister. Nayler says that the Spirit witnessed against this, but he consulted 'another' and 'so let the creatures into my affections, then his temple was defiled through lust . . . and he gave me up, and his light he withdrew, and his judgment took away'. In this state Nayler had lost his own guide and 'my adversary so prevailed that all things was turned and perverted against my right seeing'.[28] This reminds me of Nayler's account of the fall, where Adam and Eve looked to 'another' and ate of the tree of good and evil. Damrosch sees this too and writes:

> Seeking to escape from self and re-enact the passion of Christ, Nayler had instead tasted the forbidden fruit of good and evil and had been cut off from the tree of life.[29]

Nayler viewed his 'fall' as similar to that of Adam and Eve, who sought outer knowledge and were sucked into worldly things. He found the world a pit of darkness, with

> many wild spirits, ranters and suchlike, acting many evil things against the life of truth and name of Christ, his light and people that walk therein, on purpose to bring reproach thereon, and set themselves to break and disquiet the meetings of the people of God.[30]

In this work and others, Nayler expresses his contrition that his actions saddened the innocent and harmless people of God and enabled their opponents to rejoice at their divisions. Yet, he says he has no evil in his heart 'against him that sought my life in that day', nor does he ask for the darkness to pass quickly because he found that

> the Spirit of Christ Jesus which thinks not evil for evil, and when all visible help was removed afar off, and I in the depth of the pit, then this was with me and in me

before God, which often appeared when all else was gone, and many a time stayed by soul in secret that it sunk not under the accuser and the weight of his temptations when I was alone from any creature.[31]

Nayler is not talking of a human person but of the devil, against whom he bears no animosity, for the Spirit of Christ does not speak evil to evil.

A short tract titled *To All the People of the Lord*, written in Bridewell prison in early 1658 and published in 1659, is sometimes thought of as Nayler's confession. A pirated version with the same text but the title *James Nayler's Recantation* was published after it, and Nayler issued a paper disclaiming the work. Nayler opens his tract by saying he is oppressed by the unclean spirits that have deceived simple souls and bred disunity. He warns the simple ones that

> [t]hrough me these spirits have got much head and entrance into the minds of some who were simple towards God's truth. And this the envious one hath done, in the night of my trial . . . [w]hen my judgment was taken away, and I led captive under the power of darkness.[32]

The evil spirits steal into simple minds under the pretence of humility, promising great things but once there cause the person to think themselves above God. An evil spirit can be recognised:

> It will secretly withdraw your entire love from the flock of God already gathered, and cool your affections and zeal towards their present meetings, and if you judge it not there, it grow on with an evil eye, to spy out their failings, and delight to hear of them and talk of them, with a hidden joy, whispering them to others, and adding thereunto.[33]

This is an astute description of the sort of words and actions that continue in Quaker meetings today: unpleasant remarks leading to a withdrawal from meeting and the company of

Friends. Nayler warns that once this spirit has entered someone it is very hard to get it out again.

In this short tract, Nayler accuses himself of spiritual pride. It had entered him, and his failure had led 'simple minds' astray. This could mean that simple minds are prone to pride. Or, that they are susceptible to those (like himself in former times) who claim spiritual authority over others. If the second, then he is describing the development of factions within early Quakerism. There was a faction in London in 1657 and 1658 that supported Nayler. Fox called them 'Ranters and loose persons'. George Whitehead, in his 1716 introduction to Nayler's works, remembers that '[p]ersons of a loose Ranting spirit got up and frequently disturbed our Friends meetings in London'.[34] If so, then this tract is an indirect attack on those who claim leadership of 'simple minds' and a warning against taking sides — it is not an apology or recantation.

Nayler kept to his understanding of the 'sign'. Questioned in Bristol about his entry to the city, he said,

> It was for the praises of my Father and I may not refuse anything that is moved of the Lord; and that their Father commanded them to do it.[35]

He told the parliamentary committee that examined him:

> [I]t pleased the Lord to set me up as a sign of the coming of the Righteous One, and what has been done as I passed through these towns, I was commanded by the Lord to suffer such things to be done by me, as to the outward, as a sign, not as I am a creature.[36]

Dorcas Ebury claimed Nayler had raised her from the dead when she was seriously ill while in Exeter jail with Nayler. Nayler, however, said that power was not in him.

> [A]s a creature that hath a beginning and an ending, that I utterly deny, but that that any see of God in me, by the same spirit that revealed anything to them, that I

do not deny. . . . There cannot be a more abominable thing than to take from the Creator and give to the creature.[37]

Nayler, Simmonds, and others continued performing the 'sign' until the end. Before the authorities bore through his tongue and branded the letter 'B' for blasphemy on his forehead, Nayler spent two hours in the pillory. Hannah Stranger, Martha Simmonds, and Dorcus Ebury arranged themselves around him in imitation of the three Marys at the crucifixion, with Robert Rich beside them.[38] This seems to have been the last time they were together in public. Nayler's wife Ann cared for him in Bridewell prison. Rebecca Travers nursed Nayler after the London punishments. And after Nayler's release in late 1659, Travers gave him a home.

It is probable that Simmonds was accepted back into the Quaker community at some point. Hubberthorne reported to Margaret Fell in 1657 that 'there was something of God stirring in her'.[39] Her last appearance in print was as one of the authors of *O England thy time is come* (December 1656), for which she wrote three short sections (Nayler also contributed). The first section she wrote is the longest and gives a warning. The Christ she writes about in this section is clearly the inner Christ, not Nayler. The second section praises God for the mercies God has shown her in her life. God gave her a rod to smite the backslider and the hard-hearted, but now it is taken away and she needs only to enjoy his blessings,

> O Lord, thou knowest it was thy will, I did not resist thee. Oh that they might know it, the rod, and who it was that did appoint it! And now thou hast taken it out of my hand, and bowed me to thy will, and hath opened a door of mercy to all sorts of people; oh let thy mercy shower down abundantly, and fill the earth with thy blessing that thy works may praise thee, for now praises are ready for thee, and many hearts panteth after thee that have long lain amongst the pots.[40]

The third section by Simmonds, starting 'Oh my beloved', is described by Bernadette Smith as 'the culmination of her entire literary output' in which her spiritual search is completed.

> I sought for the way to all that pretended to direct the way; but they had stolen thy words, & had not thy life, so they wearied me and profited me not; but now thou hast revealed thy Son in me. Oh! how am I overcome with thy presence? and now I shall live with thee forever.[41]

Stranger's contribution to this pamphlet is short but interesting.

> I would not have you ignorant of the mighty day of the Lord, and of his glorious appearing amongst the sons of men. [God could fill another] vessel fit for himself to dwell in all righteousness, meekness, and longsuffering. . . . So friends consider, that if it had pleased him, he could have prayed to his Father, and he would have sent him legions of angels; but he chose rather to suffer, and thereby to cross his own will, and also all men's wills; for surely he is the same now as he was in former ages, who always appeared contrary to the expectations of all the world . . . for as he suffered at his going away, so doth he at his coming again, for so saith the Scripture, "he shall come in like manner as he went" [Acts 1:11].[42]

Are her words about Christ or about James Nayler? Did the women, and Nayler, chose to remain 'in character' during the whole sequence of events? Once arrested and obviously intended to be used as a public example, did they decide on a deliberately maintained 'performance' so that everyone in England would experience for themselves the shock of the second coming and their own sinful unpreparedness?

Nayler, Simmonds, and Hannah Stranger were not the only people enacting a show. The entire episode — from Nayler's entrance and silence at the St James's Fair in Bristol to the final second whipping in the same city — was a public spectacle and political drama. The 'sign' had already been shown twice, in Glastonbury and Wells, without incident. The local authorities in Bristol, perhaps alerted by the Bristol priest Ralph Farmer, made preparations for the group's reception in Bristol. The key people (Nayler, Simmonds, and Hannah Stranger) were swiftly transferred to Parliament, even though the local magistrates had the authority to try cases of blasphemy. The protector, Oliver Cromwell, and the Parliament used Nayler's trial as an opportunity to air a contest about the wider question of religious liberty versus conformity. The law under which Cromwell governed, the Instrument of Government, had religious liberty (for Protestants) at the heart of it. Parliament set that aside as not applying to Quakers. It also ignored the fact that it was not a court of law. Cromwell questioned the legality of the trial, but he did not intervene further.

Within the Quaker community, Fox saw Nayler as a threat to the cohesion of the community and to his own leadership. Nayler was gaining a fervent group of disciples around himself 'that gave him a strength and prestige independent of Fox'. Fox's biographer Larry Ingle continues, 'Nayler posed a threat of major proportions to Fox. No movement can follow two masters, as Fox realised'.[43] Fox's careful arrangements, after the visit to Exeter, to ensure that Nayler was carrying letters disowning Fox ensured that Fox was not personally implicated and preserved the wider movement from guilt by association. George Bishop used his influence in Bristol to keep Quakers away from Nayler so that not a single Friend brought him food in prison (see chapter 18), although Ralph Farmer's account of events in *Satan Enthroned* contradicts this.

Simmonds died in 1665, either in May on board a ship traveling to Maryland or in Southwark on 27 September. The affair of James Nayler was an episode in her life. She seems to have made peace with herself and with Quakers. Braithwaite wrote that she was

> a woman of much enthusiasm and little judgment, who took an unhelpful part in meetings and engaged in service away from London against the judgment of Friends.[44]

To me, Martha Simmonds was a resourceful person, persuading Desborough to release Nayler from Exeter jail; an energetic minister willing to risk imprisonment; and a woman willing to challenge the male patriarchy of early Quaker leadership. Her enthusiasm would not be to the taste of later Friends, and undoubtedly Hubberthorne, Burrough, and Howgill found her difficult. But I do not think she was a temptress or deliberately manipulative. The authorities chose to ignore her central role, if she played such a role. I am struck by a remark made by Colonel Sydenham, a soldier in Cromwell's army and a member of Parliament, recorded at the end of Thomas Burton's diary:

> I cannot but wonder to see the strange temper of the House in this business; how zealous they were for that high sentence against Nayler, though there was no law for it at all . . . and now how different a punishment far lesser would content them against these women; who in my opinion committed idolatry. He [Nayler] denied all honour to himself.[45]

It seems the Parliament men and the Quaker men had one thing in common. The women may have been idolaters and witches speaking filthiness, but because they were women, they were not considered dangerous enough to merit severe punishment. It could all have been very much worse for Martha Simmonds.

A brief chronology of mid-1656 is as follows:

May: apparently open dispute between Simmonds and Howgill and Dewsbury.

June: Nayler traveling to Yorkshire and back via Lincoln.

July (first week): Burrough and Howgill leave London for a short tour which ends in Bristol at the St James's Fair (26 July)

12 July: Howgill writes a loving letter to Nayler from Oxford.

July (second week?): Simmonds and Hannah Stranger complain (again) to Nayler about the treatment they received at the hands of Howgill and Burrough. Nayler reverses his judgment about the correctness of Simmonds's complaint. This change of mind seems to have triggered a 'breakdown', physically and mentally.

July (third or fourth week): Nayler taken by friends to Bristol in order to get him away from Simmonds, who they think is an unhealthy influence on him. Simmonds follows him, and they meet again in Bristol. Nayler does not preach at the fair.

August: Nayler leaves Bristol without Simmonds to see Fox at Launceston. Arrested on the way and sent to Exeter jail (by the 13th). Simmonds and Stranger do reach Fox at Launceston and accuse him of wanting to be leader. Fox is now fully aware of the seriousness of the divisions in London. Simmonds then finds General Desborough (responsible for order in the southwest) and agrees to nurse Desborough's wife for free if he will sign a release for Nayler and other Quakers. At some point she meets Hubberthorne, probably in London, who questions her.

13 August: Howgill writes to Margaret Fell.

23 August: Hubberthorne writes to Margaret Fell.

15. On James Nayler and Martha Simmonds

12 September: Fox is released from Launceston jail (not as a result of Simmonds's efforts). Travels with Friends to Exeter to see Nayler.

20 September: Fox arrives in Exeter. Sees Nayler the next day, a Sunday. Hubberthorne is now in Exeter too.

23 September: final breach between Nayler and Fox. Fox leaves for London via Bristol.

October (early): The order for the release of Nayler and others is signed. This order is carried from London by Thomas Simmonds. Fox writes a letter to Nayler casting Nayler out of his company.

4 October: Hubberthorne writes a letter to Margaret Fell with his account of the meetings between Fox and Nayler at Exeter.

20 October: Nayler is released from prison and begins his journey to Bristol via Glastonbury and Wells.

24 October: Nayler and others enter Bristol and are arrested.

16. 'Concerning Redemption'

I find redemption the hardest theological concept to understand. The orthodox teaching on redemption is that the death of Christ on the cross paid for our sins as someone might 'redeem' a slave: *In him we have redemption through his blood, the forgiveness of our trespasses, according to the riches of his grace* (Ephesians 1:7 NRSV); *And he is the propitiation for our sins: and not for ours only, but also for the sins of the whole world* (1 John 2:2 KJV). These are two of the biblical texts used to explain this doctrine. Quakers also used this language. For example, George Fox and others wrote in the letter 'For the Governour' of Barbados in 1671:

> And that Jesus Christ is his Beloved and Only Begotten Son . . . in whom we have redemption, through his blood, even the Forgiveness of Sins.[1]

In 1693, the Religious Society of Friends issued a *Declaration of Christian Doctrine* which included this sentence:

> He [Christ] having been in his dying for all, that one great universal offering and sacrifice for peace, atonement, and reconciliation between God and man; and He is the propitiation not for our sins only, but also the sins of the whole world. (BoD 1887, p. 7)[2]

Nayler in 1656 does not start with any of this explanation. He assumes his audience knows the orthodox belief in redemption, and he is quick to say they may be mistaken about their own redemption.

> This is that which many boast on and glory in, who never knew what it is to be redeemed further than in words and imagination thereof; nay, there are few who are come so far as to know what it is that wants redemption and that the promise is to, wherein only it is seen and received, for there is a seed to which the

promise of redemption is, but you who take delight in sin and plead for it, art not he. (LL 3:113–14)

The ability to quote Scripture and boast of being saved is not enough. Nayler continues, 'Talk of redemption little changes thy condition'. There follows a passage in which Nayler says if someone finds within them that which cries 'woe to thee because of thy wickedness, and mourns because of the abominations of thy times,' that takes no delight in show and vanities, and that is choked by riches and pleasures, then

> that is the seed of the kingdom, to which the promise is; and no further than that principle is raised to reign in thee above all that is contrary to it, no further art thou redeemed by Christ Jesus; for that's the plant of God's renown, the lily among the thorns; which with the cares of this world, and the deceitfulness of riches, and pleasures, is choked, that it may not bring forth to God, who hath placed it in thee for himself . . . and from thence those might receive wisdom and strength, yea, all that is needful for thee in thy measure to which thou art called.

> And this I say to all you that find such a thing as is holy thus moving in you against your lusts and worldly pleasures: take heed and do not deceive yourselves with a talk of redemption while this is in prison and not brought above all your lusts; but in the light of Christ wait, which lets you see this, that you may see his power in Spirit to raise this to reign above all in you that is contrary, and so shall you reign with it over all the world and its wicked ways; but if you have found this breathing towards God, and you have no regard thereto, take heed, lest he that gave this for thy salvation take it away from thee in wrath and leave thee to thy lusts without reproof (for his Spirit will not always strive with you). And then it had been good you had not been born. (LL 3:114–16)

The seed is within us but is not part of us; it has been placed there by God. It is the seed that holds the promise of salvation, not the earthly man or woman. The metaphor of the seed is used in the Bible to mean first the descendants of Abraham and then by extension everyone of faith: *and I will make an everlasting covenant with them. And their seed shall be known among the Gentiles, and their offspring among the people: all that see them shall acknowledge them, that they are the seed which the LORD hath blessed* (Isaiah 61:8–9 KJV). Mark also Nayler's reminder that God's 'breathings, or encouragements' to salvation can be taken away. And he goes on to say that this has happened to many and notes that

> the greatest profession now set up by many is to make the redemption of Christ a cover for all licentiousness and fleshly liberty, and say they are to that end redeemed. (LL 3:117)

This is an attack on the Ranters. In 1654, Ephraim Pagitt described the Ranters as 'more open and less sour than a Quaker'.[3] They frequented ale houses, smoked, and believed that as there was no resurrection there was no danger in 'sin'. George Fox met Ranters who said they were God. Hill summarizes some of their beliefs:

> The world is not a vale of tears to be endured, expecting our reward hereafter. . . . For Ranters Christ in us is far more important than the historical Christ who died at Jerusalem. . . . Since all men are now freed of the curse, they are also free from the commandments; our will is God's will.[4]

The Ranters' salutation to one another was 'my one flesh'. The popular voice in the 1650s confused Ranters and Quakers. Ranter(ish) behaviour might also be practised by those who believed they were the elect, chosen by God for salvation and incapable of sin. This was a doctrine known as antinomianism, which means 'opposed to law'. The respectable elect had no need to demonstrate their salvation by actions; equally, they taught that all were sinful and incapable of salvation except for a few who were already chosen. Nayler spoke against this 'preaching up sin', by which he meant telling people they would always be sinners. Nayler makes it clear the elect will only know of their election if they follow the Light that checks their sin:

> So read your condemnation, you vain babblers, who spend your time disputing about election with your reprobate minds. When ye find that the light of Christ condemns you for your lusts and earthly delights, and the Spirit of God moves in you against your evil deeds, but you will not be obedient thereto; but still harden your hearts again the light, that is the reprobate state. (from 'Concerning Election', LL 3:96)

Having dealt with the Ranters for bad behaviour and thinking themselves Christ and the elect for assuming salvation without attending to the Light within, Nayler had a third party to contend with. Arminianism is the doctrine that God is willing to save any who turn to God and that salvation is to some extent a matter of human choice and is influenced by one's own efforts — 'justification by good works'. This requires a church and a priesthood to guide the steps of the sinful towards effective good works. Archbishop Laud in the 1630s had attempted to move the Anglican Church away from Calvinism towards this gentler and more inclusive approach. It was rejected by many as being too much like Catholicism (especially as Laud also championed a 'high church' approach to clothing and sacraments). Nayler, who joined an independent church, probably rejected Arminianism. However, the Quaker message to turn to the Light within was considered by some opponents to be a 'good works' argument. The result of Quakers picking their way between these three parties was that they were variously branded as Ranters or crypto-Catholics or perfectionists. Nayler wrote:

And this is true redemption to all that know it, whereby this seed hath received redemption for us, who were transgressors, even to purge the conscience from dead works to serve the living God. And for this end he gave himself for us, to redeem us from all iniquity, and to purify unto himself a peculiar people zealous of good works: who hath redeemed us to God by his blood [Romans 5:9], out of kindreds, tongues [Revelation 13:7], and fashions, from amongst men, to follow the Lamb [John 1:29] and not the lust. And all whose redemption leads not out of this world will fail you, when you look for one another, and this all that are redeemed know. . . .

So with the light of Christ which lets you see your transgressions, search your hearts, that you may see if the just principle that moves to righteousness be not oppressed and burdened, and overpowered by the seed of the evildoer, and that nature which loves carnal delights; and so you be led captive to do the works of Satan; then what redemption have you further than a talk? (LL 3:117)

We are to give up 'dead works' (avoiding Arminianism) and become a peculiar people, the chosen elect but a people zealous of 'good works' (avoiding antinomianism). However, if we behave as if we are sure of salvation and ignore the Light of our conscience (Ranterism), then all that is left of our redemption is idle talk. Nayler's argument carefully distinguishes the seed or Light within as receiving redemption, but only if the earthly human waits for that Light and follows its guide. Changed behaviour is the result, from which others will understand that the person is redeemed. Once again, Nayler has shown that the thin 'Lightline' of our connection with God is our lifeline.

17. 'Concerning Christ Jesus'

This is he whom the world much talk of, but few there be that know him, though it be he by whom all things were made [John 1:3], who is the life of all creatures, who was before all creatures, without beginning of days or end of life [Hebrews 7:3], a priest forever [Hebrews 5:6, 7:17], and a king of whose dominion there is no end; by him kings reign, and dominions are cast down [Colossians 1:16]. . . . [Y]et doth he reveal himself to such as walk in his light [1 John 1:7], . . . [those] who deny themselves that they may learn the way of the Lord, to such he freely reveals his way for their return, that he may bring them down from the seat of exaltation and make known to them their beginning and from whence they are digged [dug out from the earth]; that they may see him who bears up the pillars of the earth [1 Samuel 2:8; Psalms 75:3] and hath laid the foundation thereof; who have set the world in their hearts, . . . who is the eternal word [John 6:68], before all time, glorified in the heavens [Isaiah 44:23] with the Father, who in time was manifest, which word became flesh and dwelt among us [John 1:14], and took upon him the form of a servant [Mark 10:44], and was made in the likeness of men [Philippians 2:7]; and being found in fashion as a man, he humbled himself and became obedient to the death [Philippians 2:8], that he might become a living example to all generations, which no creature could be, the whole creation being in the fall; and having finished the work of redemption, given him of the Father to do, and for which he was begotten [John 3:16], he ascended far above all heavens [Ephesians 4:10], to prepare a place [John 14:2] for all that follow him by faith in his light; and that from thence all such as wait for him may see his appearance as a savior [John 4:42]. And only such know him for their redeemer [Isaiah 54:5] who know him for their judge and lawgiver [James 4:12], who love him and keep his commands; to such he comes, and the Father also, and make their abode with him.

And this is he who is the light of the world [John 8:12, 9:5], and lighteth every man that comes into the world [John 1:9]; who stands at the door and knocks [Matthew 7:7]; and if any hear his voice and open he will come in and sup with him [Revelation 3:20]; and such know him, and he knows them who hear his voice, by which they are quickened out of the trespasses and sins, and the seed of God raised out of death in man [1 John 3:9]. (LL 3:125–126)

I inserted as many biblical references into the above quotation as I could reasonably make fit, using an online concordance, just to illustrate how rooted in the King James Bible Nayler's language was. For the Old Testament references, Nayler uses similar words; the New Testament references, especially those from John and Paul's letters, are close paraphrases. This is an example of what Leo Damrosch describes as an interweaving of Scripture and key words to overwhelm resistance (see my discussion of this on p. 22). Nayler's description of Christ is biblically based, but that does not mean it is orthodox. Puritan opponents thought the Quakers' Light was not Christ but a principle—a theory not a man. Quakers also deviated from orthodoxy by believing there was no salvation without an intimate knowledge of the inward workings of Christ.[1] Carole Spencer notes that Nayler believed that

deity could unite with humanity, not only uniquely in the flesh of Jesus, but also that saints' "bodies can become fit temples for God to dwell in." Nayler's theology echoed the apostle Paul who said that he would labour until "Christ be formed in you," (Gal.

4:19) and "your bodies are the temples of God" (1 Cor. 3:16).[2]

After quoting a section from 'The Fall of Man' in *Love to the Lost* (3:52–53), Spencer writes,

> Perfection is a process, a journey, not an event. It begins with repentance, a turning of the mind to the living God, surrender of self-wisdom, and a standing still in the light with "the mind stayed to wait". . . . Life and strength then erupts from the 'the word' which becomes the seed raised out of death, which is nourished and grows into the 'new creation' and is reconciled to God. . . . After repentance, the Word-seed brings wisdom and empowerment, purification, reconciliation, and union with God.[3]

This is a very helpful sketch of how Nayler's writings follow a logic of transformation from corrupt human to immortal being. Fox would have described such a sketch as a 'notion', that is an intellectual idea without a basis in his experience. I think it is important to treat Nayler's writings not as a devised theology of outward words but as an attempt to put into words his experience of the workings of God's spirit within him that were beyond words. Did Nayler think he was or could be perfect: I doubt it. But perhaps sometimes he experienced such an inrush of God that he felt he might be.

For Nayler, Christ existed before the creation and had a part in the creation. He became the Word manifest and also the Light and a living seed in humans to reveal God to humans and bring them back to God. This is closer to John's gospel than the synoptic gospels, which were of less interest to early Quakers. As Rosemary Moore says, Nayler in the section 'Concerning Christ Jesus' is writing about the pre-existent Christ.

> The Quakers' intense experience of Christ, or the light of Christ, which led them to blur the distinction

between Christ and themselves, was difficult to reconcile with a belief in Jesus as man.[4]

Moore also gives the example of Edward Burrough saying to John Bunyan, 'That body which was begotten of the Holy Ghost is not so carnal as thou supposest'.[5]

Later Quaker writers explaining Quakerism to the public tried to reconcile more orthodox teachings about the blood of Christ redeeming humanity with the distinctive Quaker message of Christ within working to save each and every individual. Quaker universality, the belief that Christ could reach anyone of any era or country (Colossians 1:23), was condemned by Nayler's contemporaries.

Early Quakers taught that we all have an everlasting mediator and priest within, so we have no need of priests without. How are we to reach this inner priest?

> [T]hen mind that light in you which thus witnesseth; for as Christ is, so is his light that leads to him; . . . And as thou follows the light out of the world, thou wilt come to see the seed. . . . And as that seed is raised, therein is the Father revealed, and his power and Godhead in his Son Jesus Christ which in him dwells, [Colossians 2:9] and without him is not revealed, but being known is life eternal, and eternal power, and eternal glory and riches, made manifest in the light [Ephesians 5:13]; for as you know this seed raised by the same spirit that raised Jesus Christ from the death; so shall you see him to whom all power and judgment is committed in heaven and earth, and for whom, and by whom all things were made in heaven and earth [John 1:3] . . .

> And to all that are yet in the night shall he appear, if you look towards the place of his rising, which is not, Lo here, lo there [Mark 15:21]; but within you in your hearts. (LL 3:126–27)

Up to now, I have not quoted the passages of condemnation in this section. Nayler is clear that a lot of people 'have got the words of the Lord, and Christ, and Jesus, yet they know not his light, his power, his kingdom', and it is the devil that rules in them. He knows this because they use these words as a cover for their sin and, more particularly, because those who claim to know Christ but do not keep his commandments 'abide not in the truth' (that is, their outward life does not conform to Nayler's understanding of a redeemed soul's behaviour).

> So all that know Christ, know the seed, the promise, the word of life, the covenant, the heritage, the righteousness, the kingdom, the power, the glory which is not of this world, and the Father of all; which you that commits sin have not seen. Neither can any say that Jesus is Lord, but by the Spirit; so you whose knowledge is without, another lord ruleth within. (LL 3:129)

And so Nayler ends this section on Christ.

It might be helpful to briefly summarize the course of Quakers' relationship with Christ since the 1650s. During the last two decades of the seventeenth century, Friends moved from thinking of Christ as within a person both as a spiritual and physical presence (as Nayler demonstrated in his ride into Bristol) to a more orthodox view of Christ. Stephen Angell comments that 'Much of the evidence of the first generation's more extreme identification with Christ was suppressed', only to be recovered later by academics.[6] Moore views the Quakers as moving from being the most radical of sects looking for God on earth to a Society more concerned with its inner life and processes.[7] As the books of discipline reveal, their theology began to use the language of traditional Christianity and became more concerned about the maintenance of their community. For some Quakers in the eighteenth century, the Light became something that influenced the noble faculty of reason, and their writings moved towards deism and Unitarianism but without losing a mystical colouring. Christ became more a principle than a person. John Woolman (1720–1771) in 1761 used the idea of a pure, universal, and inner principle to argue that all humanity were brethren:

> There is a principle which is pure, placed in the human mind, which in different places and ages hath had different names. It is, however, pure and proceeds from God. It is deep and inward, confined to no forms of religion nor excluded from any, where the heart stands in perfect sincerity. In whomsoever this takes root and grows, of whatever nation soever, they become brethren in the best sense of the expression.[8]

To knowingly contravene such a pure principle by keeping slaves not only wronged your brethren but also depraved the owner's mind to the extent that their hearts and those of their children are 'shut up against the gentle movings of uncreated Purity'.[9]

Job Scott (1751–93) wrote about salvation by Christ, and his writings were published in 1825 well after his death. The delay was because his American monthly meeting had doubts about the orthodoxy of his message. He does sound similar to Nayler:

> "Christ in us" has been in every age and nation the only true and solid ground and hope of glory. Nothing but a true and living birth of God in the soul, of the divine and incorruptible seed, a real and substantial union of the divinity and humanity in one holy offspring, has ever brought salvation. . . . None can be a true child of God without this divine birth, this true brother and sister of Christ, this real offspring of God.[10]

We are the 'Sons of God' as Christ was. Our regeneration, which sometimes Scott seems to visualize as almost physical (in contrast to Nayler), grows within us. Scott writes,

And even in the case of our Lord's conception in the virgin, it was not without the hearty assent of her mind; . . . The conception even of the body not being without the cordial submission, faith, and acquiescence of the virgin; which is a lively display of that state which invariably takes place in every soul that becomes the *mother of Christ*, which every one doth that is born again, or is born of God. For this new birth, or birth in man, "of the incorruptible seed of God" is as real a birth as is our first birth, or birth into this world.[11]

I find this a remarkable and disturbing vision of a Christ that physically grows within our bodies. Elias Hicks (1748–1830) echoes Woolman when he writes that

the law and covenant is spiritual and universal — written in the heart of every rational being under heaven — and is therefore invisible to all the external senses and is only manifested [shown or known] by its fruits. . . . and is universally manifested to all the children of men the world over, and by whom the gospel is preached in every rational creature.[12]

By contrast, nineteenth-century evangelical Quakers such as Joseph John Gurney (1788–1847) regarded the Light as irrelevant. Gurney wrote in 1840 that it was wrong to think that

because Christ is called the light (i.e., the enlightener), he is therefore to be identified with the influence which he bestows; in short that the light of the spirit of God in the heart of man, is itself actually *Christ*. The obvious tendency of this mistake, is to deprive the Saviour of his personal attributes, and to reduce him to the rank of a *principle*.[13]

Although Christ is called 'the light', that did not mean the light in the heart of a person was Christ. In 1879, London Yearly Meeting stated clearly that the light that shines into man's heart is not of man, and must ever be distinguished both from the conscience which it enlightens, and from the natural faculty of reason which, when unsubjected to its holy influences, is, in the things of God, very foolishness. As the eye is to the body, so is conscience to our inner nature, the organ by which we see; and as both light and life are essential to sight in the natural eye, so conscience, as the inward eye, cannot see aright without the quickening and illumination of the Spirit of God. (BoD 1883, p. 18; reprinted in CFP 1959, para. 170)

Here the Spirit of God, or the Light, is outside humanity, coming in. Christ is not within, as Nayler thought he was, but is an external source of salvation and an object of belief. The division between those who held to the inner workings of the Light, or Christ, within us and those who depended upon the external agency of God's Spirit grew and caused splits within Quakerism. The New England Quaker John Wilbur (1774–1856) became the main leader of those opposed to the Gurneyite view, standing firmly by early Quaker statements about the Light and arguing that Quaker distinctiveness would be dead if the 'true light' signified no more than 'Christ the Enlightener'. [14] This developed into a major split in American Quaker society between 'orthodox' Gurneyites and others. In London Yearly Meeting, there was a smaller schism in 1836 when a group led by Isaac Crewdson (1780–1844) completely repudiated the Light of Christ. This had little impact in the long-term on British Quakers. They were a smaller body united by ties of family, class, and friendship and would not survive a major schism. They adopted the orthodox views of Gurney but refused to adopt the 1887 'Richmond Declaration of Faith', which stated,

We own no principle of spiritual light, life, or holiness, inherent by nature in the mind or heart of man. We believe in no principle of spiritual light, life, or holiness, but the influence of the Holy Spirit of God, bestowed on mankind, in various measures and degrees, through Jesus Christ our Lord.[15]

The variety of Quaker views on Christ, the Light, and the Spirit of God is immense. Angell concludes:

One might well wonder to what degree any or all such changes are brought about by response to the Holy Spirit or response to an outward non-Quaker culture; indeed, they may be occasioned by some of both, as Spirit perhaps can work through outward cultures.[16]

I like the idea that the Spirit can move through culture and, as I have discussed in chapter 2, that different cultures produce different understandings of God's truth.

British Quakers moved from 'Christ within' towards 'Christ without' and back again; simultaneously, they moved away from 'Christ the principle' and towards 'Jesus the person'. The 1822 book of discipline has the following:

We earnestly exhort, that ye hold fast the profession of faith in our Lord Jesus Christ, without wavering; both in respect to his outward coming in the flesh, his sufferings, death resurrection, ascension, mediation, and inter-cession at the right hand of the Father; and to the inward manifestation of his grace and Holy Spirit in our hearts, powerfully working in the soul of man, to the subduing of every evil affection and lust, and to the purifying of our consciences from dead works, to serve the living God. (a 1736 epistle, as quoted in Extracts 1822, p. 82)

In addition, a cross-reference to the section on discipline says:

If there be any such gross errors, false doctrines, or mistakes held by any professing truth, as are either against the validity of Christ's sufferings, blood, resurrection, ascension, or glory in the heavens according as they are set forth in the scriptures; or any ways tending to the denial of the heavenly man Christ; such persons ought to be diligently instructed and admonished by faith friends. (Extracts 1822, p. 50)

Such Friends were to be instructed and, if they did not change their minds, 'disowned', although they could still attend a meeting for worship. There is no mention of how the example of Jesus' life and the Holy Spirit assist the inward manifestation of Christ. The 1834 book of discipline begins with advices, and the first one reads:

> Take heed, dear friends, we intreat you, to the convictions of the Holy Spirit, who leads, through unfeigned repentance and living faith in the Son of God, to reconciliation with our Heavenly Father, and to the blessed hope of eternal life, purchased for us by the one offering of our Lord and Saviour Jesus Christ. (BoD 1834, p. 1)

This is repeated in the 1883 book of discipline. The effective agent in salvation is the Holy Spirit and belief in Christ, which is a different emphasis compared with Nayler's writings that focus on the workings of the Light or of the seed or of Christ within. In 1928, the advices were revised. This language is more familiar to liberal British Friends, especially the opening:

> Take heed, dear Friends, to the promptings of love and truth in your hearts, which are the leadings of the Holy Spirit of God. Resist not His strivings within you. It is His light that shows us our darkness and leads to true repentance. It is God's love that draws us to Him, a redemptive love shown forth in Jesus Christ in all His life and above all on the cross. He is the Way, the Truth, the Life. (CG 1931, p. 40)

The theology is both inner and outer. The promptings of the Holy Spirit are within our hearts and should not be resisted as it is this light that leads us from darkness to light. However, Christ is external. The advice urges us to follow the example of Jesus' life and states that it is his death that is redemptive. I am left asking whether we are saved by following the leadings of the Holy Spirit, as understood by our heart, or by following Jesus' example together with a belief in his redemptive death.

In 1964 the advices were revised again, following the 1959 revision of *Christian Faith and Practice*. The opening of the 1964 edition of the advices draws heavily on the 1928 edition.

> Take heed, dear Friends, to the promptings of love and truth in your hearts, which are the leadings of God. Resist not his strivings within you. It is his light that shows us our darkness and leads to true repentance. The love of God draws us to him, a redemptive love shown forth by Jesus Christ in his life and on the cross. He is the Way, the Truth and the Life. As his disciples, we are called to live in the life and power of the Holy Spirit. (AQ 1964, p. 9)

As before, Christ's suffering on the cross is redemptive. However, in this advice the love he showed in his life is also redemptive. There is also a reference to the Light leading us to true repentance.

In the 1980s came another revision. As a trial run, the revision committee produced an early draft of the advices called *Questions and Counsel* (1987). I remember this being read in our meetings. I was naïve and unpractised in Quaker-speak then. I had no difficulties with *Questions and Counsel* save that perhaps it was a little short. I quote the first two.

> 1. Trust, dear Friends, the promptings of love and truth in your hearts, which are the leadings of God. There is a light in each one of us that shows us our darkness and brings us to new life. 2. Bring the whole of your life before God. Can you yield to the healing power of love, and the forgiveness it brings? (QC 1988)

This is about the Light; it contains no mention of the Holy Spirit and no mention of the promptings leading towards belief in a redeemer, although the reference to the healing power of love might be an acknowledgement of that. We are to bring our lives before God, not Christ. *Questions and Counsel* was rejected. Perhaps it limited too greatly the role of Jesus. Number 4 read:

> The life and death of Jesus show us the reality and cost of obedience to God, and the mystery of resurrection. How does Jesus speak to us today? Does his closeness to God challenge you to put what you have learnt from worship into daily practice? Be faithful in your inspiration. (QC 1988)

The life and death of Jesus are held up as an example of one who has followed the promptings of love and truth, maybe to excess. The counsel suggests Jesus is not within us and is not the path to salvation. The resurrection is a mystery and not within us. Although the historical Jesus is close to God, he is not God's son. We learn our living faith from worship, not from leadings of the Holy Spirit. The 1987 *Questions and Counsel* was perhaps too far away from the Quakers' starting point at the Light of Christ. In 1994, London Yearly Meeting approved a new revision of *Advices and Queries* which is still in use today. This edition opens with words familiar from earlier iterations.

> 1. Take heed, dear Friends, to the promptings of love and truth in your hearts. Trust them as the leadings of God whose Light shows us our darkness and brings us new life. 2 Bring the whole of your life under the ordering of the spirit of Christ. Are you open to the healing power of God's love? Cherish that of God within you, so that this love may grow in you and guide you. Let your worship and daily life enrich each other. Treasure your experience of God, however it comes to you. Remember that Christianity is not a notion but a way. (QFP 2013, 1.02)

This revision cleverly brings together disparate elements of Quaker thinking about Christ. The opening is plain and simple and keeps the directness of the earlier revision. The phrase 'under the ordering of the spirit of Christ' in the second advice might mean Christ within us reorders our lives and changes our priorities. Are we to go about doing good as Christ did? This phrase echoes Nayler's words:

> And only such know him [Christ] for their redeemer who know him for their judge and lawgiver, who love him and keep his commands; to such he comes, and the Father also, and make their abode with him. (LL 3:126)

Or is it about 'corporate holiness? The advice continues. We are 'to cherish that of God within us' (not Christ). This is more definite than 'leadings' and could include Christ or the Light or the Seed as well. Then there is the reference to the healing power of God's love. Is that a mention of redemption or a secular understanding of the psychological healing that worship and belief can bring? Finally, there is the reference to Fox's expression 'not a notion but a way', which effectively dismisses all theological questions as irrelevant, including any questions about the theological meaning of the advice!

The role of Christ in Quaker theology has taken many forms. We have seen how British Quakers have moved back and forth along the spectrum. Other yearly meetings are on the same journey but are in different places. If treated with respect and sampled without prejudice, this diversity gives all of us a varied diet. Here are queries from Northwest Yearly Meeting in America, a 'covenantal community of evangelical Friends churches':

> Do you live in vital relationship with God, trusting in Jesus Christ as your saving Lord and obeying the leadings of the Holy Spirit? Is Christ's presence evident in your life?[17]

And this is a slightly more familiar (to British Friends) query from Conservative Friends in Ohio:

Use vigilant care, dear Friends, not to overlook those promptings of love and truth which you may feel in your hearts; for these are the tender leadings of the Spirit of God. Nor should any of us resist God's workings within us, for it is His redemptive love which strives to show us our darkness, and to lead us to true repentance, and to His marvelous light. "Behold, I stand at the door and knock: if any man hear my voice and open the door, I will come in to him, and will sup with him, and he with me" (Rev. 3:20).[18]

In all this theology, from every age, it is attending to the knock at the door of the heart that is important.

18. On the Exercise of Power 1656 to 1661

Contemporaries and historians have often viewed the Nayler episode as a struggle between George Fox and James Nayler for control of the Quaker movement. It should be emphasised, however, that Nayler and Fox were close. Nayler deferred to Fox. He wrote constantly (at least once a week) to him and usually addressed Fox as 'Dear Brother' (once as 'My Father, My Father'). He used phrases such as 'thou art in my heart, I am often with thee. I am much refreshed when I hear from thee', 'It is my desire to see my way & be obedient. Let me hear from thee as soon as thou canst conveniently', 'pray for me that I may be kept in the power of the Lord & humble before him', and 'My dear brother, how dear thou art to me words cannot now declare'.[1]

There is little evidence that a struggle was planned by either party. Historian Larry Ingle remarks that Fox later said he had concerns about leaving Nayler in London, but 'not a syllable has survived'. However,

> high levels of lingering acrimony suggest that the matter remained to fester and was whispered about privately among those who know of the difficulties.[2]

For a long time, Fox appears to have thought Martha Simmonds had 'run out' and would cease doing so if not noticed. He made little of it and said no Friends should be discouraged (presumably from speaking in meetings for worship). It was not until Martha Simmonds and Hannah Strange came to Launceston prison and accused Fox of trying to take absolute power that he suspected Nayler might be attempting the same. After his meeting with Nayler in Exeter jail, Fox seemed to be certain of this. In his journal he describes these meetings in a quite perfunctory way:

> That night that we came to Exeter, I spoke with James Nayler, for I saw he was out and wrong and so was his

company. Next day, being the First-day [21 September 1656] we went to the prison to visit the prisoners and had a meeting with them in the prison; and I did admonish them. But James Nayler and some of them could not stay the meeting but kept their hats on when I prayed. And they were the first that gave that bad example amongst Friends. So after I had been warring with the world, now there was a wicked spirit risen up amongst Friends to war against. . . .

And the next day I spoke to James Nayler again, and he slighted it and was dark and much out; nevertheless he would have come and kissed me, but I said, seeing he had turned against the power of God, 'It is my foot' and so the Lord God moved me to slight him and to set the power of God over him.[3]

A letter from Richard Hubberthorne to Margaret Fox gives a much fuller account. On the Monday there were four visits between the prison and the inn where Fox and Hubberthorne were staying: it seems Nayler could get passes to leave prison. First, Nayler went up to the inn and 'was tender and broken and dear love went out from G [George Fox] to him & in tenderness he spoke to him'. Then Hubberthorne walked back with Nayler to the prison and tried to persuade him to give up his present company. The 'present company' accused Hubberthorne of being a fair-weather friend and said 'when he was on the cross I spised him'. Hubberthorne told them to beware what they sowed and accused them of being envious of those Friends 'that were in the truth and power of God, and that we were not to look for any other fruit nor any other power than that which we had received a measure of'. Fox came into the prison at this point, but Nayler would not speak to him. The final meeting that day came when Nayler went back to the inn and told Fox 'there was that which could never be separated from him; and much love and tenderness was from Geo. to him'. Nayler offered Fox an apple, which Fox refused.[4]

18. On the Exercise of Power 1656 to 1661

The final break came with two meetings on the Tuesday. First, by a misunderstanding, Nayler got a pass for the castle, whereas Fox wanted him to come to the inn to talk privately. Nayler refused to ask the jailor to change his destination, and they ended up talking in the street at the castle entrance. Nayler shouted at Fox 'Take heed of lying and false accusing', so loudly that bystanders gathered. Both walked away. Later, Hubberthorne was sent by Fox to ask Nayler what he meant by those words, and Nayler said it was not Fox who was the false accuser but others. Hubberthorne argued that Fox was right to raise questions when he received reports, but he had 'not judged things by the reports'. Nayler asked why he should say anything to Hubberthorne when 'I sought to catch him in my wisdom and subtlety'.[5]

Fox came one last time to the prison room, where Nayler sat in a place lower than the rest of the room and Fox stood above him. Nayler again professed great love to Fox and again offered him an apple. Fox said,

> 'If thou can say thou are moved of the Lord to give me it.' Ja. said, 'Would thou have me to lie?' Then Ja. having Geo. by the hand, he asked him if he might kiss him. Geo. standing above the low place would have drawn Ja. out to him, but he would not come out; but Geo. standing still could not bow down to him at his asking of him in that thing which if he had come out he could have suffered him to have done it. Then Geo. gave him his hand to kiss, but he would not; and then George said unto him, 'It is my foot'. So with a few more words we passed away.[6]

These encounters are very sad. Fox and Nayler are using hierarchical symbols — hats on or off, the kissing of a hand (as one would a bishop's) or a hand pretending to be a foot and high and low places where they met — in a society founded on equality. Fox challenges Nayler over the offer of an apple (possibly an apple that had spent a lot of time in Nayler's pocket), asking, in effect, Are all your casual gestures inspired by God; are you always Christ? Nayler knows the difference between God's love and the offer of an apple and replies, Why would you want me to lie? We both know the difference between an action led by God and one led by human love.

Indeed, they can love each other but not their respective associates, whose influence they fear might lead to a betrayal. Ingle suggests that Simmonds's influence meant Nayler could not function. Fox would agree with this. The lying and false 'reports', Ingle thinks, were broadsheets and papers organised by the clique around Simmonds who in Fox's view were creating a party within a party. Nayler was not willing to distance himself from this group in London, either because he thought there was truth in the broadsheets or because he was under the spell of Simmonds.[7]

Fox left with Hubberthorne and held a large meeting in Bristol, where he collected George Bishop. At Reading, Fox dictated a letter to Bishop for him to send to Nayler in the expectation that it would be found by magistrates in Nayler's pockets. And that is in fact what happened. It started by casting Nayler out of his company:

> Thou must bear thy own burden, & the company with thee while iniquity doth increase & by thee is not cried against. Thou hast satisfied the world, yea their desires [which] they labour for, & thou & thy disciples are with the whole world joined against truth, it is manifest through your wilfulness, & stubbornness, & this is the word of the Lord God to thee.

Then he reproves Nayler:

> Many did not expect that thou wouldst have been an encourager of such as do cry against the power & life of truth, but wouldst have been a nourisher of truth, & not trained up a company against it.

Finally, he warns Nayler against believing that the women are led by God. Instead, he says, they are fulfilling the world's prophecy that the movement is Ranterism and madness:

> And what is that which doth fulfil the world's prophecy, & their desires? Therefore consider, & search thyself if this be innocency. The light of God is all I own, but this I judge.[8]

Fox probably intended the Bristol magistrates to find this letter for it enabled Bristol Quakers to avoid guilt by association with Nayler.[9] Around the same time, Fox wrote a second letter to Nayler and also circulated copies of it amongst Friends. This letter contained strong accusations that Nayler was deliberately building a rival power base:

> [A]nd I saw thee at Exeter, a cloud of darkness would arise up against me, which was entered into thee . . . And now James the darkness is entered into thy disciples' vessels out of thee, & is poured abroad; and is driven home again by the life & power of truth. And as Martha cried against the truth, and Hannah, so now do thy disciples, and such as have had relation to the Ranters which are gotten up & comes & cries against the truth.   . . . [N]ow it is manifest, them that be of thy flock, begotten disciples which are turned from the power . . . Cain-like are turned against the Just, & betraying it to the world, & making tumults. . . . O James, be awakened & consider aright & shake off & come from under the cloud of earth & darkness. . . . And so all them that depart from friends to thee comes who would gather a party make a party, in the self-separation crying against the truth, which formerly they were convinced by. . . .
>
> All friends whom this comes to, dwell in the light of life & power, which comprehends darkness.[10]

Margaret Fell wrote to Nayler on 15 October 1656 in a letter carried by a Friend and given to George Bishop who sent it back unopened, for fear the Magistrates might find it and draw her into the affair. She had heard that

> thou would not be subject to him [Fox] to whom all nations shall bow; it hath grieved my spirit. Thou hath confessed him to be thy father and thy life bound up in him, and when he sent for thee and thou would not come to him, where was thy life then?[11]

The 'sending for him' appears to be a reference to the misunderstanding about meeting at the inn or the castle. Francis Howgill wrote to Margaret Fell on 21 October with news from Bristol of Nayler's release.

> [T]ruly my dear J.N. is bad, and he hath written private letters to some in the city who were in deceit, & told them, G.F. tempted him but he had withstood him, and resisted him, and there is such filthy things acted in there in such havoc & spoil & such madness among them, as I cannot write; but there is about 10 of them in all with him, & they call him "I am" and the "Lamb." . . . [T]ruly my dear G.F. bore it so long, and stood so of us, that it's become a mountain, and he sees he suffered it too long now; I saw thy letter which James sent thee [presumably the one to which Fell replied on 15 October]; & I saw it full of cunning subtlety, and repented I had sent it thee.[12]

Nayler's letter to Margaret Fell is lost. By the time Nayler reached Bristol, the Quakers there had been warned not to welcome him, and George Bishop made it clear to the magistrates that the Bristol Quakers had denied Nayler. And so two parties were created for the protection of those not with Nayler. But what was the substance of their difference? Ralph Farmer in his account of events at Bristol makes the point that Nayler's imitation of Christ was no different from Fox's behaviour:

> Is not this (as before) the natural and genuine issue of their opinions and principles? . . . [A]nd did not he

[Fox] avow himself to be the Christ? yea, the Way, the Truth and the Life? . . .

. . . Now then, if we may judge George Fox (whom we do not so well know here) by his companions and their practices (even in this matter) we may well conceive their quarrel against James is not real but feigned; for although our Quakers there did seem publicly to disclaim him and his, . . . yet secretly many of them owned them and cherished them, in sending in supplies unto them in the prison, although necessaries were not (otherwise) wanting to them.[13]

This flatly contradicts Bishop's assertion to Margaret Fell 'none go to visit them as I can tell' in his letter of 27 October. As Farmer sees it, the reason for this pretend quarrel is that Fox's disciples think it is not yet time for a Quaker leader to accept homage as Christ; therefore, their opposition is feigned.[14] That seems unlikely, but the theological point is acute.

This brings us back to the suggestion that the row with Martha Simmonds in London developed further because it was a struggle for control. To have people treating you as Christ is one way of demonstrating authority and power, and Fox did have to rebuke Friends for worshipping him. There was no formal understanding about where authority lay in the movement. There had not yet been a yearly meeting of Friends. Kate Peters does argue that as early as 1653 there was a central organisation, based first at Swarthmore (Margaret Fell's home in Westmoreland) and then in London. It primarily directed minsters were to go and assessed and paid for publications. Peters considers the very tight control Fox had on publications and public statements during Nayler's arrest and trial is evidence of 'the very tight organisation which lay behind Quaker pamphleteering and the organisation as a whole'.[15] Nayler would have been a member of this circle, but just how close he was to Fox, as compared to Margaret Fell, Howgill, and others, we cannot tell. There are only a few letters from Fox to Nayler; others may have been destroyed. Ingle says that amongst the senior Quakers there was a tacit understanding that, when decisions were needed about who would go where and do what, Fox's view prevailed. Nayler does not seem to have disputed this. But, as Ingle says,

> Sects based on personal experience . . . always find it difficult to forestall determined adherents from insisting that their own special revelation is more valid than others'.[16]

Nayler's great personal success in London starting in mid-1655, and Fox's absence traveling or in Launceston jail, meant Nayler was creating a separate base. Leading Quakers would ask him to 'look over' their pamphlets, and it was he who received the invitations to dispute with Baptists and Independents. A vacuum opened within the leadership. Nayler's decision to change his mind about Simmonds and dispute the discernment of Burrough and Howgill created the possibility of divided counsels in London, a situation which Richard Roper as late as October 1656 described in a letter to Margaret Fell as similar to Corinth when Paul was there.[17] The danger to Fox and to the movement is obvious.

Nayler was embarrassed by, or allowed, a further indication of authority. 'Hat honour' is now disregarded amongst Friends, but it meant a lot to early Quakers. Friends were jailed for not taking off their hat to judges. The only time a man took his hat off in Quaker circles was when another Friend was ministering. But a few Friends kept their hat off in Nayler's presence —something that made Fox truly angry. Nobody took their hat off to Fox. When Nayler was brought into the great Bristol fair in order to speak (but did not), he was preceded by a bareheaded Friend, Thomas Wedlock from Ely. Francis Howgill, who was speaking at the time, was almost struck dead, and Edward Burrough had to stand up and take over the meeting.

John Stranger walked bareheaded — in the pouring rain — in front of Nayler when they entered Bristol.[18] Then there was Nayler's physical appearance. When Nayler and the others were arrested, one of the women was found to have on her a copy of an ancient fake letter allegedly from the Roman Senator Publius Lentulus to Tiberius Caesar describing the appearance of Jesus. Farmer writes:

> This wretch James Nayler being somewhat fitted for it by bodily shape, colour of hair, and some other advantages of nature endeavours artificially to compose and dispose himself as much as he may to this description, parting the hair of his head, cutting his beard forked, assuming an affected gravity, and other the like as is there expressed. And this they no doubt make use of amongst simple clowns and silly women . . . and now does it not appear that these Quakers are most horrid and abominable blasphemers.[19]

Farmer is using the coincidence of Nayler's appearance being similar to a fake image of Jesus in a fake letter to bolster his claim that Nayler was guilty of blasphemy. Nayler's charisma and personal charm and his ability to suit his manners to his audience were not lost on Fox nor on the supporters of either side.

For Fox, the break with Nayler at Exeter in October 1656 appears to have been final. His attitude towards Nayler was unforgiving. Neither he nor other leading London Quakers signed a petition asking for Nayler's punishment to be remitted, and a paper he wrote on religious liberty 'was heartlessly neutral regarding Nayler's case'.[20] Ingle considers this was not Fox's finest hour, as he could have supported Nayler with no danger to himself. Indeed, Fox did less than Nayler's old commanding officer, General Lambert, who took the trouble to tell the House of Commons on the first day of the trial that

[h]e was two years my quartermaster and a very useful person. We parted with him with great regret. He was a man of very unblamable life and conversation, a member of a very sweet society of an Independent church. How he comes (by pride or otherwise) to be puffed up to his opinion I cannot determine.[21]

Lambert was also one of the members of Parliament who supported petitioners to the House to postpone the second part of Nayler's punishment in London (the boring through of his tongue, branding a 'B' on his forehead, and additional whipping). The House refused the request.

It took a lot of persuasion for Fox to agree to meet Nayler after his release in September 1659. Bittle says that Howgill came from Yorkshire to persuade him and that a meeting was arranged in January 1660, at which Fox required Nayler to kneel before him, which he did.[22] Nayler was, therefore, prepared to accept Fox's authority, and Fox achieved the submission he had failed to obtain in Exeter jail. The meeting is not recorded in his journal.

Much more can be said about the exercise of power amongst Friends. At this early stage in the movement, power was dependent entirely on personality and the authority given a single person by others. Historians generally agree that the Nayler episode was a turning point in the exercise of power among early Quakers. Fox saw the urgency of creating proper structures so that disputes would no longer threaten the movement with disintegration. The sect needed a mechanism by which Quakers who were in danger of 'running out' could be identified and controlled. The system of monthly and quarterly meetings charged with managing Friends in their geographic areas was built up laboriously during the severe persecution of the 1660s. How Nayler would have accommodated himself to these structures I do not know. In *Concerning Magistracy*, he distinguishes between Christians who exercise power in God's will and heathens who exercise lordship in their own wills which 'they set up in their selfish principle'.[23] This is the same selfish principle that Nayler saw in himself and which he later wrote let in the adversary and created spiritual pride.[24] If Friends were to embrace such a spirit, possibly unavoidable in any authority structure, what would Nayler have thought? It is not clear that Nayler would have been willing to accept a Friend's exercise of spiritual oversight by virtue of appointment to an office.

19. 'Concerning the Resurrection'

The section on the resurrection was not included in the first printing of *Love to the Lost*. Maybe Nayler thought the resurrection unnecessary to cover, or perhaps the pages were lost. It does, however, seem a suitable topic with which to end a survey of Christian beliefs.

> "I am the resurrection and the life," saith Christ, "he that believes in me though he were dead, yet shall he live"; and "whosoever liveth and believeth in me shall never die" [John 11:25–26]. Blessed is he that this knoweth and believeth, "which is the first resurrection, for on such the second death shall have no power [Revelation 20:6]. Yet the day cometh, in which all that are in the graves shall hear the voice of the judge, and shall come forth: they that have done good unto the resurrection of life, and they that have done evil unto the resurrection of condemnation" [John 5:29]. (LL 3:135)

I have inserted the biblical references to show how Nayler combined passages from John and Revelation. It is unusual for *Love to the Lost* in that Nayler (or the printer) has inserted quotation marks to show that the words are scriptural. The result, even in the opening words, puts a certain spin on the biblical texts. In Revelation, the reference to the first resurrection is explicitly to those martyrs who were beheaded for their faith [Revelation 20:4]; it is not, as Nayler would have it, to the first 'resurrection' of the seed of Christ in the heart of man. Nayler's interest is in the spiritual resurrection in individuals, not Christ's physical resurrection or the necessity to believe in that for salvation. The opening is followed by a section listing those who believe they are saved but who are not.

19. 'Concerning the Resurrection'

A terrible day will this be to you that die in your sins; and this the children of light knows, whom your envious minds is accusing as though they denied the resurrection, though you see them preparing for it by casting off the deeds of darkness and works of the flesh, and all the ungodly ways of the world, the pleasures and vanities thereof, and esteeming more of the cross of Christ and the reproach of the world. (LL 3:135)

In 1656, Quakers were thought to deny the resurrection because they placed emphasis not on the saving power of Christ's death and resurrection but more on the power of the Light within to bring about a spiritual resurrection. Consequently, they were accused of devaluing the human Christ. Nayler continues:

And we know that a city is prepared for us, whose maker is God, a durable habitation in the heavens, which such who love the world cannot receive: and . . . therefore hath God appointed a day wherein he will judge the world in righteousness. . . . [W]oe to you who die in your sins at that day, who neither live nor die in the faith of Christ; and you are they who live and die in that faith that you cannot be set free from sin while you live; for this is not the faith of Christ, nor did ever any of his profess it or die in it, but believe him that is able to save the uttermost all that come to him. (LL 3:136)

The city 'prepared for us' is a reference to the heavenly city that appears in Revelation 21:10 and also in Galatians and Hebrews, where it is talked of as the city of the living God, heavenly Jerusalem (Hebrews 12:22). This is a place where those who live out of the world are safe. Nayler writes that Christ will save everyone who professes him. This is a rejection of the view that only those who are 'elect' or 'justified' are saved and resurrected, although he may well have held that view earlier. He uses words from Hebrews 7:25: *Wherefore he is able also to save them to the uttermost that come unto God by him, seeing he ever liveth to make intercession for them* (KJV). Those who believed, as many did, that it was impossible to cast off one's sin in this life were described by Quakers as 'preaching up sin' — in modern language, telling people they are permanently inadequate and without potential.

Nayler then continues by addressing the question that 'busy minds' always ask about resurrection: With what bodies will we come back? Paul addresses the same question, and Nayler says, 'You that are wise in your eyes, you may read the 1 Cor. 15, and you may see the apostle speaks plain words to that purpose; and if you cannot understand his speech, neither can you do mine' (LL 3:137). Like Paul in 1 Corinthians:37–38, Nayler uses the analogy of a seed. Indeed, some of this section draws on 1 Corinthians directly, as my interpolations in square brackets show.

> [Y]et doth the sons of God (who are born of the incorruptible seed) know the incorruptible body that shall never wax old: therefore doth give up the corruptible to be tortured by the wills of the wicked and bloody persecutors [as Paul fought wild beasts at Ephesus 1 Corinthians 15:32], for the honor of him who hath called us thereto, by whom the inward man is daily renewed, though the outward man perish, and from who we have assurance that when this earthly tabernacle is dissolved we shall be clothed on from above; which clothing we see from faith, not by what the carnal can see or comprehend; for that which is seen is temporal, but that which is not seen is eternal; and all flesh is not the same [as the flesh of men differs from birds, beasts, and fishes 1 Corinthians 15:39], nor is all flesh from the earth, for there is heavenly bodies [as the sun, moon, and stars 1 Corinthians 15:40], and there is earthly bodies; yet cannot the earthly reveal the heavenly nor judge of them; even so is the resurrection of the dead: he that hath an ear let him hear; but flesh and blood cannot inherit the kingdom of God [this is

straight from Paul, who continues, 'nor doth corruption inherit incorruption' [1 Corinthians 15:48]. (LL 3:137)

Paul's words are not sufficient to convey the message that Nayler has about the resurrection. Perhaps the insertion 'he that hath an ear let him hear', which is often found after the parables of Jesus, was put there by Nayler to suggest that this resurrection is also a parable. Paul is clear that his faith is entirely bound up with Christ's physical resurrection; if there is no resurrection of the dead, then Christ has not risen and *then is our preaching vain, and your faith is also vain* (1 Corinthians 15:14 NRSV). The last paragraph *of Love to the Lost* has a different view:

> And this I say to all who desire to attain the resurrection from the dead and to be counted worthy thereof, consult not with flesh and blood about it, nor seek to comprehend it in thy reason, lest thou lose it and become brutish in thy judgment; but in the light wait, which shows the old man's deeds, that out of darkness thou may be led, to obtain the new birth and first resurrection; and as thou becomes conformable to that body which came down from heaven and ascended into heaven, so shalt thou see the resurrection, the form and power and purity thereof: but the woeful estate of the wicked, who die not in the Lord, who are talking of the resurrection but the old man still living, so live and so die, that resurrection is to eternal destruction. Hearken all you busy minds, whose ear is open to mischief. (LL 3:137)

Paul would say that the resurrection, like a seed, is sown in dishonour, raised in glory; sown in weakness, raised in power; sown in a natural body, raised in a spiritual body: and as the first man (Adam) was a living soul, so the second (Christ) is a quickening spirit (1 Corinthians 15:42–45). Nayler says that we will all see the resurrection. We will see it in ourselves as we change with the growth of the Light (or with the quickening spirit of Christ) within us; we will then feel more powerful and will no longer suffer weakness and sin. Our bodies will become spiritual, by which Nayler means that Quakers will no longer be 'of the world', and, because the bodies are spiritual in motivation (yet still corporal), their actions will not be comprehended by the earthly world. We will also see this in others; as the Light grows in them there will be companies of Friends resurrected together and meeting together in this world instead of waiting for the day of judgment as described in Revelation and elsewhere. For Nayler, the resurrection happens once we are prepared to accept the new birth that God offers us. A theoretical belief in resurrection is not enough. Nayler advises us not to think about resurrection because it is too fine and delicate for our brutish minds to understand. We should obtain the new birth and grow into that new body, the same body (Jesus) that descended from heaven and ascended again.

It is not clear whether Nayler believed in the physical resurrection of Jesus the man. In the penultimate paragraph he says the 'Sons of God (who are born of the incorruptible seed) know the incorruptible body that shall never wax old' (LL 3:137). The old man will perish as the 'inner man' is 'daily renewed' and 'when this earthly tabernacle is dissolved we shall be clothed on from above' (LL 3:137) and see that which is eternal. This could mean we will become living spirits after death. But it could also be interpreted as happening on earth during our temporal lives. Nayler used the metaphor of 'clothing' in his chapter on love, and perhaps he means here that incorruptibility will be placed over us. The renewal of the 'inner man' reminds me of Job Scott's image of rebirth in our earthly bodies (see chapter 17).

In 1693, London Yearly Meeting produced a *Declaration of Christian Doctrine given forth on behalf of the Society*. This was designed to reassure the authorities that Quakers were orthodox Christians. On the resurrection, it says simply,

> Concerning the resurrection of the dead, and the great day of judgement yet to come . . . what the Holy

Scriptures plainly declare and testify in these matters, we have been always ready to embrace. (BoD 1834, p. xi; reprinted in BoD 1883, p. 8)

Later British Quakers did not often use 'resurrection' as a metaphor for personal transformation. It was more likely to be used in the context of a life after death. The 1922 *Christian Life, Faith and Thought* does not list resurrection in its index. This is the edition in which selections from Friends' writing first appear, and the opening pages have the famous 'last words' of Nayler beginning 'There is a spirit that delights to do no evil . . . . ', which has in it these sentences,

It is conceived in sorrow, and brought forth without any to pity it, nor doth it murmur at grief and oppression. . . . I found it alone, being forsaken. I have fellowship therein with them who lived in dens and desolate places of the earth, who through death obtained this resurrection and eternal holy life. (James Nayler, 1660, as quoted in CLFT 1922, p. 16)

Nayler had come back into favour by 1922, and his 'last words' are quoted in each subsequent book of discipline. The opening pages of the 1922 edition also contain a quotation from William Dewsbury, convinced with James Nayler, which illustrates the more radical 1650s interpretation of resurrection.

I lay waiting for the coming of Christ Jesus, who, in the appointed time of the Father appeared to my soul, as the lightnings from the east to the west [Luke 17:24]. And my dead soul heard His voice, and by His voice was made to live, who created in me a lively hope, and sealed me up in the everlasting covenant of life with His blood [Ephesians 1:13, 4:30]. Then I witnessed the wages of sin and death, and gift of God of eternal life, through Jesus Christ my Lord. (William Dewsbury, 1655, as quoted in CLFT 1922, p. 11)

For Dewsbury, the resurrection is a radical, internal transformation that is best described using the symbolic language of the King James Bible. The 1959 book of discipline has resurrection in the index and a section on life after death, not quite the same idea as salvation through the resurrection.

> I must confess to a passionate devotion to God, as the spiritual reality par excellence, If He be real, and if He be concerned for me, I ask no more. I believe He cares, and that He continues our lives after death, in a fellowship of which we have a foretaste here. (Thomas Kelly, 1940, as quoted in CFP 1959, para. 192)

> I was very glad to hear from you, for in these days one is anxious in one sense though in another *not at all.* . . . What I mean is that ultimately whether you are in Suffolk or South Heaven, Norfolk or North Heaven, you exist and live, and it's the joy I have in the quality of your living that is important, not where you are at a given moment. (Carl Heath, 1940, as quoted in CFP 1959, para. 194)

I wonder how many contemporary British Friends believe that God continues our lives after death? The 2013 book of discipline has a short section on death which contains passages about the resurrection. William Littleboy is most explicit:

> Death is not an end but a beginning. It is but an incident in the 'life of the ages', which is God's gift to us now. It is the escape of the spirit from its old limitations and its freeing for a larger and more glorious career. . . . The dear one returns with us to our home, ready and able, as never before, to comfort, encourage, and beckon us onward. (William Littleboy, 1917, as quoted in QFP 2013, 21.54)

These are surprisingly warm and encouraging words from a Friend whom most know as a forbidding profile in a portrait hanging in the hall at Woodbrooke. *Quaker faith and practice*, in a section on the world family of Friends, reminds us that 'many Friends have a vivid experience of personal salvation through the teaching, life, death and resurrection of Jesus Christ' (QFP 2013, 9.02). Resurrection has become for British Friends a metaphor, a gesture towards the mystery, a powerful image of renewal. Their attention is drawn to the exemplary nature of Jesus' life, not the literal truth of his resurrection (see Kathleen Lonsdale as quoted in QFP 2013, 20.26). A member of the Quaker Women's Group writes in 1986 of a night vigil against the cruise missile base at Greenham Common. A police officer asks,

> 'What are you doing then, love? Not cutting the fence are you?' 'No, just praying at it.' A soldier with a dog walks up and down inside, suspicious, watching me watching him. . . . I wait, not knowing what I'm waiting for. The kingdoms of the Lord? A hundred yards to my left, women cut the wire, roll away the stone, and walk through into the tomb. No angels greet them; no resurrection yet. (QFP 2013, 24.28)

Was there no resurrection there? Would not the actions of those women cutting the wire and braving the soldiers with the dogs bring about a resurrection within them, a rebirth in their hearts? Nayler might say so.

Today, Friends also associate resurrection with illness, with death, and with pain, and in those circumstances it gives hope:

> The resurrection, however literally or otherwise we interpret it, demonstrates the power of God, to bring life out of brokenness; not just to take the hurt out of brokenness but to add something to the world. It helps us to sense the usefulness, the possible meaning in our suffering, and to turn it into a gift. The resurrection affirms me with my pain and my anger at what has happened. It does not take away my pain, it still hurts. But I sense that I am being transfigured; I am being

enabled to begin again to love confidently and to remake the spirit of my world. (S. Jocelyn Burnell, 1989, as quoted in QFP 2013, 26.56)

From her experience of a near-fatal illness, Jenifer Faulkner wrote:

> From the closeness to my own dying, I know *God is*. Death is not a negation of life but complements it: however terrible the actual dying, life and death are both parts of the whole and that wholeness is God. I still fight the conventional words of 'resurrection and life everlasting' but I know that after Jesus died the overwhelming certainty of his presence released his disciples from fear. I believe eternal life is in each moment of life, here and now; the real tragedy is not how or when we die but if we do not live the life we are given to our full potential. (Jennifer Faulkner, 1982, as quoted in QFP 2013, 21.57)

These are very gentle words compared with Nayler's; no threat can be found here. Nayler wrote, 'A terrible day will this be to you that die in your sins' (LL 3:135). For me, this remains the threat most to fear. Would it not be terrible to die without having made the effort to give life our full potential? Our resurrection awaits us in this life, whether or not there is a next. That I think was Nayler's message, and it remains the message of British Quakers today.

20. Defeat: September 1658 to May 1660

Oliver Cromwell died on 3 September 1658 after an illness of five weeks. The constitution allowed him to nominate his successor. It is unclear whether he did so, but a consensus soon formed around his eldest son Richard. Richard has been characterised as affable but incapable, a 'tumble-down Dick'; but the records suggest he was, if not charismatic, certainly charming, broad-minded, and capable of decision but sadly not able to resolve the contradictions he inherited. Oliver had run a personally selected broad church government based on its members' loyalty to himself. Its fall revealed its cracks; any elected Parliament would fail to meet the wishes of the army regarding a religious settlement but would be suspended if it did not; military rule alone was too expensive and the Parliament was unlikely to vote more taxes; and the traditional gentry rulers were beginning to reassert themselves. If this is reminiscent of Charles I's problems, then that is because the social composition of the country remained broadly the same. The specific problems for Richard Cromwell were, as Ronald Hutton summarises:

> Richard had to please Parliament to pay the army, but the former provoked the latter to mutiny; the junior officers forced their commanders to accept the purged Parliament on the strength of promises . . . that Parliament was never inclined to keep . . . [and] they provoked the army to another mutiny [yet the religious dynamic that had driven the army to form a commonwealth was still present in 1659]. The radical pamphleteering of 1659 showed as much vigour as that ten years before, and possessed in the Quaker movement a base which the earlier reformers had apparently lacked, covering almost all the country and representing both town and country. . . . The saints of

the 1640's had been overtaken on the road to the new Jerusalem by the Quakers. There is an air of limpness, of intangibility, about many of the republicans of 1659, in comparison with their earlier selves.[1]

It is certain that Quakers did enlist or re-enlist in 1659 in the hope that Jerusalem could be saved. Their hopes were highest from May 1659 when the Rump Parliament (now only around forty-two strong), previously expelled but not dissolved by Oliver, returned. The Quakers and other sectaries felt God was at last vindicating them. Moore writes that

> [f]ierce apocalyptic warnings, and a feeling of excitement because God was at last about to act, were characteristic of the majority of Quaker pamphlets of 1659. Dorothy White [wrote to Parliament] . . . , 'The Lord will overturn you by his powerful arm, for the decree of God and his purpose is . . . to throw down and break up Parliaments. . . . God himself will rule and bear rule in the hearts of men'.[2]

Ingle views Quakers as being clearly on the side of the army, and they petitioned Fleetwood, the commander in chief, in support of this blessed cause and said they would 'cheerfully afford our further assistance to the hazard of our lives and all our earthly concernments'. [3] Quakers prepared petitions against tithes, wrote against an upper chamber of lords, and collected the names of Quakers who could be justices of the peace. A Gloucestershire member of Parliament said in April 1659, 'There is one [Quaker justice of the peace] in my county that could lead out three or four hundred with him at any time'[4]. On 1 August 1659 came a Royalist uprising in Cheshire (uprisings in other parts of the country had been stood down at the last minute) in which the Royalists encouraged Presbyterians to join them by playing on their fears that Quakers were about to rise and massacre them in their beds.[5] Lambert put down the uprising with no difficulty, and the sectaries' hopes rose higher. In late August or early September, the Rump agreed to an amnesty for some imprisoned Quakers, including James Nayler. The Rump was about to increase taxation to pay the army when it also voted against increased religious toleration. This coincided with further pressure from the army for a more radical programme, which was clearly not forthcoming. On 13 October 1659, junior officers excluded the Rump Parliament from the House of Commons. The generals were unprepared for this but established on 20 October a Committee of Safety, with a majority of civilians as members, to run the country and decide on a form of government. As Hutton writes, 'Despite the lobbying of sectaries and Quakers, it was no more a group of reformers than the preceding executives'.[6] Fox retired to Reading, and Burrough fulminated.

So, what did the Quakers in 1659 think they were doing? Hill has no doubt — they thought they were fighting for 'the good old cause', a term frequently in Quaker mouths in 1659 as they stared defeat in the face. As Howgill said, 'Many precious men ventured their lives and lost their blood and consumed their estates to win liberty as men and as Christians',[7] and he added that it was the Quakers that stood by Parliament in its time of greatest danger in 1659. Religious freedom and a wider representative parliamentary democracy is the 'good old cause'. George Bishop said this cause was 'the highest on which men were ever engaged in the field'. Hubberthorne thought the war had been 'for our rights and liberties', and Anthony Pearson said 'tithes should have been cut off with the King's head'.[8]

The expulsion of the Rump Parliament split the army. General Lambert supported the expulsion, and his army was the most cohesive in Britain, apart from that in Scotland. There General George Monck, the military commander and a former Royalist, promoted by Oliver Cromwell for his military skill, not his politics, declared for the expelled members of Parliament. His motives are uncertain. It is possible that he believed the Quakers were attempting to take over the government. In 1657 Fox had preached in Scotland, and the number of Quakers there had grown and by 1659 'aboundit and drew themselssis in companyis throw the cuntrie without contolment', as one contemporary Scottish diarist put it.[9] Monck's wife was a Presbyterian, and later he described his actions as intended to save the country from fanatics (Quakers). It is clear Monk was in favour of a conservative religious settlement. It was also clear that if army rule continued, it would mean (as it had in the past) a more radical religious regime. Monck told a correspondent he had risked everything to save the country from the 'fanatical party who blasphemed against Christ'.[10]

Lambert moved slowly north to counter this threat, enlisting new men, including Quakers, as he went; Monck purged his army of Quakers and waited. Meanwhile, in other parts of the country the army was falling apart. In London and elsewhere, without the leadership of Lambert, calls for the return of the Rump Parliament increased, and it was reinstated on 24 December. Lambert's army, now at Newcastle, disintegrated, and Monck began his advance into England on 2 January 1660, the Rump rewarding him with lands worth £1000 a year. On 2 February, Monck's army marched into Whitehall in front of silent crowds, found a group of Quakers worshipping in Palace Yard, and promptly beat them up, saying they had come to rid England of sectaries.[11] Hutton argues that the Commonwealth 'did not die naturally, but was murdered with great skill and force'.[12] The death of 'the good old cause' still resonates in British politics today.

It is worth emphasising how quickly this happened. In December 1659, some Quakers were still expecting, or hoping, that Lambert could secure the republic. Fox produced in December a pamphlet with fifty-nine propositions for a better government which he hoped the Rump would enact. Five months later, a Royalist 'convention Parliament' restored the monarchy and Charles II been welcomed into London in scenes described as 'fantastical' by Quaker William Caton in a letter to Fox. Quakers were a group 'entirely set apart from a populace absolutely ecstatic with joy and celebration'. As Burrough said, 'The days are evil and the times are perilous'.[13]

It is not known whether Nayler was in London to see this transformation for himself. On his release from prison, he had been given a home by Rebecca and William Travers. He seemed in reasonable health. Francis Howgill arranged a public reconciliation between Fox and Nayler. Although neither seemed particularly keen, Nayler did as requested and knelt at Fox's feet. Nayler wrote two political tracts during this period of confusion. One was titled a *Warning to the Rulers, in the Year 1659, Wherein a Just Liberty of Conscience is Pleaded*. When Whitehead included this in his 1716 edition of Nayler's pamphlets, he said it was 'never before printed'. The title sums up the contents. A letter Nayler wrote to Charles II on 3 June 1660 was published that same year. In it, Nayler explains that God had gathered to himself in England a people 'known to himself better than to men' who do not receive their laws from men and who have suffered grievous persecution. But, he writes,

> though we cannot swear and unswear, covenant and uncovenant with every change that comes, as men do that know the everlasting covenant and decree of God, yet this hath God sealed in our hearts, to seek the good of all men, plot against none, but study to live quietly and exercise our conscience faithfully towards whatever government our God shall set up. . . .
>
> Wherefore O King . . . do justice and judgment in this thy day, relieve the helpless oppressed and break the yoke of bondage that lies upon the poor, and bring judgment into the gates, and let not justice be sold, lest the meek of the earth cry to God against thee.[14]

Initially, some Commonwealth men were included in the ministry appointed by Charles II, and a few managed to survive with their lands intact. However, the change was dramatic: most of the lands sequestrated during the wars were restored to the original owners, the original vicars were given back their livings, all the laws passed during the 'interregnum' were repealed, and Charles II's reign was backdated to his father's death in 1649. It was as if the days of the Lord (the commonwealth) had never been. Reviewing these events 140 years later, a radical Whig condemned Monck:

> It is impossible in reviewing the whole of this transaction, not to remark that a general [Monck] who had gained his rank, reputation, and station in the service of a republic, and of what he, as well as others, called, however falsely, the cause of liberty, made no scruple to lay the nation prostrate at the feet of a monarch, without a single provision in favour of that cause; and if the promise of indemnity may seem to argue that there was some attention, at least, paid to the safety of his associates in arms, his subsequent conduct gives reason to suppose, that even this provision was owing to any other cause, rather than any generous feeling of his breast.[15]

Defeat was complete. The Quaker history of the next decade is one of the deaths of leaders (Burrough, Hubberthorne, Audland, Camm, Howgill, Farnsworth, and Nayler), imprisonment, and heavy financial penalties. By the end of 1660, despite Charles II's own willingness to offer some toleration, Quakers were being put into prison faster than he could free them.[16] At the same time, over the subsequent decade Fox was able to consolidate and remodel the Religious Society of Friends, giving it an organisational framework that remained broadly the same until the turn of the twenty-first century.

In October 1660, while Charles II and his advisers continued arranging the settlement of the country, Nayler was asked by Fox, or decided himself, to travel north towards home and possibly on to Durham, where he might have been safer from arrest. He had not gone far when he was set upon by thieves and was beaten and robbed. He died at the house of Thomas Parnell, a Quaker physician in Kings Ripon near Huntingdon. He was buried on 21 October 1660 in an unmarked grave that now lies under fruit trees in a private garden.

Fox did not remark on Nayler's death. Nayler's biographers do not mention public mourning or reports of his death. Nayler had been the best-known Quaker in England; foreign ambassadors commented on his trial; his picture was sold abroad; and John Deacon wrote his biography (unauthorised and hostile) in 1656. But, after 1660 he disappeared from public knowledge and from the thoughts of Quakers. A history of the early Quakers published in 1712 (William Crouch's *Posthuma Christiana*) makes no mention of Nayler.[17] In 1716, George Whitehead published a collection of his pamphlets, a faithful reprint of most of them. This must have been approved by a committee, and they must have thought the 'second generation' of Quakers would find his writings useful. It might also have been an act of piety; Whitehead had grown up in Sunbiggin, a tiny hamlet just a few miles from Orton, where Nayler was first arrested in 1652, where Whitehead may well have seen him. This was the last published edition of Nayler's writings for nearly three hundred years. He disappeared from view.

In the early twentieth century, there was renewed interest in James Nayler. Mabel Richmond Brailsford wrote a biography in 1927, followed by Emilia Fogelklou in 1931. However, Christopher Hill's 1972 history of civil war radicals, *The World Turned Upside Down*, provided the first modern academic account of Nayler and placed him in context. Hill saw Nayler through the twin lenses of 1930s Marxism and the 1960s counterculture. His account of Nayler as a political radical is very attractive but does not convince me. There were others more radical and more willing to act as Quaker politicians (George Bishop, Edward Burrough, George Fox himself). There are today more biographies of Nayler than of other early Quakers. He has been glamourized, psychoanalysed, reinterpreted, and portrayed as a theologian or a revolutionary, and writers have continued to debate what he meant by his sign in Bristol on the afternoon of 24 October 1656.

Charisma is a fascinating attribute. Why do some people have it and some do not? Why are some who have it willing to use it, whereas others are awkward and avoid publicity? Nayler certainly had charisma. He might not have always had it, but certainly as a minister, preacher, and leader he did. This brought him fame and notoriety. Nayler, when in 'the world', received respect from his social superiors — Margaret's husband Judge Fell, Anthony Pearson, one of the magistrates at Appleby who converted to Quakerism, and General Lambert. But this respect seems to have meant little to him, and from his writings and actions it is clear he did not enjoy its possession.

Being respected ran counter to the spiritual abnegation of the self and submission to the inner Christ Nayler sought. He convicted himself of spiritual pride and worried that he often felt 'exalted above' and 'pretending a greater thing to come another way', a possible allusion to his power of leadership and ability to move humanity in political ways.[18] But, without the emotional certainty of Christ's guidance, he was at a loss: uncertain whether to leave home in 1652; uncertain about Simmonds's ministry; uncertain about 'the sign'. After his trial, he seems to have found a greater certainty that what he knew in his spiritual heart was the Truth. He writes in *To the Life of God in All* (1659):

> It is in my heart to praise thee O my God, let me never forget thee, what thou hast been to me in the night, by thy presence in the day of trial, when I was beset in darkness, when I was cast out as a wandering bird, when I was assaulted by strong temptations, then thy presence in secret did preserve me, and in a low estate I felt thee near me.[19]

Nayler was a prophet whose life and soul had been turned inside out by God's revelation. He hoped his own words and actions would challenge others to change. He asked them constantly to examine and then discard the realities of their material lives and seek instead the inner life they were given by God. At Bristol he asked, through a damp and small procession: 'If Christ were living today how would you — landlords, merchants, priests deceiving the people, and magistrates oppressing the poor — account for your actions?' Hannah Stranger wrote later that Christ had appeared (in Bristol) and that the people were found to be 'the blindest of all sorts'.[20] For future generations, this procession of James Nayler into Bristol proved to be fatal for his message and ministry.

Appendix A: The British Wars 1637 to 1653

Charles I ruled three kingdoms: England and Wales, Scotland, and Ireland. Each had a different political and economic system and a different religious settlement. There were tariffs between them, and the colonisation of Catholic Ireland from Calvinist Scotland was encouraged. England was dominant in every way, and the others undoubtedly resented this. However, England was not a settled country. There were tensions between local power elites and the central government, as well as religious conflict between Puritans and Anglicans. The transfer of property and prestige in previous generations had led to stronger local elites and a richer, more confident merchant class that challenged old monopolies and absolute rule.

Charles believed — and this is fundamental to understanding his choices — in the divine right of kings. He had been given his role(s) by God, and he answered to no one but God. This included parliaments, for although two of the kingdoms had a form of representative democracy, he preferred to rule without consulting them. The disadvantage of this, particularly in England, was that he never had enough money (only Parliament could grant permission for new taxes), so he resorted to 'illegal' (as claimed by his opponents) taxes and forced loans on city merchants. But this did not mean his government was inadequate or unable to run the country in peacetime. He was insistent that his divine role meant that all his people should worship in the manner most acceptable to God. For Charles, this was a reformed Anglicanism, closer to Catholicism in its rituals than the Elizabethan settlement. This reformed Anglicanism was championed by Archbishop William Laud.

The immediate cause of the wars was Charles's decision to impose on the more Calvinistic and Presbyterian Scottish church the Laudian prayer book. This prayer book was first used on 23 July 1637 in Edinburgh, and a riot ensued after a parishioner threw her stool at the unfortunate priest. [1] Reconciliation between Charles and his Scottish subjects failed. The Scots organised a National Covenant in which they pledged to uphold their own religious settlement, and on 15 February 1638 they invaded England. Charles had no army (because of the lack of funds) and quickly agreed to a truce. He was then obliged to call a meeting of Parliament in England to raise money to pay off the Scots — he was going to tax one of his kingdoms so that he could pay another for invading the first. The first 'short' Parliament lasted one month — April to May 1640. The Scots re-invaded, and Charles was forced into another treaty with one of his kingdoms, in which he agreed to pay the Scots £860 a day for every day they were in England. He called another English Parliament, the 'Long Parliament', to raise the money and made political sacrifices (Laud was imprisoned), but reconciliation with England became increasingly difficult.

In October 1641, the Catholic majority in his third kingdom, Ireland, rebelled and massacred Protestant settlers in the north. In a final attempt to control England, Charles attempted to arrest five of his most determined Parliamentary opponents (4 January 1642). They escaped, London burst into violence, and the king left his capital. On 23 February, his queen, Henrietta, left for Holland to pawn the crown jewels to raise money for an army. Charles moved north, attempted and failed to seize the City of Hull which had armaments stored there, failed to persuade the landowners of Yorkshire of his case (Nayler may have been present), and finally raised the Royal Standard at Nottingham on 22 August 1642. Charles was now fighting a civil war in one country while repelling an invasion from the second and putting down a rebellion in the third.

The first civil war battle was Edgehill (23 October 1642), at which Prince Rupert and his cavalry smashed one wing of the parliamentary army and rode on to pillage their baggage train. When they returned, they found their opponents, led by the Earl of Essex, in possession of the battlefield. Both sides still sought a political settlement in England and Scotland, though neither would accept a settlement in Ireland, where matters went badly for the Catholics. Nayler, under the command of Fairfax in Yorkshire, helped clear the West Riding of Royalists. In England and Scotland, strategically inconclusive battles and indeterminate negotiations characterised the coming years. The English Parliament and the Scottish Presbyterians agreed to a Solemn League and Covenant (25 September 1643) whereby the religion in both kingdoms would be Presbyterian. The Irish agreed to a truce (15 September 1643), which allowed Charles to reinforce his army with Royalist Catholics from Ireland. However, a Parliamentary army under Fairfax defeated Charles's Irish reinforcements in England at Nantwich, Cheshire (24 January 1644; Nayler was present). The Presbyterian Scots invaded England on the same day. At their back, Montrose landed in Scotland, rallied the Royalists there, and defeated a Scottish Presbyterian army.

Parliament was beginning to get the upper hand in England. The Battle of Marston Moor (just outside York) was won by Cromwell (2 July 1644; Nayler was present). The Queen left for France on 15 July to find European support for her husband, and York surrendered to Parliament (16 July). But the Royalists took the southwest of England from Essex, who surrendered at Fowey in September 1644. In early 1645, Parliament finally achieved its aim of unifying most of its army; the New Model Army cost £6000 a month and was paid for by taxes from areas controlled by Parliament. Nayler remained part of the Northern Army under General Lambert. On 14 June, the New Model Army under the command of Cromwell defeated the Royalists at the Battle of Naseby, then took Langport, Somerset, on 10 July, Prince Rupert surrendered at Bristol on 10 September, and on the 15th Montrose was defeated in Scotland and fled to the Continent.

Charles I by now had few options, and he surrendered to the Scots on 5 May 1646. He hoped for better terms from them than from Parliament. However, he failed to reach an agreement with the Scots, and they, having no further use for Charles at that time, 'sold' him to Parliament for £400,000. They had found someone to pay for their army. But although the New Model Army and Parliament were in control on the field, the king was still the king, and the victors began to quarrel. In May 1647, Parliament voted to disband the army without acceding to their demands regarding back pay. Crucially, Cromwell sided with the army when on 4 June 1647 Cornet Joyce seized Charles from Parliamentary control. Charles, while imprisoned, began a double set of negotiations — openly with Parliament and its allies the Scottish Presbyterians and secretly with the Scottish Royalists. Parliament rejected his proposals on 24 December 1647. Charles reached a secret agreement with the Scottish Royalists.

In 1648, attitudes hardened as Parliament set out Charles's 'misdeeds' (11 February 1648) and Cromwell called for 'no allegiance' to the king. On 1 May, the Scots invaded England yet again, starting the 'second civil war'. However, Cromwell and the New Model Army defeated them at Preston, Lancashire (17–20 August). Nayler may have been there as a member of Lambert's Northern Army. Parliamentary negotiations with Charles continued. Meanwhile, the army had become increasingly radicalised, and the obstinacy of Charles towards Parliament was replicated by the obstinacy of Parliament towards the army, part of which was now camped in Hyde Park, London. Finally, on 6 December, Colonel Pride stood at the door of the House of Commons with a list in his hand and turned away those on it. Roughly eighty members were allowed in. Parliament had lost to the army. When informed of 'Pride's Purge', Cromwell (who was a member of Parliament throughout the civil wars) remarked that he was glad of it and would endeavour to maintain it. On 23 December, Parliament voted to bring Charles to trial. On 30 January 1649, he was executed.

The Scottish Parliament (5 February 1649) declared Charles's son king as Charles II. The Irish rebelled again under Ormond in support of Charles II. The remains of the Long Parliament (known as the 'Rump') abolished the House of Lords (17 March) and the monarchy (19 March) and declared England a Commonwealth on 19 May. Cromwell was ordered to crush the Irish, which he did in a bitter war called by some a genocide, the memory of which continues to harm relations between Ireland and England. Montrose, the Scottish Royalist, was defeated at Carbisdale (27 April), captured, and executed. Cromwell found it necessary to go to Scotland to continue the war with the Scots. At the battle of Dunbar on 3 September, Cromwell fell upon the unsuspecting Scots, who lost three thousand dead and ten thousand taken prisoner. Lambert was there, as was Nayler. This was probably Nayler's last military engagement.

Dunbar was not the end of Royalist resistance. Cromwell captured Perth on 2 August and pursued Charles II down the country towards Worcester. Some of the troops paused on the way at Derby to try to persuade Fox (imprisoned there) to become an officer. He refused. Without Fox, on 3 September 1651, Cromwell defeated Charles II at Worcester. On 27 October 1651, his son-in-law Henry Ireton defeated the Royalist Catholic Irish at Limerick. The 'Long Parliament' was finally expelled by Cromwell on 20 April 1653 because it was seeking to perpetuate itself indefinitely. Oliver Cromwell, a man unknown in 1642, had become the absolute ruler of the three kingdoms. But, in the process, huge constitutional questions about relations between the kingdoms, the role of Parliament, who could vote, and accessibility to the law and the land were opened up. This subversive underground stream fed British political discourse for the next three hundred years.

Appendix B: James Nayler Chronology

Adapted from David Neelon's *James Nayler: Revolutionary to Prophet.* Neelon's timeline is a product of collaboration between Neelon and Jane Orion Smith, now of Canadian Yearly Meeting.

1616–1618: Birth of Nayler in Woodkirk Parish, West Ardsley, Yorkshire.

1623, 10 January: Martha Simmonds born at Meare, Somerset.

1624: George Fox born at Drayton-in-the-Clay, Leicestershire.

1634: First mention of a separated church at Woodkirk.

1637: First invasion of England by Scotland.

1639: Nayler marries Ann(e) and moves to Wakefield.

1639: Martha Simmonds and her mother Ann move to London, where her brother Giles is a bookseller at Black-Spread Eagle, St Paul's churchyard.

1639: Second invasion of England by Scotland. The north of England is occupied by Scots waiting for reparations.

1640–1643: Three daughters, Mary, Jane, and Sarah, are born to Nayler and Ann(e) in Wakefield.

1640–1642: Political conflict between the English Parliament and Charles I.

1640, 3 November: The 'Long Parliament' opens. Scots are allied with the Presbyterian party in the English Parliament.

1642: King Charles I attempts the arrest of parliamentary leaders and fails. Leaves London. Royalist blockade of towns near West Ardsley.

1642, 23 October: Battle of Edgehill.

1643 January: Nayler leads a brave charge to relieve the siege of Leeds by Royalist troops.

May 20: Nayler joins Copley's cavalry as a corporal. Records of him being paid at Barnsley and Gainsborough.

1644, May 27: Nayler promoted to quartermaster of Copley's cavalry.

1644, July 2: Nayler present at Marston Moor.

1645: Pontefract captured by Parliament, lost to the Royalists, and then recaptured by General Lambert on 9 July. Nayler present at all these engagements.

1645, April: New Model Army formed.

1645, 14 June: Battle of Naseby, won by Cromwell.

1646: The Northern Army is consolidated under Lambert's command, and Nayler becomes Lambert's quartermaster.

1646: 5 May: Charles I surrenders to the Scots.

1647: Nayler probably still in York and Pontefract.

1647 January: Charles I handed over by the Scots to the English in return for £400,000.

1648 May: Scots invade England in support of Charles I. Start of the second civil war.

1648, 17–19 August: Battle of Preston between Scots Royalists, the New Model Army, and some of the Northern Army results in a decisive defeat for the Scots and the end of the second civil war.

1648, 6 December: The 'Long Parliament', which had sat continuously since 1640, is 'purged' of supporters of a settlement with Charles I. The remnant was known as the 'Rump'.

1648, 12 December: Nayler present at Lambert's Army Council in Pontefract, which votes for the trial of Charles I as a criminal.

1649, 20–26 January: Trial of Charles I on charges of 'high treason' and other 'high crimes'.

1649, 31 January: Charles I executed for treason.

1649–1652: Continued fighting to suppress revolts in Ireland and Scotland.

1650: First Blasphemy Act passed against Ranters and Quakers and other troublesome sects. George Fox imprisoned in Derby.

1650, 3 September: Nayler in Cromwell's Army at the Battle of Dunbar, a defeat for the Scottish Royalists. Nayler leaves the army soon afterwards because of ill health.

1651, 3 September: Battle of Worcester. The end of the Royalists in England. The young Charles II flees for France.

1651 October: George Fox is released from prison in Derby. Fox probably meets Nayler and William and Mary Dewsbury at Stanley near Wakefield. Nayler hears the call to leave his father's house but delays; the precise date of his departure is not known.

1652: Joins Farnsworth in Westmoreland and is present at Swarthmore Hall when George Fox first visits. According to Margaret Fell, Nayler persuades her husband, Judge Fell, to speak to Fox and allow him to stay. Nayler is arrested for vagrancy (date uncertain) and imprisoned at Appleby with Francis Howgill. Nayler writes his first pamphlet.

1653 January: Trial of Howgill and Nayler at Appleby. They are sentenced to indefinite imprisonment. Nayler visited by his wife.

1653 April: Howgill and Nayler released from jail.

1653–1656: The period of Nayler's traveling and preaching. In these years, he wrote some fifty pamphlets.

1653 July: Nayler in Westmoreland.

1653 August: Nayler at Rampshaw Hall, West Auckland, Durham, the home of Justice Anthony Pearson.

1653 September: Nayler at Newby, southwest of Penrith.

1654 March–April: Nayler at Rampshaw Hall again and the Durham and Yorkshire coast.

1654 July: Burrough and Howgill commence London mission. Martha Simmonds convinced.

1654 July–August: Nayler in Yorkshire near Bradford.

1654 November: Nayler in Nottingham.

1654 December: Nayler in Chesterfield.

1655 June: Nayler arrives in London and is known as the 'head Quaker' by some of the public.

1655 July: Howgill and Burrough go to Ireland. George Fox and Alexander Parker are in London with Nayler.

1655 September: Audland and Camm begin a highly successful ministry in Bristol amongst Seekers, Baptists, and Independents. Meetings of up to three thousand people.

1655 December: Martha Simmonds mentioned in a letter from James Parnell in Colchester as going naked as a sign and being imprisoned.

1656 January: George Fox imprisoned at Launceston, Cornwall.

1656, 6 February: Nayler's pamphlet *Love to the Lost* is published.

1656 April: Nayler asks Howgill and Burrough to return to London. Burrough comes that month.

1656 April–July: A split develops between Nayler and the London leadership of the Religious Society of Friends. Simmonds and Nayler meet once or twice during the first two weeks of July. Nayler has a physical and mental collapse. Nayler is taken to Bristol.

1656 August: Nayler and others are arrested at Oakhampton on their way to see Fox and are jailed in Exeter.

1656, 12 September: Fox released from Launceston prison.

1656, 20 September: Fox and Hubberthorne arrive at Exeter to visit Nayler. Decisive split between Fox and Nayler.

1656 October: Nayler released from jail.

1656, 24 October: Nayler and others enter Bristol, re-enacting Christ's entry into Jerusalem. Arrested and taken to London.

1656, 15 November: Examination by Parliament begins.

1656 December: James Nayler, Martha Simmonds, and Hannah Stranger publish *O England thy time has come*.

1656, 6–17 December: Nayler tried by Parliament for 'horrid blasphemy'. Found guilty.

1656 18 December: Nayler stands in the Westminster pillory for two hours. Then taken through London tied to the back of a cart and whipped at every cross street — 310 lashes in total. Confined in Newgate prison.

1656, 27 December Nayler stands in the City pillory for two hours, during which Martha Simmonds, Hannah Stranger and Dorcas Ebury arrange themselves as the three Marys around him. Richard Rich sits at his feet. Nayler's tongue is bored through with a hot rod and the letter 'B' for blasphemy is branded on his forehead. Confined in Newgate prison.

1657, 17 January: Nayler is taken to Bristol, where he enters the town mounted backwards on a horse and is whipped and pilloried again. A Quaker coppersmith checks the beadle's arm at each lash, and the damage to his back is less than in London. Nayler is returned to solitary confinement in Bridewell prison, London. Visited by his wife, who petitions Parliament, and his prison conditions improve.

1657 summer: Nayler can receive visitors and has pen, ink, and paper. Starts to write again.

1658: Nayler in prison, writing.

1658, 3 September: Oliver Cromwell dies. Richard Cromwell succeeds him as lord protector.

1659, 6 May: Army removes Richard Cromwell and reinstates the 'Rump' Parliament. A series of Royalist uprisings is suppressed by the parliamentary army under Lambert.

1659, early September: Rump Parliament releases Nayler and other Quakers. Nayler lives with William and Rebecca Travers and resumes ministry in London.

1659, 13 October: Rump Parliament expelled again by junior officers because of its rejection of more radical policies. General Monck in Edinburgh moves towards the English border.

1659 November: Lambert leaves London with an army to counter General Monck's threat and recruits new men, including Quakers, on the way.

1659, 24 December: Rump Parliament reinstated. Lambert halts in York, and his army starts to disintegrate.

1660, 2 January: General Monck invades England from Scotland in support of Charles II. Collapse of the parliamentary army.

1660, 2 February: General Monck enters London.

1660, 21 February: The members purged in 1648 return to Parliament. The reinstated 'Long Parliament' agrees to elections to a 'Convention' Parliament to settle the government of the country and dissolves itself on 13 March.

1660, 4 April: Charles II issues the Declaration of Breda promising a general pardon for crimes committed during the civil wars.

1660, 25 April: Convention Parliament opens with a Royalist majority. Parliament debates Charles II's Declaration of Breda.

1660, 8 May: Convention Parliament declares that Charles II has been king since his father died.

1660, 29 May: Charles II enters London to great rejoicing.

1660 October: Nayler leaves London for West Ardsley and is attacked on the road near Huntingdon. Taken to a Quaker's house, he dies and is buried in an unmarked grave on 21 October.

Acknowledgements

My debt to past and present Quaker historians will be immediately obvious; without their research, this book would have been impossible to write. I owe a special debt to Licia Kuenning of the Quaker Heritage Press, who edited the four volumes of Nayler's works. Charles Martin of Inner Light Books and Kathy McKay, the copy editor, gave invaluable suggestions and made many corrections to the manuscript. It is a better book for their attention. I would like to thank Penelope Cummings and Lizz Roe for encouraging me to continue with this project. My wife, Jane Lewis, all too often found me with my mind not in the present, and I thank her for her patience and understanding, which helped immensely during difficult times. Any mistakes and errors that remain are my own.

Notes

Introduction to James Nayler (pp. 1–18)

[1] Hill, *World Turned Upside Down*, 231.

[2] Hill, *World Turned Upside Down*, 250.

[3] This account comes from two contemporary sources, a letter from George Bishop to Margaret Fell dated 27 October 1656 and a hostile pamphlet by Ralph Farmer, *Satan Enthroned in his Chair of Pestilence* published in early 1657. Farmer has Welbeck leading the horse bareheaded. I prefer Bishop's account as he knew those involved. It is not clear whether another man from Ely, Simon Carter, was also there.

[4] Farmer, *Satan Enthroned*, in Nayler, *Works*, 3:558.

[5] Bishop to Margaret Fell, 27 October 1656, Nayler, *Works*, 3:551.

[6] Neelon, *James Nayler*, 178.

[7] Moore, *Light in Their Consciences*, 34.

[8] The analysis that follows comes from Stone, *Causes of the English Revolution*, 67–76.

[9] The Diggers, also known as True Levellers, were an uncoordinated movement of the landless and the poor living mostly in southern and middle England. They believed in abolishing land ownership; they pulled down enclosures and dug up common land, hence the term 'diggers'. On 1 April 1649 they took over the common land on St George's Hill, Kingston, Surrey, and it was a year before the army turned them off. Other encampments were set up in Kent, Buckinghamshire, Northamptonshire, Bedfordshire, and Leicestershire. They survived for only a few months. Their best-known intellectual leader was George Winstanley (1609–1676), whose pamphlet *More Light Shining in Buckinghamshire* was published just before the St George's Hill camp began. It is thought that Winstanley later became a Quaker. The Diggers should not be confused with the Levellers, a primarily army organisation

concerned with extending the franchise to tenants and freeholders of small farms.

10 Hill, *English Revolution* 28.

11 Stone, *Causes of the English Revolution*, 72. 'Gentry' and 'gentleman' in the 1600s were inexact terms used to indicate someone with land who had the capacity to govern locally and was deserving of respect.

12 Hoskins, *Making of the English Landscape*, 163.

13 Stone, *Causes of the English Revolution*, 74.

14 Andrew Nutter was an old man by the time James Nayler met him. His first parish appointment was Drayton-in-the-Clay (George Fox's birthplace) in the 1580s. He would have known Christopher Fox, George's father. His appointment there was also due to a local Presbyterian family buying the right to nominate the vicar.

15 Stone, *Causes of the English Revolution*, 93.

16 Stone, *Causes of the English Revolution*, 78.

17 Parker, *Global Crisis*, xv.

18 Parker, *Global Crisis*, 327–33.

19 Parker, *Global Crisis*, 374.

20 As quoted in Parker, *Global Crisis*, 385.

21 Parker, *Global Crisis*, 385.

22 Martyn Bennett, *The Civil Wars Experienced: Britain and Ireland 1638–1661*. London: Routledge, 2000), as quoted in Parker, *Global Crisis,* 359.

23 Parker, *Global Crisis*, 359–60.

24 See the chronology in Neelon, *James Nayler*, xxiv–xxviii.

25 Neelon, *James Nayler*, 62.

26 Moore, *The Light in Their Consciences*, 172.

27 Neelon, *James Nayler*, 45.

28 Neelon, *James Nayler*, 4.

29 Hill, *English Revolution 1640*, 30.

30 Morrill, *Nature of the English Revolution*, 15.

31 Morrill, *Nature of the English Revolution*, 388.

[32] Morrill, *Nature of the English Revolution*, 388.

[33] Morrill, *Nature of the English Revolution*, 389. Morrill's argument is that the 'revolution' was really a search for a government that could ensure order.

[34] Hill, *Experience of Defeat*, 131.

[35] Spufford, *Contrasting Communities*, 283.

[36] Spufford, *Contrasting Communities*, 283.

[37] Nayler, *Lamb's War*, in Nayler, *Works*, 4:3.

[38] Gwyn, 'Seventeenth-Century Context', 19.

[39] Neelon, *James Nayler*, 71.

[40] 'An account of early travels', in Nayler, *Works*, 3:761–62. This is an unpublished manuscript with a title given by the editor.

[41] Neelon, *James Nayler*, 118.

Introduction to *Love to the Lost* (pp. 19–25)

[1] James Nayler to George Fox, April or May 1656, in Nayler, *Works*, 3:757–58.

[2] Nayler to Margaret Fell, 1 June 1656, in Nayler, *Works*, 3:759.

[3] Nayler, *To the Life of God in All*, in Nayler, *Works*, 4:261.

[4] John Deacon *An exact history of the life of James Nayler* (1657), as quoted in Damrosch, *Sorrows of the Quaker Jesus*, 82.

[5] Damrosch, *Sorrows of the Quaker Jesus*, 84.

[6] Spencer, 'James Nayler', 72–73.

[7] Spencer, 'James Nayler', 75–76.

[8] Peters, *Print Culture*, 22.

[9] Edward Burrough, *A warning from the Lord to the inhabitants of Underbarrow, and so to all the inhabitants in England*, as quoted in Peters, *Print Culture*, 23.

[10] Damrosch, *Sorrows of the Quaker Jesus*, 80–81. The quote at the end of the paragraph comes from Richard Bauman, *Let Your Words Be Few*.

1. 'Concerning the Fall of Man' (pp. 26–36)

[1] Thomas, *Only Fellow-Voyagers*, 64–65.

[2] Fox, *The Power of the Lord* 435.

Notes

3 Fox, *Journal*, 27.

4 Ambler, *The Quaker Way*, 26.

5 Fox, *The Power of the Lord*, 357.

6 Thomas, *Only Fellow-Voyagers*, 75.

2. 'Concerning Light and Life' (pp. 37–48)

1 Neelon, *James Nayler*, 13.

2 James Nayler, *Letter to them of the independent society* (1654), in Nayler, *Works*, 1:319–22.

3 Nayler, *Letter to them of the independent society* (1654), in *Works*, 1:321.

4 Nayler, *Saul's Errand to Damascus*, in Nayler, *Works*, 1:33–34.

5 Simmonds, *Lamentation For The Lost Sheep*, 55–56 The quote is the last sentence of the six-page pamphlet.

6 Rowntree, 'Faith and Life,' 403.

3. 'Concerning the Word (pp. 49–57)

1 I use the King James Version of the Bible as that may be the closest to the words Nayler read.

2 James Nayler to George Fox, April or May 1656, in Nayler, *Works*, 3:757.

3 A note to 2013 *Quaker faith and practice* (2013), 19.24, explains that George Fox, 'after justifying women's meetings by abundant quotation from scripture, concluded with the words: "If there was no scripture . . . Christ is sufficient"'.

4 Ashworth, *Paul's Necessary Sin*, 139–44. Ashworth has a fascinating discussion of the use by Paul of the Greek equivalent of 'earnest' and how it has been translated and described by later theologians. I think Nayler's and other Quaker writers' use of the word 'measure' is similar to Paul's use of 'earnest'.

4. 'Concerning Worship' (pp. 58–68)

1 Northwest Yearly Meeting, *Faith and Practice*, 11.

2 North Carolina Yearly Meeting (Conservative), *Faith and Practice*, 'Worship and the Spiritual Life,' section iii.

3 Punshon *Reasons for Hope*, 208–9.

4 Punshon *Reasons for Hope*, 209.

[5] James Nayler, 'A General Epistle to all Friends', 1 April 1656, in Nayler, *Works*, 3:756.

[6] Dandelion, *Open for Transformation*, 88.

5. On Women (pp. 69–78)

[1] See chapter 5, 'Women's Speaking Justified', in Peters, *Print Culture and the Early Quakers*

[2] Peters, *Print Culture and the Early Quakers*, 143.

[3] Peters, *Print Culture and the Early Quakers*, 131–34. The second paragraph is a quotation from Farnsworth. There is a short discussion of his pamphlet in Birkel and Angell, 'The Witness of Richard Farnworth', 87.

[4] Peters, *Print Culture and the Early Quakers*, 140.

[5] Peters, *Print Culture and the Early Quakers*, 124.

[6] Peters, *Print Culture and the Early Quakers*, 137–41.

[7] Mack, *Visionary Women*, 168.

[8] Mack, *Visionary Women*, 167.

[9] Trevett, *Women and Quakerism*, 73.

[10] Mack, *Visionary Women*, 212.

[11] Moore, *Light in Their Consciences*, 137

[12] Mack, *Visionary Women*, 204.

[13] As quoted in Mack, *Visionary Women*, 177.

[14] Peters, *Print Culture and the Early Quakers*, 145.

[15] Peters, *Print Culture and the Early Quakers*, 149.

[16] Peters, *Print Culture and the Early Quakers*, 135.

[17] Mack, *Visionary Women*, 275–76.

[18] White, *Six Weeks Meeting*, 5, 7.

[19] Quaker Women's Group, *Bringing the Invisible*, 16.

[20] Quaker Women's Group, *Bringing the Invisible*, 17–18.

[21] Quaker Women's Group, *Bringing the Invisible*, 18.

[22] Garman, *Quaker Women's Lives*, 238.

7. On Ann Nayler (pp. 84–88)

Notes

[1] Neelon, *James Nayler*, 4.

[2] Neelon, *James Nayler*, 2–3.

[3] Hill, *Defeat*, 138.

[4] Neelon, *James Nayler*, 75.

[5] James Nayler to George Fox, February 1653, in Nayler, *Works*, 2:572.

[6] Weld, *The Perfect Pharisee*, in Nayler, *Works*, 1:364.

[7] Peters, *Print Culture and the Early Quakers*, 146.

[8] Farmer, *Satan Enthroned*, in Nayler, *Works*, 3:568.

[9] Nimmo, *Testimony to the Grace of God*. The extracts are from pages 8 (two extracts), 13, 41, and 48, respectively.

8. 'Concerning Hope' (pp. 89–94)

[1] Scott, *What Canst Thou Say?*, 27–35.

[2] Scott, *What Canst Thou Say?*, 31.

[3] Moore, *The Light in their Consciences*, 63.

[4] Moore, *The Light in their Consciences*, 68.

[5] Scott, *What Canst Thou Say?* 35.

9. 'Concerning Love' (pp. 95–104)

[1] Weld, *The Perfect Pharisee* 1:359.

[2] Nayler, *Answer to 'The Perfect Pharisee'*, in Nayler, *Works*, 1:389.

[3] Nuttall, *James Nayler*, 18.

[4] Nayler, *A Message from the Spirit of Truth*, 4:55.

[5] Nayler, *A Message from the Spirit of Truth*, 4:55.

[6] Ashworth, *Paul's Necessary Sin*, 128–29.

[7] Law, *Selected Mystical Writings of William Law*, 139–40.

10. 'Concerning Perfection' (pp. 105–13)

[1] Fox, *Journal*, 27.

[2] Tousley, 'Sin, Convincement, Purity, and Perfection', 173.

[3] Tousley, 'Sin, Convincement, Purity, and Perfection', 173.

[4] Fox, *Journal*, 18.

[5] Tousley, 'Sin, Convincement, Purity, and Perfection', 177.

[6] Tousley, 'Sin, Convincement, Purity, and Perfection', 178.

[7] Tousley, 'Sin, Convincement, Purity, and Perfection', 177.

[8] Paul Buckley, introduction to Hicks, *The Journal*, xix.

[9] Hicks, *The Journal*, 129.

[10] The citation in *Quaker faith and practice* indicates that this comes from Joshua Rowntree's *Social Service: Its Place in the Society of Friends* (Swarthmore Lecture of 1913). An eirenicon is a proposition that harmonises conflicting viewpoints.

11. 'Concerning Government or Magistracy' (pp. 114–25)

[1] James II, deposed by the Revolution of 1688, was a friend of William Penn and had appointed dissenters, including Quakers, to positions of civil authority within their communities. The local landowners objected, and this practice was reversed once they had control. The episode left Quakers with mixed loyalties towards the new monarchs William and Mary.

[2] T. J. Nossiter, *Influence, Opinion and Political Idioms in Reformed England: Case Studies from the North East 1832–74* (1975), as quoted in Kirby, *Men of Business*, 57.

[3] In 1832, these Quakers were still Whigs, the party that had driven out James II in 1688 and had prospered during the eighteenth century. As the nineteenth century progressed and more of the population were able to vote, Whigs turned into Liberals who espoused free trade and religious freedom and supported manufacturers rather than landed aristocracy. They drew their support from urban dissenters led by old Whig aristocratic families, such as the Russells, the Greys, and the Grenvilles. John Bright, a Liberal and a Quaker, led the campaign for free trade. Gradually, they adopted more 'social' policies around old-age pensions, free education, public housing, and free health care. Their greatest reforming government was that immediately before the First World War, led by Herbert Asquith and containing both Lloyd George and Winston Churchill. After the war, internal divisions and an increase in the number of working men and women elected to Parliament led to their decline. The Labour Party led by Clement Attlee became the 'socially progressive' party, and its government from 1945 to 1951 founded the National Health Service and nationalised transport, utilities, and some industries, in effect continuing the 'planned economy' needed to win the Second World War. However, the Liberals slowly made a comeback, doing well when socially liberal voters disliked Conservative social policies. After the indecisive election of 2010, the Liberals denied Labour power by

forming a coalition with the Conservatives led by David Cameron. The Liberals were destroyed at the 2015 election because they had not understood that their voters wanted to keep the Conservatives out! Cameron's unexpected victory forced him to make good on his promise to hold an in/out referendum on membership in the European Union. This split both the Conservative and Labour Parties and led to deadlock in Parliament. British Quakers support all the current political parties but in the present circumstances (2019) are more likely to vote 'progressively'.

4 Introduction to CFP 1959, para. 547.

5 Alton, *Changing Ourselves*, 29.

12. On Nayler's Politics (pp. 126–36)

1 Nayler, *Saul's Errand to Damascus* (12 March 1653), in Nayler, *Works*, 1:36–37.

2 Nayler, *Love to the Lost*, Nayler, *Works*, 3:84–85.

3 Nayler, *Behold You Rulers*, Nayler, *Works*, 4:44–45.

4 Nayler, *Works*, 1:5–6; Fox's counterattack is in Nayler, *Works*, 1:6–18.

5 Nayler, *Saul's Errand to Damascus*, Nayler, *Works*, 1:4–5.

6 Nayler, *A discovery of the First Wisdom* (25 April 1653), in Nayler, *Works*, 1:66–67.

7 Nayler, *Several papers* (1653), in Nayler, *Works*, 1:230.

8 Nayler, *A Few Words Occasioned* (17 March 1654), in Nayler, *Works*, 1:141–42.

9. Nayler, *A Few Words Occasioned* (17 March 1654), in Nayler, *Works*, 1:143–44.

10 Nayler and Fox, *Lamentation*, in Nayler, *Works*, 1:196–97.

11 Nayler and Fox, Lamentations, in Nayler, *Works*, 1:203.

12 Nayler, *To Thee Oliver Cromwell* (1655), in Nayler, *Works*, 2:258.

13 Nayler, *To Thee Oliver Cromwell* (1655), in Nayler, *Works*, 2:259.

14 Nayler, *To Thee Oliver Cromwell* (1655), in Nayler, *Works*, 2:260.

15 Nayler, *To Thee Oliver Cromwell* (1655), in Nayler, *Works*, 2:261.

16 Nayler, *To Thee Oliver Cromwell* (1655), in Nayler, *Works*, 2:261.

17 Moore, *The Light in their Consciences*, 71.

[18] Nayler, *To Thee Oliver Cromwell* (1655), in Nayler, *Works*, 2:262

[19] See chapter 9, 'The Army and the Radicals', in Hill, *Experience of Defeat*.

[20] Neelon, *James Nayler*, 124.

[21] Gwyn, *The Covenant Crucified*, 150.

[22] Hutton, *Restoration*, 122–23.

14. 'Concerning the Lord's Supper' (pp. 145–51)

[1] As quoted in Duffy, *Stripping of the Altars*, 102. See chapter 3 titled 'The Mass' for accounts of reverse transubstantiation.

[2] MacCulloch, *A History of Christianity*, 635–36.

[3] Wyclif (1320?–1384) was an Oxford philosopher who thought that the Bible was the only source of divine truth and that the Eucharist was a clerical deception. He was supported by powerful political patrons and died peacefully. However, his followers, nicknamed 'Lollards' (meaning 'mumblers who talk rubbish'), were mixed up with the losing side in early-fifteenth-century English politics and were severely persecuted. Part of that persecution was to ban, in 1407, the possession of any English translation of the Bible. Lollards continued meeting in secret to read the partial and tattered copies they had hidden. They were particularly influential in the east Midlands (George Fox's birthplace), east Anglia, and parts of Yorkshire.

[4] "The Twelve Conclusions of the Lollards," The Geoffrey Chaucer Page, Harvard University, htp://sites.fas.harvard.edu/~chaucer/special/varia/lollards/ lollconc.htm, accessed 18 March 2019.

[5] See Farrow and Wildwood, *Universe as Revelation*.

15. On James Nayler and Martha Simmonds (pp. 152–75)

[1] For information on Simmonds's early life, see Smith, *Martha Simmon[d]s*, 9–13.

[2] Haggland, 'Quakers and the Printing Press', 36.

[3] Smith, *Martha Simmon[d]s*, 49.

[4] Smith, *Martha Simmon[d]s*, 49–50.

[5] Nayler, *Works*, 3:529.

[6] Neelon, *James Nayler*, 132.

[7] The two pamphlets are James Nayler, *Weakness above Wickedness*, in Nayler, *Works*, 3:449–74, and Jeremiah Ives,

Innocency above Impudency, in Nayler, *Works*, 3:475–508. Bittle, in *James Nayler 1618–1660*, quotes another by Ives titled *The Quakers quaking*.

8 Bittle, *James Nayler 1618–1660*, 94.

9 Farmer, *Satan Enthroned*, in Nayler, *Works*, 3:564.

10 Edward Burrough to Martha Simmonds, [May] 1656, in Nayler, *Works*, 3:530–31.

11 William Dewsbury to Martha Simmonds, ca. May 1656, in Nayler, *Works*, 3:532.

12 James Nayler to London Friends, June 1656, in Nayler, *Works*, 3:760.

13 Braithwaite, *The Beginnings of Quakerism*, 244n2.

14 Edward Burrough and Francis Howgill to Margaret Fell, 13 August 1656, in Nayler, *Works*, 3:534–36.

15 Richard Hubberthorne to Margaret Fell, 26 August 1656, in Nayler, *Works*, 3:538–39.

16 Richard Hubberthorne to Margaret Fell, 26 August 1656, in Nayler, *Works*, 3:539.

17 Howgill to Margaret Fell, 13 August 1656, in Nayler, *Works*, 3:535.

18 Fox to Nayler, probably after the meeting in Exeter, in Nayler, *Works*, 3:541.

19 Farmer, *Satan Enthroned*, in Nayler, *Works*, 3:564–65.

20 Nayler, *Works*, *Love to the Lost* 3:64.

21 Nayler, *To all the People of the Lord* (1659), 4:65. This was also printed as *James Nailor's Recantation*, which Nayler refused to recognise as his work.

22 Mack, *Visionary Women*, 200.

23 Neelon, *James Nayler*, 149.

24 Hubberthorne to Margaret Fell, 25 November 1656, *Works*, 3:553.

25 Carroll, *Martha Simmonds*, 49.

26 Carroll, *Martha Simmonds*, 45.

27 Nayler, *To the Life of God in All* (1659), in Nayler, *Works*, in Nayler, *Works*, 4:261.

28 Nayler, *To the Life of God in All* (1659), in Nayler, *Works*, in Nayler, *Works*, 4:261-2.

29 Damrosch *The Sorrows of the Quaker Jesus* 254.

30 Nayler, *To the Life of God in All* (1659), in Nayler, *Works*, 4:263.

31 Nayler, *To the Life of God in All* (1659), in Nayler, *Works*, 4:266.

32 Nayler, *To All the People of the Lord* (1659), in Nayler, *Works*, 4:63.

33 Nayler, *To All the People of the Lord* (1659), in Nayler, *Works*, 4:64.

34 Braithwaite, *The Beginnings of Quakerism*, 269–70.

35 Farmer, *Satan Enthroned*, Works, 3:568.

36 Burton, *Diary of Thomas Burton*, in Nayler, *Works*, 3:601.

37 Rich, *True narrative*, in Nayler, *Works*, 3:700–01.

38 Bittle, *James Nayler*, 142.

39 Carroll, 'Martha Simmonds', 51.

40 Simmonds et al., *O England*, in Nayler, *Works*, 3:592; see also Smith, *Martha Simmon[d]s*, 63. The phrase 'lain amongst the pots' is probably a reference to the washpot of Moab; see Psalm 60:8.

41 Simmonds et al., *O England*, *Works*, 3:593; see also Smith, *Martha Simmon[d]s*, 64.

42 Simmonds et al., *O England*, in Nayler, *Works*, 3:590–91.

43 Ingle, *First among Friends*, 132.

44 Braithwaite, *Beginnings of Quakerism*, 244.

45 Burton, *Diary of Thomas Burton*, in Nayler, *Works*, 3:691.

16. 'Concerning Redemption' (pp. 176–80)

1 This letter is quoted in the 1883 *Book of Christian Discipline* on page 3, the opening page of 'Christian Doctrine'. However, there are doubts about how involved Fox was in the authorship of this letter, which was written in 1671 on board a ship to Barbados. The letter was designed to reassure the Barbadian authorities that Quaker planters and slave owners were not going to overturn the government's authority; hence, Quakers needed to appear as orthodox as possible. See Angell, 'An Early Version'. The orthodoxy of this letter was noticed by nineteenth-century American Friends

and used by evangelical and Gurneyite Quakers to support their evangelical understanding of the Quaker message.

2 Angell explains that the 1690s saw renewed questioning of the toleration given to Quakers in Britain. As a result, leaders such as Thomas Ellwood and George Whitefield issued statements that were almost creeds, interpreting Quaker beliefs in an orthodox light. Angell, 'An Early Version'.

3 Hill, *World Turned Upside Down*, 205.

4 Hill, *World Turned Upside Down*, 206–7.

17. 'Concerning Christ Jesus' (pp. 181–93)

1 See Angell, 'God, Christ, and the Light' 159. This section (158–61) has a very helpful summary of the ways in which Quaker thinking differed from Protestant Christianity.

2 Spencer, 'James Nayler', 72. The first quotation in this passage is from *Saul's Errand to Damascus* (Nayler, *Works*, 1:19) and refers to 1 Corinthians 3:16–17.

3 Spencer, 'James Nayler', 73.

4 Moore, *Light in Their Consciences*, 105–6.

5 Moore, *Light in Their Consciences*, 106.

6 Angell, 'God, Christ, and the Light', 160.

7 Moore, *Light in Their Consciences*, 214.

8 Woolman, 'On Keeping Negroes: Part Second', 236.

9 Woolman, 'On Keeping Negroes: Part Second', 237.

10 Scott, *On Salvation by Christ*, 7.

11 Scott, *On Salvation by Christ*, 41, emphasis in the original.

12 Buckley, *The Essential Elias Hicks*, 60.

13 John Joseph Gurney, as quoted in Angell, 'God, Christ, and the Light', 165, emphasis in the original.

14 Angell, 'God, Christ, and the Light', 167.

15 'Richmond Declaration of Faith,' as quoted in Angell, 'God, Christ, and the Light', 165.

16 Angell, 'God, Christ, and the Light', 171.

17 Northwest Friends, *Faith and Practice*, 15.

18 Ohio Yearly Meeting, *Book of Discipline*, 25.

18. On the Exercise of Power 1656 to 1661 (pp. 194–204)

[1] These quotes are from various letters from Nayler to Fox found in Nayler, *Works*, 2:568–77.

[2] Ingle, *First among Friends*, 132.

[3] Fox, *Journal*, 268–69.

[4] Richard Hubberthorne to Margaret Fell, 4 October 1656, in Nayler, *Works*, 3:544.

[5] Richard Hubberthorne to Margaret Fell 4 October 1656, in Nayler, *Works*, 3:545.

[6] Richard Hubberthorne to Margaret Fell 4 October 1656, in Nayler, *Works*, 3:546.

[7] Ingle, *First among Friends* 142.

[8] George Fox to James Nayler, n.d., in Nayler, *Works*, 3:541.

[9] See a letter from George Bishop to Margaret Fell dated 27 October 1656 which gives a full account of events and includes, 'And with these were other letters taken. . . . One that GF, which were written with my hand, and sent to him [Nayler] about the 12th instant'. Nayler, *Works*, 3:550.

[10] George Fox to James Nayler, not dated, in Nayler, *Works*, 3:542–43.

[11] Margaret Fell to James Nayler, 15 October 1656, in Nayler, *Works*, 3:547.

[12] Francis Howgill to Margaret Fell, 21 October 1656, in Nayler, *Works*, 3:549.

[13] Farmer, *Satan Enthroned*, in Nayler, *Works*, 3:580–81.

[14] Farmer, *Satan Enthroned*, in Nayler, *Works*, 3:581.

[15] Peters, *Print Culture and the Early Quakers*, 239.

[16] Ingle, *First among Friends*, 141.

[17] Richard Roper to Margaret Fell, 20 October 1656, in Nayler, *Works*, 3:548.

[18] Farmer, *Satan Enthroned*, in Nayler, *Works*, 3:568.

[19] Farmer, *Satan Enthroned*, in Nayler, *Works*, 3:575.

[20] Ingle, *First among Friends*, 149.

[21] Bittle, *James Nayler*, 120.

Notes

22 Bittle, *James Nayler,* 173.

23 Nayler, *Love to the Lost*, in Nayler, *Works*, 3:86.

24 See also chapter 15 above.

20. Defeat: September 1658 to May 1660 (pp. 214–22)

1 Hutton, *Restoration*, 121–23.

2 Moore, *The Light in Their Consciences* 168–69.

3 Ingle, *First among Friends* 171.

4 Hill, *Experience of Defeat*, 135.

5 Hutton, *Restoration*, 57.

6 Hutton, *Restoration*, 67.

7 As quoted in Hill, *Experience of Defeat*, 132.

8 As quoted in Hill, *Experience of Defeat,* 133.

9 As quoted in Hutton, *Restoration*, 71. The quotation is taken from the diary of John Nicoll.

10 As quoted in Hutton, *Restoration*, 71.

11 Hutton, *Restoration*, 91.

12 Hutton, *Restoration*, 122.

13 See Ingle, *First among Friends*, 187. Fox was wisely travelling outside London at this time.

14 James Nayler to Charles II, 3 June 1660, in Nayler, *Works*, 4:406, 408–9.

15 Fox, *History of the Early Part of the Reign*, 21.

16 Hutton, *Restoration*, 147.

17 Damrosch, *The Sorrows of the Quaker Jesus*, 6.

18 Nayler, *To All the People of the Lord*, in Nayler, *Works*, 4:64.

19 Nayler, *To the Life of God in All* (1659), in Nayler, *Works*, 4:267.

20 As quoted in Simmonds, *O England, thy Time is Come*, in Nayler, *Works*, 3:591.

Appendix A: The British Wars 1637 to 1653 (pp. 223–27)

1 The dates in this appendix are primarily from Williams, *Chronology of the Expanding World*.

Bibliography

Books of Discipline

I have drawn on the British Quakers' books of discipline published between 1822 and 2013.[†] These were known first as 'extracts' because they were manuscript books held by each monthly and quarterly meeting in which were copied out extracts from yearly meeting minutes and epistles. They also gave instruction and advice on personal and communal behaviour and how to run a Quaker meeting. The extracts were first printed in 1782 (Quakers are slow to adopt new technology!). This was revised in 1802 and then republished in 1822 with an additional supplement. The 1822 edition is the first book of discipline from which I quote. In 1834, it was revised again and called *Rules of Discipline of the Religious Society of Friends;* my copy has a supplement of extracts approved by the yearly meeting in 1848 bound in with it. The discipline was revised again in 1861 and in 1883, when the name was changed to *Book of Christian Discipline of the Religious Society of Friends.*

The books of discipline described above contain extracts from the entire life-span of London Yearly Meeting minutes and epistles. British Quakers took care to demonstrate the continuity of their advice to members and of their theology. I have often noted that, for example, an extract in the 1883 discipline was also in the 1822 edition and may have been written decades before that. It is useful to know just how old some of the advice is.

[†] For a useful history of London Yearly Meeting's books of discipline, see Olver, 'The History of *Quaker Faith and Practice'*.

Bibliography

At the start of the twentieth century, during the transition from an evangelical to a more liberal theology, London Yearly Meeting decided to divide the discipline into three parts: administration or government, practice, and finally faith and thought – which was described as part one. The yearly meeting addressed the easiest part first and approved *Church Government* in 1906. *Christian Practice* came in 1911, which dealt with devotional life, the family, and what we now would call Quaker witness in the world. This was revised again in 1925, and that is the edition I have used.

The last part of the new discipline to be published, called *Christian Life, Faith and Thought: Being the First Part of Christian Discipline of the Religious Society of Friends in Great Britain,* was published in 1922 and was utterly unlike the Christian doctrine sections of the 1883 *Book of Christian Discipline* which it replaced. It was the first edition to include extracts from the writings of individual Friends rather than limiting the content to statements from yearly meetings. This practice has continued, allowing a range of Quaker views to be published with the approval of yearly meeting. The books reflect more accurately the movement of the Spirit in the Religious Society of Friends, and this practice allows a wider range of spiritual belief than can be shown through minutes and epistles.

In 1928, this tri-partite structure had a fourth pillar added to it, the separate publication of *Advices and Queries.* My edition of these advices is printed in the 1931 edition of *Church Government.* By the 1950s it was clear that Quaker faith and thought had moved on, and in 1959 the yearly meeting approved a book of discipline that brought together both doctrine and practice in a single volume called *Christian Faith and Practice in the Experience of the Society of Friends.* In 1964, the *Advices and Queries* were again revised. I was given a copy of that edition in 1980 when I started attending the Quaker meeting in Rochester, Kent. The third revision of *Church Government* since 1906 was approved in 1967.

In 1994, all three books and *Advices and Queries* were brought together in *Quaker faith and practice: The Book of Christian Discipline of the Yearly Meeting of the Religious Society of Friends (Quakers) in Britain*. The chapters on church government remained unrevised, but the doctrine and practice sections were newly minted, and the revised advices and queries appeared as chapter 1. This book has gone through five editions because of later changes to the church government chapters, but the other sections remain unchanged. I cite the fifth edition of 2013.

In 2018, Britain Yearly Meeting, as it is now called, decided to undertake a full revision of the entire work. It remains to be seen how the revision will describe the doctrine and practice of British Quakers and how broad a range of extracts it will contain. We live in exciting times.

Abbreviations

AQ 1964

Advices and Queries Addressed to the Meetings and Members of the Religious Society of Friends, and to those who meet with them in public worship. London: The Society of Friends, 1964.

BoD 1834

Rules of Discipline of the Religious Society of Friends with advices. 3rd ed. London: Darton and Harvey, 1834.

BoD 1883

Book of Christian Discipline of the Religious Society of Friends in Great Britain. London: S. Harris, 1883.

CFP 1959

Christian Faith and Practice in the Experience of the Society of Friends. London: London Yearly Meeting of the Religious Society of Friends, 1959. Note that citations of this work reference the paragraph numbers, not the page numbers.

CG 1931

Church Government: Being the Third Part of Christian Discipline of the Religious Society of Friends in Great Britain. London: Friends' Book Centre, 1931.

CLFT 1922

Christian Life, Faith and Thought in the Society of Friends: Being the First Part of Christian Discipline of the Religious Society of Friends in Great Britain. London: Friends' Bookshop, 1922.

CP 1925

Christian Practice: Being the Second Part of Christian Discipline in the Religious Society of Friends in Great Britain. London: London Yearly Meeting, 1925.

Extracts 1822

Extracts from Minutes and Advices of the Yearly Meeting of Friends, held in London, from its first institution. 2nd ed. London: 1802, with supplement printed in 1822.

QC 1988

Questions and Counsel: A Provisional Document Offered by the Book of Discipline Revision Committee. London: The Religious Society of Friends, 1988

QFP 2013

Quaker faith and practice: The Book of Christian Discipline of the Yearly Meeting of the Religious Society of Friends (Quakers) in Britain. 5th ed. London: Quaker Books, 2013. https://qfp.quaker.org.uk/. The 1994 *Advices and Queries* are cited using this edition. Note that citations of this work reference the chapters and section numbers, not the page numbers.

Other Works Cited

Alton, Chris. *Changing Ourselves, Changing the World.* The 2018 Swarthmore Lecture. London: Quaker Books, 2018.

Ambler, Rex. *The Quaker Way: A Rediscovery*. Winchester, England: Christian Alternative, 2013.

Angell, Stephen W. 'An Early Version of George Fox's "Letter to the Governor of Barbados"'. *Quaker Studies* 19, no. 2 (March 2015): 277–94.

———. 'God, Christ, and the Light'. In *The Oxford Handbook of Quaker Studies*, edited by Stephen W. Angell and Pink Dandelion, 158–71. New York: Oxford University Press, 2013.

Ashworth, Timothy. *Paul's Necessary Sin: The Experience of Liberation*. Aldershot, England: Ashgate, 2006.

Birkel, Michael, and Stephen W. Angell. 'The Witness of Richard Farnworth: Prophet of Light, Apostle of Church Order'. In *Early Quakers and Their Theological Thought, 1647–1723*, edited by Stephen W. Angell and Pink Dandelion, 83–101. Cambridge: Cambridge University Press, 2015.

Bittle, William G. *James Nayler, 1618–1660: The Quaker Indicted by Parliament*. York: William Sessions, 1986.

Braithwaite, William C. *The Beginnings of Quakerism to 1660*. 2nd ed., revised by Henry J. Cadbury. York: Williams Sessions, 1981.

Buckley, Paul. *The Essential Elias Hicks*. San Francisco: Inner Light Books, 2013.

Burton, Thomas. *The Diary of Thomas Burton Esq*. Edited by John Towill Rutt. London: H. Colburn, 1828. In Nayler, *Works*, 3:600–91.

Carroll, Kenneth L. 'Martha Simmonds, a Quaker Enigma'. *Journal of the Friends Historical Society* 53, no. 1 (1972): 31–52.

Damrosch, Leo. *The Sorrows of the Quaker Jesus: James Nayler and the Puritan Crackdown on the Free Spirit*. Cambridge, MA: Harvard University Press, 1996.

Dandelion, Ben Pink. *Open for Transformation: Being Quaker*. The 2014 Swarthmore Lecture. London: Quaker Books, 2014.

Duffy, Eamon. *The Stripping of the Altars: Traditional Religion in England, 1400–1580*. New Haven, CT: Yale University Press, 1992.

Farmer, Richard. *Satan Enthroned in his Chair of Pestilence* (1656). In Nayler, *Works*, 3:557–84.

Bibliography

Farrow, Jo, and Alex Wildwood. *The Universe as Revelation: An Ecomystical Theology for Friends*. Jo Farrow and Alex Wildwood. London: Pronoun Press, 2013.

Fox, Charles James. *A History of the Early Part of the Reign of James the Second*. London: William Miller, 1808.

Fox, George. *The Journal of George Fox*. Edited by John L. Nickalls. London: Religious Society of Friends, 1975.

———. *The Power of the Lord Is Over All: The Pastoral Letters of George Fox*. Edited by T. Canby Jones. Richmond, IN: Friends United Press, 1989.

Garman, Mary van Vleck. 'Quaker Women's Lives and Spiritualities'. In *The Oxford Handbook of Quaker Studies*, edited by Stephen W. Angell and Pink Dandelion, 232–44. New York: Oxford University Press, 2013.

Gwyn, Douglas. *The Covenant Crucified: Quakers and the Rise of Capitalism*. Wallingford, PA: Pendle Hill Publications, 1995.

———. 'Seventeenth-Century Context and Quaker Beginnings'. In *Early Quakers and Their Theological Thought, 1647–1723*. Edited by Stephen W. Angell and Pink Dandelion, 13–31. Cambridge: Cambridge University Press, 2015.

Haggland, Betty. 'Quakers and the Printing Press'. In *Early Quakers and Their Theological Thought, 1647–1723*, edited by Stephen W. Angell and Pink Dandelion, 32–48. Cambridge: Cambridge University Press, 2015.

Hicks, Elias. *The Journal of Elias Hicks*. Edited by Paul Buckley. San Francisco: Inner Light Books, 2009.

Hill, Christopher. *The English Revolution 1640*. London: Lawrence & Wishart, 1985.

———. *The Experience of Defeat: Milton and Some Contemporaries*. London: Faber and Faber, 1984.

———. *The World Turned Upside Down: Radical Ideas during the English Revolution*. London: Penguin Books, 1975.

Hoskins, W. G. *The Making of the English Landscape*. London: Penguin Books UK, 1985.

Hutton, Ronald. *The Restoration: A Political and Religious History of England and Wales 1658–1667*. Oxford: Oxford University Press, 1987.

Ingle, H. Larry. *First among Friends: George Fox and the Creation of Quakerism*. New York: Oxford University Press, 1994.

Kirby, M. W. *Men of Business and Politics: The Rise and Fall of the Quaker Pease Dynasty in North-East England, 1700–1943*. London: George Allen & Unwin, 1984.

Law, William. *Selected Mystical Writings of William Law.* Edited by Stephen Hobhouse. London. C. W. Daniel Co., 1938.

MacCulloch, Diarmaid. *A History of Christianity: The First Three Thousand Years.* London: Allen Lane 2009.

Mack, Phyllis. *Visionary Women: Ecstatic Prophecy in Seventeenth-Century England.* Berkeley: University of California Press, 1992.

Moore, Rosemary. *The Light in Their Consciences: The Early Quakers in Britain, 1646–1666.* University Park: Pennsylvania State University Press, 2000.

Morrill, John S. *The Nature of the English Revolution: Essays.* London: Longman, 1993.

Nayler, James. *Answer to 'The Perfect Pharisee'* (1654). In Nayler, *Works* 1:365–95.

——. *Behold You Rulers* (1658). In Nayler, *Works,* 4:43–49.

——. *A discovery of the First Wisdom from Beneath and the Second Wisdom from Above* (1653). In Nayler, *Works,* 1:41–71 .

——. *A Few Words Occasioned by a Paper Lately Printed* (1654). Nayler, *Works,* 1:120–149.

——. *The Lamb's War* (1657). In Nayler, *Works,* 4:1–20.

——. *Love to the Lost* (1656). In Nayler, *Works,* 3:47–137.

——. *A Message from the Spirit of Truth, unto the Holy Seed* (1658). In Nayler, *Works,* 4:50–62.

——. *Saul's Errand to Damascus* (1653). In Nayler, *Works,* 1:1–40.

——. *To all the People of the Lord, everywhere gathered or scattered* (1659). In Nayler, *Works,* 4:63–65.

——. *To Thee Oliver Cromwell into whose hands God hath committed the sword of justice* (1655). In Nayler, *Works,* 2:258–62.

——. *To the Life of God in All* (1659). In Nayler *Works,* 4: 260–69.

——. *The Works of James Nayler (1618–1660).* 4 vols. Farmington, ME: Quaker Heritage Press, 2003–2009.

Nayler, James, and George Fox. *A Lamentation (by one of England's Prophets) over the Ruins of this Oppressed Nation* (1653). In Nayler, *Works,* 1:196–204.

Bibliography

——. *Several papers some of them given forth by George Fox and others by James Nayler* (1653). In Nayler, *Works*, 1:208–43.

Neelon, David. *James Nayler: Revolutionary to Prophet.* Becket, MA: Leadings Press, 2009.

Nimmo, Dorothy. *A Testimony to the Grace of God in the Life of James Nayler.* Master Print, 1991.

North Carolina Yearly Meeting (Conservative). *Faith and Practice: Book of Discipline of the North Carolina Yearly Meeting.* 1983. https://www.ncymc.org/home/faith-and-practice.

Northwest Yearly Meeting of Friends Church. *Faith and Practice: A Book of Christian Discipline.* Newberg, OR: Barclay Press, 1987.

Nuttall, Geoffrey F. *James Nayler: A Fresh Approach.* Presidential address to the Friends' Historical Society. London: Friends House, 1954.

Ohio Yearly Meeting. *The Book of Discipline of Ohio Yearly Meeting of the Religious Society of Friends.* Barnesville, OH: Ohio Yearly Meeting, 2018.

Olver, David. 'The History of *Quaker faith and practice*'. *Friends Quarterly* 42, no. 3 (August 2014): 12–22.

Parker, Geoffrey. *Global Crisis: War, Climate Change and Catastrophe in the Seventeenth Century.* New Haven, CT: Yale University Press, 2013.

Peters, Kate. *Print Culture and the Early Quakers.* Cambridge: Cambridge University Press, 2005.

Punshon, John. *Reasons for Hope: The Faith and Future of the Friends Church.* Richmond, IN: Friends United Press, 2001.

Quaker Women's Group. *Bringing the Invisible into the Light.* London: Quaker Home Service, 1986.

Rich, Robert. *A True Narrative of the Examination, Trial and Sufferings of James Nayler* (1657). In Nayler, *Works*, 3:692–746.

Rowntree, J. W. 'Faith and Life'. In *Essays and Addresses*, edited by Joshua Rowntree, 384–405. London: Headley Brothers. 1905.

Scott, Janet. *What Canst Thou Say? Towards a Quaker Theology.* London: Quaker Home Service, 1980.

Scott, Job. *Essays On Salvation by Christ and the debate which followed their publication.* 2nd ed. Farmington, ME: Quaker Heritage Press, 2010.

Simmonds, Martha. *A Lamentation For The Lost Sheep of the House* (1655). In Smith, *Martha Simmon[d]s*, 52–57.

Simmonds, Martha, Hannah Stranger, James Nayler, and N. T. *O England thy time is come* (1656). In Nayler, *Works*, 3:592–93.

Smith, Bernadette. *Martha Simmon[d]s 1624–1665: Her Life and Quaker Writings and 'the Fall' of James Nayler.* York, England: Sessions Book Trust, 2009.

Spencer, Carole Dale. 'James Nayler'. In *Early Quakers and Their Theological Thought, 1647–1723,* edited by Stephen W. Angell and Pink Dandelion, 64–82. Cambridge: Cambridge University Press, 2015.

Spufford, Margaret. *Contrasting Communities: English Villagers in the Sixteenth and Seventeenth Centuries.* Sutton History Handbooks. Stroud, Gloucestershire: Sutton Publishing, 2000.

Stone, Lawrence. *The Causes of the English Revolution 1529–1642.* London: Routledge and Kegan Paul, 1972.

Thomas, Anne. *Only Fellow-Voyagers: Creation Stories as Guides for the Journey.* Swarthmore Lectures. London: Quaker Home Service and Woodbrooke College, 1995.

Tousley, Nikki Coffey. 'Sin, Convincement, Purity, and Perfection'. In *The Oxford Handbook of Quaker Studies,* edited by Stephen W. Angell and Pink Dandelion, 172–86. New York: Oxford University Press, 2013.

Trevett, Christine. *Women and Quakerism in the Seventeenth Century.* York, England: Sessions Book Trust, 1991.

Weld, Thomas, Richard Prideaux, Sam Hammon, Will Cole, and Wil. Durant, *The Perfect Pharisee under Monkish Holiness Opposing The Fundamental Principles of the Doctrine of the Gospel* (1654). In Nayler, *Works*, 1:323–64.

White, Winifred M. *Six Weeks Meeting 1671–1971.* London: Six Weeks Meeting, Religious Society of Friends, 1971.

Williams, Neville. *Chronology of the Expanding World 1492 to 1762.* London: Barrie & Rockliff, The Cresset Press, 1969.

Bibliography

Woolman, John. 'Considerations on Keeping Negroes: Part Second' (1761). In *The Journal and Major Essays of John Woolman*, edited by Phillips P. Moulton, 198–237. New York: Oxford University Press, 1971.

Also available from Inner Light Books

William Penn's 'Holy Experiment'
by James Proud
> ISBN 978-0-9998332-9-2 (hardcover)
> ISBN 978-1-7328239-3-8 (paperback)

A Guide to Faithfulness Groups
By Marcelle Martin
> ISBN 978-1-7328239-4-5 (hardcover)
> ISBN 978-1-7328239-5-2 (paperback)
> ISBN 978-1-7328239-6-9 (eBook) $10

In the Stillness: Poems, prayers, reflections
by Elizabeth Mills
> ISBN 978-1-7328239-0-7 (hardcover)
> ISBN 978-1-7328239-1-4 (paperback)
> ISBN 978-1-7328239-2-1 (eBook)

Walk Humbly, Serve Boldly: Modern Quakers as Everyday Prophets
by Margery Post Abbott
> ISBN 978-0-9998332-6-1 (hardcover)
> ISBN 978-0-9998332-7-8 (paperback)
> ISBN 978-0-9998332-8-5 (eBook)

Primitive Quakerism Revived
by Paul Buckley
> ISBN 978-0-9998332-2-3 (hardcover)
> ISBN 978-0-9998332-3-0 (paperback)
> ISBN 978-0-9998332-5-4 (eBook)

Primitive Christianity Revived
by William Penn
Translated into Modern English by Paul Buckley
> ISBN 978-0-9998332-0-9 (hardcover)
> ISBN 978-0-9998332-1-6 (paperback)
> ISBN 978-0-9998332-4-7 (eBook)

Jesus, Christ and Servant of God
Meditations on the Gospel According to John
by David Johnson
> ISBN 978–0–9970604–6–1 (hardcover)
> ISBN 978–0–9970604–7–8 (paperback)
> ISBN 978–0–9970604–8–5 (eBook)

The Anti-War
by Douglas Gwyn
> ISBN 978-0-9970604-3-0 (hardcover)
> ISBN 978-0-9970604-4-7 (paperback)
> ISBN 978-0-9970604-5-4 (eBook)

Our Life Is Love, the Quaker Spiritual Journey
by Marcelle Martin
> ISBN 978-0-9970604-0-9 (hardcover)
> ISBN 978-0-9970604-1-6 (paperback)
> ISBN 978-0-9970604-2-3 (eBook)

A Quaker Prayer Life
by David Johnson
> ISBN 978-0-9834980-5-6 (hardcover)
> ISBN 978-0-9834980-6-3 (paperback)
> ISBN 978-0-9834980-7-0 (eBook))

The Essential Elias Hicks
by Paul Buckley
> ISBN 978-0-9834980-8-7 (hardcover)
> ISBN 978-0-9834980-9-4 (paperback)
> ISBN 978-0-9970604-9-2 (eBook)

The Journal of Elias Hicks
edited by Paul Buckley
> ISBN 978-0-9797110-4-6 (hardcover)
> ISBN 978-0-9797110-5-3 (paperback)

Dear Friend: The Letters and Essays of Elias Hicks
edited by Paul Buckley
> ISBN 978-0-9834980-0-1 (hardcover)
> ISBN 978-0-9834980-1-8 (paperback)

The Early Quakers and 'the Kingdom of God'
by Gerard Guiton
> ISBN 978-0-9834980-2-5 (hardcover)
> ISBN 978-0-9834980-3-2 (paperback)
> ISBN 978-0-9834980-4-9 (eBook)

John Woolman and the Affairs of Truth
edited by James Proud
> ISBN 978-0-9797110-6-0 (hardcover)
> ISBN 978-0-9797110-7-7 (paperback)

Cousin Ann's Stories for Children by Ann Preston
edited by Richard Beards
illustrated by Stevie French
> ISBN 978-0-9797110-8-4 (hardcover),
> ISBN 978-0-9797110-9-1 (paperback)

Counsel to the Christian-Traveller: also Meditations and Experiences
by William Shewen
> ISBN 978-0-9797110-0-8 (hardcover)
> ISBN 978-0-9797110-1-5 (paperback)